Reviewers' Praise for:

We're in the Mountains Not Over the Hill

"Informative, engaging, and inspiring... *We're in the Mountains, Not over the Hill* never loses sight of the author's underlying theme... 'Honor yourself.' She reminds us that the first challenge for women who want to backpack is to set their own goals and then to savor their successes. In the second half of her book, Alcorn deals with the practical details of backpacking — equipment, safety, staying healthy..." Barbara Sloane, *Montclarion* (Oakland)

"The title amused me. How often are women aged 60+ asked, 'Aren't you too old to be doing that?' They have backpacked on their own, with family members, or with clubs, carrying heavy packs and meeting all sort of challenges such as hungry bears, difficult llamas, every imaginable sort of weather, including blizzards and lightning strikes, but undeterred, they return, again and again to walk the many famous long walking trails in America.

"The book is an intriguing balance between practical tips to get you started and the retelling of adventures in short snippets intended to whet your appetite and arouse your interest. Although it is primarily designed to encourage older women to take up or continue hiking well into their golden years, men might also find themselves inspired to do so." *Outdoor Australia*, Barbara Darmanin

"I love to write about people and their passions. A passion, by its very nature, is a sexy thing; it draws people to it with such intoxication they're helpless to resist. Montclair writer Susan Alcorn has a passion for backpacking, and her new book challenges older women to grab a pack and 'be one with the earth.'" Ginny Pryor, *Hills Newspaper* (Oakland)

"I found plenty of interest from knee-care, diet and exercise to the experiences of the women whose backpacking is described in the book." *Backpack: Journal of the Backpackers Club*, Christine Roche, Sandbach, England

"Great Summer Read! The stories are sometimes humorous and other times serious, but most are, at the very least, inspiring." *Good News*, (Mammoth Lakes, CA)

Readers' Comments:

"We really enjoyed reading *We're in the Mountains Not over the Hill*. It inspired me to do something I'd wanted to do years ago, but had never gotten around to. Bill and I went up to Yosemite Valley Monday. On Tuesday we hiked to the top of Half Dome [4,500 feet elevation gain, 17 miles]. It was tougher than I thought, but very rewarding. Thanks, Susan for the reminder that our hiking days are not over!" Alison (San Francisco, CA)

"What a great book! I've been peeking at it since I got home and cannot wait to dive in." Ann (Berkeley, CA)

"Made me remember why backpacking is so vital. This book got me excited about the prospect of backpacking — and I'm a fairly regular backpacker already. Perhaps backpacking's most important aspects are its tendencies to inspire inner renewal and to challenge us out of our familiar ruts, and its consistent ability...to send one 'back home' with the perspective, commitment, and courage needed to effect personal change in one's 'real life.'

"I found the 'oral history' style particularly engaging, with many different voices (representing all different ages) unanimously endorsing the overall message: 'Backpacking is a priceless activity — we're fortunate to be able to do it, and we're really missing out if we neglect it.'" (A reader's review on Amazon.com)

5/10

We're in the Mountains,

Not over the Hill –

Tales and Tips

from Seasoned Women

Backpackers

by Susan

We're in the Mountains, Not over the Hill —

Tales and Tips from Seasoned Women Backpackers

Cover photo: Sierra lake in Kings Canyon National Park by Ralph Alcorn

Cover design: Marco Cardelli, Cardelli Graphics, Inc. El Granada, CA 94018. contact: www.mcardelli@rcn.com

Shepherd Canyon Books
25 Southwood Ct.
Oakland, CA 94611
510-339-3441
www. backpack45.com
Library of Congress Control Number: 2002096766

ISBN-13: 978-0-936034-02-7
ISBN-10: 0-936034-02-5

This book is dedicated to my husband, Ralph, because he has been with me every step of the way on this journey — both literally and figuratively. And, to the nearly three dozen women who graciously shared their stories to support me and encourage others.

Scene from the John Muir Trail

Preface

This book is a tribute to my "best buddy" Jean Morris who for four years climbed the most frightening, treacherous, hazard-filled mountain imaginable. We found out that Jean had Lou Gehrig's Disease (ALS) in fall, 1998. We decided we had better do some of the trips that one normally puts off until "later" — you know, retirement. In June 1999, Jean traveled extensively in Italy, France, and Germany with her oldest daughter, MaryJane. In August of that year I took her — in her wheelchair — across Sweden and Norway by plane, train, bus, boat, and car.

After the trip one of my best friends asked, "Did you have lots of deep conversations, as in 'Tuesdays with Morrie?'" I answered, "No, we were too busy. Most every day was a new city — with a hotel to locate, restaurants to try, and parks, museums, and shops to see."

I watched Jean make friends with everyone along the way. At times I even found myself envious of her because she could chitchat with people in a way that I couldn't. Every time she launched into a new round of conversation — with locals and tourists alike — she began by telling them why she was in a wheelchair, and ended up by finding out their family history. I was amazed — how could she get away with asking such personal questions? When I asked her, the reply was, "Well, they don't have to answer."

And whereas I'm not sure that I'd even have the guts to venture out in public with such a debilitating illness, Jean went wherever she wanted and managed to put others at ease. She anticipated people's curiosity, and told them what was wrong with her. "They're wondering anyway, so we might as well get it out in the open right away."

In June 2000, we took another trip — a short one to Yosemite Valley. Once again we experienced the contrast between how easily ambulatory people can travel, and how difficult every sidewalk, doorway, and bathroom is to a person in a wheelchair. Though Yosemite provides many services to the handicapped such as specially-equipped busses, designated parking spaces, and ramps leading to its public buildings and concession stands, it still presents problems to handicapped visitors.

One afternoon we naively set out on one of its paved trails to view Bridalveil Falls, a popular attraction in the park. Jean was using her new $20,000 motorized wheelchair. We followed the trail uphill a few hundred feet with the chair lurching first to one side and then the other depending on the slope of the terrain. We decided to go back downhill. As Jean started to turn her wheelchair around, it continued to lurch and the wheels on the lower side to spin. I stood by helplessly. The chair was obviously not designed for all terrain and it was much heavier than the manual one I'd pushed all over Europe. If the new chair had started to tip, I'd have been unable to right it. Finally, with the help of passersby, we were able to slowly make our way back down the trail and to the car.

In October 2000, Jean realized another dream trip; she went with friends from our high school days on a cruise through the Panama Canal with stops in the Caribbean and Costa Rica.

Throughout 2001, Jean became increasingly weak and more easily tired, but she insisted on carrying on with her normal activities as much as possible. With the help of her caregiver, Anna, or of friends, Jean continued to go shopping, to go out for lunch, to enjoy Sunday drives, and to visit the state fair. She tried to put her household affairs in order — including labeling many of her favorite dishes and collectibles with the names of future recipients.

Jean's refusal to slip into despair and her obvious delight at being with her family and friends made visits to see her bittersweet occasions. Her body was failing, but her courage was a gift to everyone who saw her. It's not that Jean was without sadness, fear, or anxiety about her situation. She cried, and allowed herself to express her emotions, but then she told herself to move on. "This is my day," she would say.

The early months of 2002 were difficult ones as Jean fought two rounds of pneumonia. But she rallied for a while and resumed her church attendance and visits to friends. I'm reminded of the line, "Only a fool is not afraid on the battlefield," but like the hero she was, Jean continued to fight her disease with courage and grace to the last. In July of 2002, she said, "I can't fight this anymore," and passed on.

Jean Evelyn Morris — May 20, 1940 to July 2, 2002.

On the Camino de Santiago, Spain

Contents

Part 2: It's Your Turn – Getting Up and Out

An Introduction to Backpacking

The first time I tried on a backpack, I immediately burst into tears. My husband Ralph and I planned to climb Mt. Whitney in two weeks' time and here I was in my living room, hardly able to stand up, much less walk. The pack was only 35 pounds — considered a modest weight by some, but I hadn't even figured out how to put the pack on by myself. It was a humbling moment; I had been determined to go, and had bragged about my upcoming adventure.

A week later we drove to the eastern side of the Sierras to the small town of Independence, California and up the 15-mile-long, steep curving road to the Onion Valley trailhead at 9,200 feet. It was dark by the time we arrived. We camped, as planned, to begin the acclimation to the high altitude. The next morning Ralph was up at daybreak to wait at the ranger station for the necessary, and rationed, wilderness passes. (It appears to me, incidentally, that in every couple there will be one "early bird" who likes to greet the dawn, and one "midnight owl" who wants to burrow deeper when the sun threatens to rise.) As I slowly packed my gear, sipped my tea, and surveyed my surroundings, all I could think was, "Here I am at 9,000 feet, and everything I'm going to climb in the next week is going to be up from here."

I missed the first round of backpacking. Though I observed its surge in popularity in the 1970s, I didn't know anyone who backpacked. I was married, and busy raising our two children, caring for our home, eventually going back to college, working part-time, writing. The TV character I admired was "Laura" from the *Dick Van Dyke Show*; the more independent "Mary" of the *Mary Tyler Moore Show* had not yet arrived on the scene.

While I loved the outdoors, and even though our family spent many weekends and every vacation camping and hiking, my first husband and I never discussed backpacking. But after we were divorced, I joined the Sierra Club and went on long hikes where the main topic of conversation was often other long hikes — and backpacking trips into the Sierra.

When I met Ralph, while on a Sierra Club camping trip, I realized that I had found someone who was knowledgeable about wilderness travel. He had grown up in Yellowstone and Kings Canyon/Sequoia National Parks, where his father had served as both ranger and naturalist. But although Ralph had spent years hiking and backpacking in the West, he hadn't backpacked in fifteen years. I could see my opportunities for outdoor adventure were expanding exponentially. I nagged him into committing to one more trip.

It was with both excitement and apprehension that I began my first backpack trip in 1989, when I was 48. I *did* make it to the top of Mt. Whitney. Most years since that first trip Ralph and I have gone on a backpacking trip — usually one or two weeks long.

We would like to go more often and for longer trips, but like everyone else we lead busy lives. We enjoy our work, our circle of family and friends, and the cultural offerings of the San Francisco Bay Area. We are also thankful that less than an hour from our house are dozens of hikes that we can enjoy because without the trails of our East Bay Regional Parks and our water district, we'd never be motivated enough to keep in condition for our backpack trips. We also find great inspiration in nearby Pt. Reyes National Seashore, Mt. Diablo, and Mt. Tamalpais, to name a few jewels.

I've always been drawn to the outdoors; walking and hiking have long been my favorite forms of exercise. As a child, I would often spend all day out-of-doors. My parents had horses that they considered too ill-tempered for me to ride, but the grassy hillsides beyond the barn were perfect for sliding down on sheets of cardboard in the spring. As I practiced running along the steep slopes, I was certain I was part goat.

It was a time when children could play outside without much concern about their safety. My friends and I entertained ourselves by riding bikes and playing "Hide and Go Seek" and "Kick-the Can" on long summer evenings.

Then my parents sold their horses and we moved closer to town. We lived two doors from my elementary school. Still, there was a huge rock outcropping nearby that could be explored and a few blocks away there was a fascinating, splashing spring that I could admire while on the way to my dreaded piano lessons.

I became a teenager. We moved again, but we still were in the El Cerrito hills. I walked the three miles home from school most days — usually with a friend or two. One day my best friend in high school, Betty (name changed), said as we walked home together, "You walk too fast for a girl." I was crushed.

It was a different era. I went to charm school; I learned how to descend stairs properly and how to sit like a lady. My mother took me to teas and fashion shows. There was always the message that these were the preferred, or at least familiar, activities for young ladies in the 1950s. But I always felt that I was being groomed for a role that didn't provide enough space.

As a teenager I noticed that preferred dinner guests were those who talked about politics, business, and travel to European cities. Women friends played bridge and conversed about shopping, collecting, antiques, and fashion. Bonnie (named changed) was a favorite family friend and a frequent visitor. I remember how she recounted with much hilarity the time she and her husband drove ten bone-jarring miles into a high Sierra wilderness camp. They were met at the entrance and offered a glass of water. I didn't get it. "What's so funny about that?" I wondered. The joke, it seemed, was that the drink was water, not Scotch. It was many years until I could accept that it was okay that Bonnie and I were worlds apart in our way of thinking — and that although I could enjoy "Happy Hour," my focus was on the outdoors.

As a young adult, I realized that my parents did not share my concerns about the environment. The camping trips that I took with my husband and children to our national parks were of fleeting interest to my parents. Since my mother practically grew up on horseback on her parents' sheep ranch in Eastern Oregon, I never could understand why she was so little interested in the outdoors. But such was the case — with her adult years, she left most of her enjoyment of the outdoors behind.

Years later, after I had taken up backpacking, I tried again to share my interest in the outdoors with acquaintances. I remember my dismay when I showed Alicia (name changed), a co-worker, the photos of a challenging summer backpack trip into the Sierra. "Yeah, I've been there," she commented. "You have, at Muir Pass?" I asked. "Well, not *there*, but after a few trips all the passes are the same."

Though my disappointment was tempered by an understanding that Alicia had a somewhat cynical outlook on life, I, with the blush of summer still on my cheeks, sun-bleached hair still more blond than grayed, wanted her to be persuaded that the steep bowl of gray granite with its held, shimmering and twinkling blue lake was a reason for faith in something mightier than ourselves. I wanted her to see our tent, a tiny orange dot, almost lost in the excesses of that moonscape. Being there had been a holy experience. We were alone, almost as insignificant as the proverbial grain of sand at the beach; but we had made it there, we had been sheltered, and we had passed safely through.

◆ ◆ ◆ ◆ ◆

Fifteen million people go backpacking a year, with 2.2 million defined as enthusiasts — adults who camp at least a quarter-mile from a trailhead, at least nine times a year, according to a study by the Outdoor Recreation Coalition of America.

I'd love to be able to say that I have set some backpacking record; I haven't. But in this book, I have recorded the stories of three women who have. I had a great time talking with Irene Cline, who holds the record as the oldest woman to walk the entire Appalachian Trail. I also was thrilled to find the written accounts of the fascinating Emma Gatewood (1887-1973), who by all accounts was a feisty, determined woman. At the age of 67, Emma was the first woman to thru hike (hike the entire trail in one trip) the AT. And it was delightful to talk to Laurie Foot, who was the first woman over 45 to hike/bike both the southern and northern routes of the cross-country American Discovery Trail

I hope you will enjoy reading the profiles of Irene, Emma, and Laurie as well as those of the 30+ other women interviewed.

About The Writing of This Book

In 1996, Ralph and I did a wonderful — beautiful and not grueling — backpack over Piute Pass (in the Sierra, south of Mammoth Lakes). I reached the natural high that every hiker, runner, and backpacker wants to experience. My stride was perfect, my pack was part of me, and I felt like I could walk forever. It was sort of like Superman's, "able to leap tall buildings with a single bound," only it was *mountains* in front of me. It was while on that trip that I decided to write this book.

I wanted to write it because I was midway through my fifties and seeing it as a stage in my life offering increased opportunities for personal growth and change. Over were the earlier choices and challenges: college and relationships in my twenties and thirties, establishing and caring for my family during my thirties and forties. While I still had responsibilities, more often than not I could make decisions of how to spend my time and money based on my needs and interests. I was joining millions of others who had found mid-life an important juncture from outer-directed to inner-directed. While we in our fifties and sixties *are* part of the sandwich generation — caught between caring for children at home or in college and caring for elderly parents, we still have more freedom than ever before in the history of humankind.

We live longer; we live healthier. And those of us in those age groupings have taken notice that lifestyle choices in diet and exercise made earlier in our lives are helping us, or taking their toll, when we enter middle age. Though we have observed too many times that, "Life isn't fair," and seen friends and family members succumb to dreaded diseases even though they took exemplary care of themselves in regard to diet and exercise, our experience has shown us that our odds are better if we eat nutritious food and keep fit. We are likely to have more strength and stamina as we age. The cliché, "Use it or lose it," has never been more accurate. We've also noticed that our friends and acquaintances who have a hard time pushing away from the dinner table, and letting go of the remote controls, have now given up active sports in favor of spectator sports.

Every time my initial enthusiasm for this book project waned, the next woman I met and talked to would rekindle it. Though some of the interviews were the results of one friend referring me to another, most were obtained by my calling, writing, or e-mailing complete strangers. I expected rejections. I expected to have phones hung up on me or, at the very least, my requests to go unanswered. Instead what I received was an outpouring of stories and kindness. I received invitations to brunches, lunches, and teas and, incredibly, the opportunity to go on a llama trek in the High Sierra.

The message was clear — women were not only willing but also enthusiastic about sharing their found pleasures of the wilderness. After all these years of wanting to share my enjoyment of the outdoors with other women, it has been exciting to find a community of women who have common interests. Finding them has helped compensate for the fact that not everyone I care about will ever, or can ever, understand the appeal of being out in nature and challenging yourself in the wild.

This book is a dream come true on many different levels. Doing the research, walking the hundreds of miles, investigating the publishing process, and promoting the book so that it would end up in readers' hands has all been a learning, enriching, and rewarding experience for me.

I hope you'll enjoy reading my story, and the stories of the many fascinating women who've contributed to the tapestry that this book has become. No doubt you will find someone whose story strikes a chord because the women

I've interviewed are real people. The almost three dozen women, all in the prime of their lives, who have shared their stories about backpacking have provided insights into why they venture in the wilderness. We have here a collection of stories of strong, gutsy women who continue to challenge themselves and thereby, inspire other women.

Just as women who were older than I am were inspiring to me, it is exciting to consider that women my age can encourage younger ones. If older women have any question about their opportunity to become role models to girls and young women, the following poem might put those doubts to rest.

The Highest and the Deepest

Not the highest mountain or deepest sea

can ever keep you from reaching your goal.

Not the scariest nightmare nor worst of all days

shall make you go no more.

For as you get higher and higher

or go deeper and deeper,

you'll make it for sure, we both know...

by Desiree R. Abad

Desiree was a student in my fifth grade class for the school year 1999-2000. A year later, when she 12 and ready to enter middle school, she sent me the poem — written in response to hearing my backpacking and trekking plans for the summer after I retired.

Quick Profiles of Our Women
Backpackers

"No coward soul is mine,
No trembler in the world's storm-troubled sphere:
I see Heaven's glories shine,
And faith shines equal, arming me from fear."

Emily Bronte

Except for Jenny Jardine and Isabella L. Bird, the three dozen women I interviewed for this book ranged in age from late forties into the seventies. They're fairly evenly divided into two groups: those who started backpacking in their teens or twenties and those who started in their forties. These quick profiles are meant to introduce you to each of the women and to enable you to begin to see each woman as an individual with a unique life story.. At book's end, you will read about each in more depth. (Note: names are in alphabetical order first name first.)

Barbara P. grew up in Alamo, California, which is in an area of oak-studded rolling hills and grassland east of San Francisco. In the 1940s, when Barbara was a child, Alamo was sparsely populated; today it is still an area of great beauty, but luxury homes increasingly encroach on the natural surroundings. Barbara's family loved the outdoors, and was athletic, but they didn't camp and backpack.

Barbara's stories are of a San Francisco Bay Area group with whom she loves to backpack — six friends who have backpacked together for 27 years.

Betty Lennox at age 75 was still backpacking when I first interviewed her in 1997. Betty and Sandra (whose introduction comes later) have taken several wilderness trips together. In 2000, the two of them spent three weeks hiking from village-to-village in France's Provence region. In 2001, then 80, Betty traveled to Switzerland and spent her days hiking extensively in the Alps.

Carmen Borrmann was in her 70s at the time of her interview and still actively backpacking. She has backpacked since college, and is an accomplished backpacker who has done most of the trails in the Sierra.

Carol Messenger, with her husband Al (Adolphus), completed the Appalachian Trail in 1995, and continues to backpack. "I had wanted to do the AT since I was in fifth grade and learning how to read a map. I saw the red dotted line going all the way up the eastern US and thought 'I'm going to do that some day.'"

Carolyn Ebel, whose trail name is "Wild Oats," is not one to give up easily. She wrote, "Backpacking is not my thing — having suffered a broken back early in life. But, one of my strengths is convincing a partner to carry much of my pack weight." She *hikes* a lot, however, and has always enjoyed the outdoors. Because Carolyn was usually day hiking when she did the Appalachian Trail, she didn't need a tent or cooking gear. This enabled her to carry a lighter load than most backpackers. With only 15-20 pounds, she could hike an average of 15-17 miles a day on the

Appalachian, whereas most backpackers would do 10-12 miles.

Debbie Collins of Alameda, California is in her 50s. She enjoys exploring the remote regions of the Sierra, particularly the North Fork of the Kings River. Nowadays, she and her husband Bill enjoy hiking in a distance from busy campgrounds, establishing a base camp, and then having a lengthy stay near a wild river.

In her mid-twenties **Della Powell** met a friend of the family, a young man just out of college, who had hiked the Appalachian Trail. She added hiking the trail to her mental list of want-to-do "sometime." Little did she know that "sometime" would take a couple of decades, but when the hospital she worked for started to downsize in the '90s, Della saw "a glimmer of hope," and retired.

On Easter Sunday, March 30, 1997, at age 52, Della set out from Springer Mountain, Georgia to hike the 2,160 miles of the Appalachian Trail. She had never been backpacking before.

Doris Klein, of Vallejo, California, now in her 70s, has backpacked for 30 years, primarily in the Sierra Nevada,. With her backpacking group, the Jane Muirs, she has covered most of the trails of the Sierra and explored many rivers to their headwaters.

My conversations with **Elizabeth Wagner** focused on her camping experiences as a child, in the early 1930s, which provided interesting historical perspective. Elizabeth resides in Orinda, California.

Emma "Grandma" Gatewood (October 25, 1887–June 4, 1973). No book on important women who have backpacked would be complete without including her story. As Emma died in 1973, my information is gleaned from previously published materials. Emma "Grandma" Gatewood was the first woman to thru-hike the Appalachian Trail, and the eighth person to finish the thru-hike — at the age of 67.

Fran Smith of Moraga, California may be a "reluctant backpacker" by her own admission, but she's an amazing one. Ralph and I met Fran on the next to the last day of our 1998 Sequoia backpacking trip. Fran was 72 at the time. She, her husband Vic, and her daughter Melanie were taking a reststop on the trail to Hamilton Lake, and headed for Mt. Whitney. They subsequently were successful at completing their trip.

Frandee Johnson grew up in St. Louis, where the prevailing attitude was, "Why hike when you can drive?" But as a child she was introduced to the outdoors through family camping and canoe trips. While at Vassar, a friend happened to show Frandee a University of Colorado yearbook. Frandee was immediately captivated by the photos of Colorado's mountains. That led to the real beginning of her backpacking experiences. She enjoys hiking with her friends Jan Robertson, Joyce Gellhorn, and Alice Bradley (Weezy). The foursome has been hiking together in the mountains near Colorado for the last 20 years. (Introductions of Jan and Joyce will follow).

Grace Lohr, the "Llama Mama," works as an escrow officer in Bishop, California several months of the year but spends most of the summer in the Sierra. Year-round her llamas keep her active and busy; during her backpacking trips they provide companionship and carry heavy packs.

Irene "Tag Along" Cline retired from teaching in 1984, at 63, and took up backpacking. She doesn't miss teaching at all. "Retirement has been the best time," she says. Irene is the oldest known woman to complete the Appalachian Trail. Irene finished the AT in April 1998 — an eight year section hike. On most of the sections, her sister, Sharon "Trip Along" Bloodgood, accompanied her. Sharon, of Fond du Lac, Wisconsin, began her section hike in 1991 and completed it in July 1998 at age 58.

Isabella L. Bird (from her book of letters to her sister) was an extraordinary English horsewoman who came to the Rocky Mountains in the fall of 1873. With no previous experience mountaineering, she climbed Colorado's challenging Longs Peak (a "fourteener") only five years after it was first climbed. Her account, *A Lady's Life in the Rocky Mountains,* is a fascinating look at pioneer spirit and at the West — as it was 125 years ago.

Jan Robertson, at the age of 16, had her first backpacking experience with her family. The equipment was "Army surplus:" mummy bags, rucksacks, and pup tents. After she married, she and her husband moved to Missouri. As their children were growing, it was hiking for several years instead of backpacking. In 1963, Jan and her husband David moved to Boulder, Colorado. "Why live in Missouri?" she commented. "We both loved the mountains, and he was a rock-climbing instructor."

Jeannine Burk has always been intrigued with adventure travel. Growing up, there were always lots of travel books; Jeannine poured over Richard Halliburton's *Book of Travel.* She was captivated by his tales of adventure in the Himalayas and she dreamt about Shangri La. She was enthralled by Halliburton's descriptions of sacrificial wells near Cancun, Mexico; when she turned 18 and started traveling, these wells were the first place she went.

Jenny Jardine is the wife of Ray Jardine, who she met on the job. "When I went to work for Ray, I soon found out that he was planning to sail around the world — which totally intrigued me. Eventually I got up enough nerve to ask if I could go with him and he said, 'Yes.'" In 1982 they sailed from San Diego, California aboard his 41-foot ketch for a three and a half-year circumnavigation. Following that adventure, they spent several years completing major backpacking trips.

Most of **Joyce Gellhorn's** backpacking experiences have been in her home state of Colorado, but she has also explored Wyoming. At present, Joyce looks forward to more hikes to the Wind River or the Tetons and to the Southwest's Escalante.

Judy Valentine married a hiker; so as they raised their four children, Judy was a good sport and went hiking and camping. (She even consented to a 40-day car camping trip, which, not surprisingly, did not turn hiking and camping into preferred activities.) It was later that she discovered the pleasures of backpacking.

Kathryn Smick of Orinda, California was the first woman I interviewed. She was originally from Wisconsin. She knew nothing about backpacking until she came to California. When she decided to learn, she joined the Sierra Club and learned the basics, at age 46. She was 79 when we met in 1997.

Kathy Morey of Mammoth Lakes, California is not only an experienced backpacker, but also a knowledgeable writer. She is the author and co-author of several Wilderness Press guidebooks.

She favors trips in the Sierra Nevada. She prefers to be in the alpine area, above timberline. Mono Pass, Yosemite to Lyell Canyon, Deadman Canyon, Shepherd Pass, as well as the headwaters of Kern Canyon are favorite areas. She has also enjoyed trips to California's San Bernardino area and to the Hawaiian Islands (of which she writes extensively).

Laurie (Laurel Ibbotson Foot) Foot is the former President of the American Discovery Trail Society. Laurie and her husband (now deceased) hiked the Appalachian Trail in the early 1990s. Then, in 1997 and 1998, Laurie and Bill bicycled and backpacked the America Discovery Trail across the United States.

Marcyn Del Clements didn't go backpacking until after she met Rick. "When I met Rick, he told me about his backpacking trip with his friend, and about going camping with his parents and fly-fishing. I feel in love on the first date. I wanted to be a part of that life! After we were married, and had our two little girls, we did go backpacking together three summers. It was hard, but it was heaven. I was in very poor physical shape in those days. But I loved the backcountry, became fascinated with everything natural, and I was getting hooked on fly-fishing — although I probably spent 30 years untying knots."

Margaret Campbell grew up in Berkeley, California and was involved in Girl Scouts. She became interested in the outdoors as a child. An adventuresome nature seems to run in the family; Barbara remembers her grandfather telling compelling stories of his time as a sourdough in Alaska and her father recounting his adventures as a civil engineer in Columbia in the 1920s.

Marilyn Morris lives in the San Francisco Bay Area and is in the legal profession.

Sandra Nicholls is in her fifties. She has backpacked with Betty (previously introduced) on California's North Coast, in the Sierra Nevada, and from village-to-village in the Provence region of France.

Sharon Hanna started backpacking in Colorado when in college, and continued while working in the Rocky Mountains. Though at first she found it scary to go without her daddy, she gradually became more self-sufficient. When she married, she introduced her husband to backpacking. Later, she and a woman friend went to Europe where they spent eight months traveling with a tent, camp kit, and not much money.

Sis Curtis has always enjoyed the outdoors. Her family had a cabin at Silver Lake near Mt. Lassen, California and also went on camping trips. She has been an enthusiastic member of the Orinda Marching Mothers since joining them in the early '70s.

Stacie Hernandez of Crockett, California loves the outdoors, but finds job and family responsibilities keep her from going often. She looks forward to a time when she can return to the wilderness because she loves its beauty and fresh air.

Sylvelin Edgerton is a university research librarian. In 1988, she moved back from the East Coast to Santa Barbara, California where she now lives. Backpacking resumed with trips to the Sierra's Mineral King area — sometimes with Valerie (whose introduction follows).

Valerie Cooley became involved with the UCLA hiking and rock-climbing club, ("mountaineers," according to Sylvelin) and went with them on her first backpacking trip. That trip was to Havasu of the Grand Canyon; it remains one of her favorites because it was her first trip and because she was with the man who was to become her husband. But in some respects it was also a difficult trip — partly because her equipment was horrible by today's standards.

❖ ❖ ❖ ❖ ❖

Now that you've been introduced to the stars of this book, I hope you will enjoy reading their adventures and advice.

Part 1: Into the Wild – *Trail Tales*

Susan at Muir Hut, JMT,
Sierra Nevada

1
Physical , Mental, Spiritual:
This is Backpacking

"The reward of a thing well done, is to have done it."
Ralph Waldo Emerson in *The Over-Soul*

Some of the reasons women go backpacking are easily expressed — "the vistas," "the fresh air," "feeling good," "fun and camaraderie," "solitude." Other experiences seem to transcend mere language: those times when the three elements that comprise our wholeness — our mind, body, and spirit — are working beautifully together.

John Muir used the word *ecstasy* to describe his wilderness adventures. Will *you* feel ecstatic? Hard to predict, but if you are healthy, adequately provisioned, and on a well-chosen trail, your backpacking trip will undoubtedly be a fulfilling experience. And if you travel into the wilderness, allow enough time to let your daily cares drop away, and open up your senses, you likely will feel such moments of splendor.

Some women have asked me, "What is backpacking and how is it different from camping?" Simply defined, backpacking is carrying the food, clothing, and equipment you'll need to survive in the outdoors. It differs from camping because it usually involves hiking to a campsite some distance from a trailhead. It likely means cars, roads, picnic tables, flush toilets, and running water are left behind. Depending on the area, the overnight stays may be at established campsites with nearby outhouses, or they may be in a wilderness area where hikers can just throw out their sleeping bags anywhere they want — subject, or course, to area restrictions on proximity to bodies of water, to delicate meadows, to hiking trails, and so forth.

The distance you carry your supplies and the time you spend outside can be as individual as you are. Some people want to hike in two or three miles from the trailhead and set up housekeeping for two weeks. Many people hike four to six miles a day and set up a new camp at each day's end. And still others enjoy covering twenty miles of mountainous terrain a day as they pursue long-distance goals.

Age need not hold women back from backpacking. In fact, older women often have the mental attitude, the experience in dealing with logistics as well as emergencies, and the common sense to make great backpackers. The only criteria should be health and desire. It can be challenging — but we can choose how daring we want to be.

When I decided to go on my first backpack trip, it was primarily because I wanted to achieve a goal. I thought it would be fun. I thought it would impress people. And, it seemed possible. "Why not? I know how to walk," I told myself. I loved the outdoors. I didn't need any special training or education. Perhaps that is why I was so upset when my first attempt to put on the loaded backpack seemed like a disaster. What an idiot I was. I thought I was going to fall over backwards! I couldn't imagine actually moving with all that weight. I'd had no concept of how 35 pounds would feel.

And, I hate to admit it, but part of why I backpack is *still* to prove something. I want to prove to others as well as myself that I can do something that I really want to do that is really difficult. In most aspects of my life, I'm a very goal-oriented person who works better with deadlines and under pressure. I pride myself on completing tasks. So, when I'm backpacking, I want to cover miles, cross passes, get to the top of peaks. I get upset about other people being able to hike faster or longer than I do. I do not like the fact that I have physical limitations. And I will reject a hike that seems too tame or has too many layover days.

When I'm backpacking, there is a lot of time to think about these things and try to sort them out. During the long nights in the tent, there are additional hours to spend in contemplation. But I'm coming to terms with these traits that I have. If I did not have these goals or benchmarks, maybe I would never get off my duff and get moving.

The women I interviewed seemed to have accepted the fact that age can slow us down. And that is wise — because if you don't modify expectations of yourself as you age, you will probably have to deal with overwhelming frustration.

A close friend recently remarked, "And they do this for fun and recreation?" Another friend remarked, "I think this is one of those things that is better in the re-telling." I love to argue with them — yet both comments contain some truth. It is, to me, not always "fun," but it is fulfilling.

It's been a long time since backpacking was the sole domain of men; many of the women who make up this book have been exploring and learning about the joy and empowerment of the art of backpacking for the last 30 or 40 years.

Nowadays, with manufacturers making better and lighter equipment — often designed for women's different body shape — women in greater numbers are quite capable of refreshing themselves, or testing themselves, in our wildest regions.

Though each journey we take is unique and every story different, you will find many common threads and instances of shared values. Just as we recognize that our bodies are made up of mind, body, and soul — each affecting the other — the reasons why we backpack are intertwined into aspects of our mental, physical, and spiritual natures.

Body

Why should you do it? Like many other forms of physical activity, backpacking has both benefits and risks. But if you're a woman who likes to hike, who would like to take a break from the demands of everyday life and venture into forests, through verdant meadows, or onto mountain tops to see vistas accessible no other way, then backpacking is something you should look into. As with beginning any new fitness routine or strenuous sports activity, you should check with your doctor before you start. Further, a cardiac screening test is recommended for women over fifty and for those with such risk factors as: smoking, obesity, high cholesterol level, family history of coronary heart disease, diabetes, hyper-thyroidism, or lung disease.

Our physical strength generally starts to decline gradually in our thirties, and to decline more rapidly in our fifties. You probably know this intuitively — think about how many people you have observed who have showed these declines at various decades of their lives. However, with regular weight training, muscle strength can be increased 15 to 30 percent, whatever your age or how long you've been inactive. After your doctor has given you an okay, you'll want to start out gradually to improve your fitness. Starting slowly means you won't get sore or suffer setbacks from injuries. You can start at home simply. Use soup cans or two-pound weights to strengthen your arm muscles. Do daily calf stretches, stomach crunches, and wall sits. If you want to begin a walking program to train for backpacking, ease into it by gradually increasing the length and steepness of your route. Then put a five-pound bag of sugar or flour in a daypack and hike with that. It will only be a few weeks before you see improvement in your muscle strength and aerobic capacity.

✦ Doris

Doris reminisces, "In earlier times, we were on our way up Mt. Whitney and Ruth said, 'Doris, I can't thank you enough for inviting me to come.' I kind of said, 'Aw shucks,' and Ruth continued, 'I did so want to climb Mt. Whitney because my father had been to Mt. Whitney, and he had always talked about climbing it because in those days it was the highest in the United States.' She had lost him at Christmas time, and then in March she'd had a double mastectomy and she was taking Chemo — and her life was way down there. She was supposed to have one more treatment, but the doctor said the mountains would be good and she skipped the last treatment. She was so gallant; she never whined, or complained, she was just one of these magnificent types — like an old pioneer. She was so precious. Sometimes I sense these things, or see a need, or intuit them. And feel, 'Gosh backpacking would be good for them.' She didn't tell me any of this before we started; I don't [usually] like these kinds of surprises, but Ruth was an athlete, and I think she was the first one up the mountain."

Doris continued, "So many people think they can't; this is why I do all this. I just want to prove to them they can do these things. A lot of women are uncertain; they're not afraid, but uncertain. So I just am very positive about what a good thing this is..."

✦ Marilyn

Marilyn likes being out in nature, seeing what nature has to offer, and the sociability of being with a group of friends — but most of all, she likes the movement.

✦ Laurie

One of Laurie's favorite memories was of the preparatory conditioning she and Bill did for hiking the Appalachian Trail. "We were in Georgia towards the end of March. Although the snow was an inch deep, Bill assured me it was no problem." They set out. A blizzard hit, and before they were three miles into the hike, the snow was five inches deep. A snowplow crew came along, so they hitched a ride into town to wait out the blizzard. After a day's layover, they were again anxious to be on their way. They were the first to break the trail.

"It was absolutely beautiful — the snow cushioning the sound — pristine, wilderness... The snow was three and four feet deep. To continue on, we had to crawl through and over drifts. It was challenging, and at the end, a real accomplishment," said Laurie.

✦ Sharon

"I love the nest-building aspect of building a home in the woods. I want to backpack just far enough to be away from the crowds, then to set up a base camp from which to take a dayhike, go swimming, or read a book," said Sharon.

✦ Valerie

Valerie backpacks because she loves the scenery, the simplicity, and getting there under her own power. She doesn't consider herself at peak-bagger — desirous of climbing every mountain she sees — but she is motivated to reach the mountain passes and to get to as many pristine lakes as she can. "I'm a summit bagger and a lake bagger," she says. At the first sign of an alpine lake, she ponders when she can go skinny-dipping.

✦ Kathryn

As a child, Kathryn was not allowed to go swimming; she was encouraged to make doilies and other needlework pieces. For her, the reward of backpacking is the accomplishment itself. "That is especially important for a woman raised not to take risks," she said.

✦ Isabella

When Isabella arrived at Estes Park in the Colorado Rockies she was enraptured by her surroundings. She wrote, "The scenery is the most glorious I have ever seen, and is above us, around us, at the very door." She was delighted that everything was filled with "… grandeur, cheerfulness, health, enjoyment, novelty, freedom, etc. I have just dropped into the very place I have been seeking, but in everything it exceeds all my dreams. There is health in every breath of air; I am much better already, and get up to a seven o'clock breakfast without difficulty. It is quite comfortable — in the fashion that I like. I have a log cabin raised on six posts, all to myself, with a skunk's lair underneath it, and a small lake close to it. There is a frost every night, and all day it is cool enough for a roaring fire."

✦ Irene

Irene made an interesting comparison that those of us who are mothers can identify with: "It's [backpacking] just like having a baby, in that you forget how hard it is." She admits she is slower going up hills than her sister is, but she and Sharon wouldn't have it any other way than to stay within sight of each other. "At least at my age, I don't feel any need to prove myself," said Irene.

Her reasons for backpacking have not changed over time. "It's where I feel most alive, most *me* because it is so special. All you need is on your back, and you go out and have a wonderful sense of accomplishment. Your body is tired, so you sleep well. You can eat whatever you want and not gain weight."

✦ Fran

Not everyone loves the physical demands of backpacking. Fran had been on several trips, and hated them, when her daughter came up with the plan to climb Mt. Whitney. "I wasn't too keen on the idea, especially such a strenuous trip as 60 miles and climbing Mt. Whitney, in part because I have osteoporosis and walk slowly. But Melanie planned the trip, and launched a campaign. The doctor okayed the trip and Melanie sent an agenda in May. I did want to see Sequoia. It's so different from Yosemite, and I was interested in seeing first hand a portion of the 882 miles Melanie's husband is responsible for maintaining within the park."

Mind

From the moment that a decision is made to take a trip — whether an overnight one close to home or a several month trek from Canada to Mexico — careful planning and common sense are essential.

✦ Betty and Sandra

Betty and Sandra have backpacked together in areas between Lake Tahoe and Yosemite a few times, with their trips lasting up to ten days at a stretch. In some respects, they have different ideas about what makes a rewarding trip. Sandra carries a heavy pack because she wants more comforts — a book, perhaps a leather-bound notebook for writing poetry. Betty wants to carry 30 pounds or less. Sandra likes a daily swim — or at least a shower at the nearest trailhead when coming out. Betty dreams of a bath at home. But in other ways their shared interests make them quite compatible. They both love to read, write in their journals, and have a great meal at the end of the trip.

✦ Doris

Doris, who leads dozens of hikes each year explains, "Your learning curve is so great when you lead. When I bumble along on other people's trips, just hiking in the rear, gossiping, I don't have to decide anything."

She added, "Another thing, I like to share. When my kids were little, I used to think, 'I'm going to be so sad when they grow up and I can't show them a giraffe at the zoo, or a ladybug, or the view from the hill.' And then of course I found that other people with the same innocence as children and with the same intellectual curiosity are just as much fun as children. And so I've been very happy with my more recent children [the people who participate in her various hikes]."

Spirit

✦ Jenny

Jenny's reasons for backpacking haven't so much changed over the years as they have expanded. "We humans are so sight-oriented that we rely mostly on visuals: the scenery, the spectacular views. There is nothing wrong with that, but there is so much more going on in nature, so much more that the natural world has to teach us. To me, now, a hike in the woods — long or short — is a walk in 'oneness' with creation and the Creator. And to do this, I simply keep all my senses open. But it's more that just the five senses. It's a combination of the "animal sense," or primal self, and the spiritual self, and of course the more fleshly input of sight, taste, smell, feel, and sound."

✦ Judy

One summer Judy went backpacking with a group of women in the Sawtooth Mountains of Idaho. In some respects, the trip began much as a previous one had. They used pack animals to carry the food and tents. It was July.

But this time the weather was too volatile to go to the original destination. They had to set up a base camp and do day trips. But the most significant difference for Judy was that there were eight women instead of four. It seemed less rewarding; the sense of intimacy of the previous year's trip was missing. She also realized that eight people make a greater impact on the environment and that fewer animals had been seen because of the increased noise as people talked.

Still, the second trip had its own rewards. One day Judy and several of the other women were following a very narrow path along the ridge of a mountain of shale. At the crest, they came to the most challenging section. Though she could have turned back, Judy overcame her fear and continued on. When she did so, she experienced a profound sense of connectedness and accomplishment.

When she returned home, she had a physical setback — a rotator cuff injury. The physical therapist had Judy lie down with alternating ice and hot packs, and told her she wanted her to put the pack on for twenty minutes. Before the therapist left the room, she set a small bell on Judy's chest with instructions to ring the bell if she needed her. As Judy lay there, tears began to flow down her face, as somehow the cold, the heat, the bell, the sense of being nurtured, while strong, somehow triggered the memories of that narrow path along the crest of the mountain of shale. When the therapist returned and saw the tears that were still flowing, she was quite alarmed, and said, "If you were uncomfortable, you should have rung the bell for me," and Judy explained that the tears were from pleasure, not pain.

✦ Frandee

When I asked Frandee what keeps her going when it's difficult, she quipped, "Once I'm on the trail I don't have much choice, and that can be a real good motivator. I feel good afterwards, knowing that I did it, and that I can do it.

It's kind of like sex. If you haven't done it, one can't explain it. You can read a book about it, but it's not the same." Regarding backpacking..."Nothing else matters — it's the flowers, the beautiful scenery, the air..."

Nowadays she usually goes with her husband and they rate their hikes, not by distance or challenge, but how few people they see. This means that of necessity most of their hikes end up being off the beaten path: cross-country and above timberline.

A day to be relished is one when she can spend the day painting. When she reflects on the hikes they have taken, she finds that rarely do they stay in one place more than one day. Frandee is re-evaluating their schedule because she wants to include painting and the pleasure it provides.

She finds that her reasons for backpacking have changed over the years, that she is less competitive and more mellow. She says, "It's not necessary to prove anything anymore. We don't really want to get exhausted or do anything scary, but inevitably there are surprises — difficult passes, bad weather — because of the cross-country and elevation hiking we do."

✦ Joyce

Joyce's reasons for backpacking have changed somewhat. Like most of the women in this book, as she gets older she goes slower. She still wants to climb the high peaks, but that's not her sole motivation. She goes to take photos and to clear her head; she no longer feels she needs to prove herself.

Luckily for Joyce, after her husband lost interest in backpacking, her sons Ben and Vincent wanted to continue. But when the opportunity to trek the Alaskan Brooks Range with them presented itself, she initially had a lot of self-doubt. She didn't want to hold them back; she wanted them to be with her for the pleasure of her company, not out of duty. "Am I in good enough shape to traverse the 120 mile route that leads through tundra, willows, and rivers? Can I carry 45 pounds hour after hour, day after day for 17 days? What if one of us is injured or becomes sick?" she wondered. Still, it was the chance of a lifetime to make the trip with her sons; since they were all at crossroads in their lives. After the trip, she said, "It was a special trip to Alaska, especially when my sons admitted they enjoyed being with me."

She's enjoyed two other trips to Alaska. One was to Denali National Park, where Mt. McKinley lived up to its reputation of hiding behind clouds most of the time. [McKinley, like many large mountains, creates its own weather]. Joyce, her son, and a friend of his spent a week backpacking, mostly in the rain, and didn't see the peak in all that time. Finally on the last day, they were rewarded with the spectacular sight of the mountain's peak from Wonder Lake.

✦ Doris

Doris and her friends photograph their trips, and as she pours over them later, her excitement is rekindled. "I was determined to climb some before our layover day. We feel so good; first we see white columbine, and that's 11,000 feet. We find sky pilot at about 12,000 to 13,000 feet. We're going up and up, rock by rock, that's the Owens Valley, you can see how rocky it is. There are two of us, a clump of black rock, and the lake. This is Mather Pass. That seemed like such a triumph. This is the Bench Lake where we stayed the next night, and our catch of fish. We've done Split Mountain at 14,007 feet."

Doris recommends Steve Roper's books. "He has a route from Kings' Canyon to Matterhorn above timberline. Once in a while he drops down to get certain places on the John Muir Trail, but basically it's a cross country route, and so sometimes we call ourselves the 'Roper Rooters' because we have done a lot of his routes. Not all 170 miles — some were just too difficult — but I find it necessary to have a goal of some sort. One was the John Muir Trail. When that was over, I kind of said 'Duh, what'll I do now, just go up and wander around?' And then another carrot in front of our nose was to explore the headwaters of everything down that way. So we explored up to the final cirque, where the snowmelt started a stream. And, oh, that is glorious! You don't see a human being for days at a time; it's so pristine.

"Well, it's the altitude; it's so incredibly beautiful up there. And so challenging, those Roper routes — there's some of those we don't go on because I know if he says it's dangerous, then it's dangerous. He's a mountaineer and he writes for mountaineers. Now there's Winnett, he writes for the multitudes. If he says it's dangerous, we find it a piece of cake — just because we're good mountaineers. We know how to handle ourselves. At least, knock on wood, we've never had any accidents. Joanne twisted her ankle on the way up through Bubb's Creek from Kearsarge to Whitney, and she walked 40 miles with a sprained ankle. Every time we'd come to a nice cold brook, she'd stick it in and ice it and say, 'Isn't it wonderful that I wasn't really hurt,' and then she'd lace her boot on. But it was a point of no return; it was as far to go back, and she wanted to do Mt. Whitney, and so she did."

Doris favors being surrounded by granite — above timberline. "I really like the wide open spaces, so I'm not that fond of going through the forest. People think I'm peculiar, and that I don't like trees. I love trees, but I want to see the grand vista…"

✦ Jenny

"Every moment out in nature is a special moment. There is always something intriguing or beautiful to be investigated or enjoyed, even in the most mundane terrain. When I hike,

I do not plod along with my mind 100 miles away; my senses and my spirit are in close contact with the ebb and flow of my surroundings. It is possible to reach a point — and Ray and I do this almost constantly when we hike — where you become 'one' with your surroundings... Your footfalls are light and almost noiseless. Your body flows along effortlessly. Your spirit reaches out and meshes with those of the surrounding earth. You notice the chickadees no longer dash away as you approach. The wind in the trees is no longer just a sound of rustling leaves, but a song that is easily understood. And when you approach a herd of elk, they do not stampede away in terror; instead they quietly acknowledge you and return to their browsing."

✦ Della

Although Della is convinced she came away from the Appalachian Trail unchanged, she did discover some important things. "I found that people are kinder than I had previously thought. I saw people help and share when there was little to share." She observed that people, including herself, would go to great lengths to help each other.

"But still, I hated hitchhiking. I figured if there was any way to get killed, that was it. This was in spite of having only positive experiences doing it." One day, she felt she had no choice; she needed provisions. She headed for the road to town. "The wind was blowing 25-35 mph. I saw an elderly man sitting on a rock near the trail entrance, going in. 'You can take my truck to get what you need,' he offered. She borrowed his truck and returned it without mishap.

✦ Carol

"I have no difficulty in naming the pleasures and rewards that we found backpacking. Number one is that we made so many friends, people that we continue to correspond with and get together with." Carol and Al joined the Keystone Trail organization in Pennsylvania, not because they live there, but because they enjoy visiting and hiking with many people they met from that state. How many people they met on the trail depended on where they hiked and what season it was. In New York in the summer, people were rarely out of sight. On other sections of the Appalachian Trail, perhaps they would see five people in two weeks. "It was extremely affirming to find that people you didn't even know would generously give up their metered-out food or water to help you. There was not a bad one in the bunch," said Carol.

✦ Carolyn

"I managed to do the Appalachian Trail day-hiking—except for five days in the Hundred Mile Wilderness [of Maine]. About one-third was done alone, constantly looking for possibilities for shuttles and sleeping in hostels and hiker hotels.

"It was the venture of a lifetime. I was rewarded by the experience of seeing all of the Appalachian Trail, by being on the trail, by learning the geography of the 14 states it goes through, and by making friends up and down the states. The trail is a network; every small town has people who form a tremendous support system. For example, in Maine, there is a spot where supporters of the trail keep a cooler full of Cokes for hikers and backpackers.

"One time I was hiking in Virginia. A man had given me a ride to the starting point of my day hike to Bald Mountain. During the day a terrible lightning storm came up. So he drove to the end point — where my car was parked — and waited to be sure that I arrived okay.

"In another instance I was hiking in Maine and it started to rain. The temperature dropped quickly. I didn't stop and change into dry clothes soon enough; I was close to hypothermia. Finally, I did take shelter and a fellow hiker got me some hot tea quickly. His quick response and kindness may have saved my life."

Along the way Carolyn and a friend found many ways to return favors they received, but one of her favorite things to do was to help backpackers hiking in the more isolated sections of Maine. She would meet people on the trail who were headed north, take "orders" for food, hike out to buy some goodies, and then drive ahead to meet them again with the potato chips or whatever else they had been craving.

✦ Betty and Sandra

Betty and Sandra had a successful backpack trip in 1993, with a bonus provided by someone they met as they were beginning their trip. A man, hiking solo, quickly out-distanced them. But before he set out each day, he would prepare a small pile of kindling for their evening campfire, and leave a friendly note.

✦ Debbie

"Backpacking for me is healing. I like being away from phones and people." For Debbie, backpacking is an ideal way to get to special places, view natural systems, and spend time with the river. Unlike some of the women in this book, it's not about covering miles, and finding new places, but the opportunity to return to special, sacred places. It's a time to eat less, activate the unconscious. Debbie's art finds inspiration in nature — she likes to paint, work with clay, and create collages. Her thought, "We have the ability to have natural wisdom if we're quiet long enough."

✦ Isabella

Of her climb of Longs Peak in Colorado, which Isabella called the "American Matterhorn," she wrote, "... had I known that the ascent was a real mountaineering feat I should not have felt the slightest ambition to perform it.

"At the 'Notch' the real business of the ascent began. Two thousand feet of solid rock towered above us, four thousand feet of broken rock shelved precipitously below; smooth granite ribs, with barely foothold, stood out here and there; melted snow refrozen several times, presented a more serious obstacle; many of the rocks were loose, and tumbled down when touched. To me it was a time of extreme terror.

"My fatigue, giddiness, and pain from bruised ankles, and arms half pulled out of the sockets, were so great that I should never have got halfway had not 'Jim,' dragged me along with a patience and skill, and withal a determination that I should ascend the Peak, which never failed.

"Above, the Peak looks nearly vertical for 400 feet; and below, the most tremendous precipice I have ever seen descends in one unbroken fall." "...But there, and on the final, and, to my thinking, the worst part of the climb, one slip, and a breathing, thinking, human being would lie 3,000 feet below, a shapeless, bloody heap!" "...Scaling, not climbing, is the correct term for this last ascent. It took one hour to accomplish 500 feet, pausing for breath every minute or two. The only foothold was in narrow cracks or on minute projections on the granite. To get a toe in these cracks, or here and there on a scarcely obvious projection, while crawling on hands and knees, all the while tortured with thirst and gasping and struggling for breath, this was the climb; but at last the Peak was won.

"From the summit were seen in unrivalled combination all the views which had rejoiced our eyes during the ascent. It was something at last to stand upon the storm rent crown of this lonely sentinel of the Rocky Range, on one of the mightiest of the vertebrae of the backbone of the North American continent, and to see the waters start for both oceans. Uplifted above love and hate and storms of passion, calm amidst the eternal silences, fanned by zephyrs and bathed in living blue, peace rested for that one bright day on the peak…"

Of the descent, Isabella wrote: "Sometimes I drew myself up on hands and knees, sometimes crawled; sometimes 'Jim' [her companion] pulled me up by my arms or a lariat, and sometimes I stood on his shoulders, or he made steps for me of his feet and hands, but at six we stood on the 'Notch' in the splendor of the sinking sun, all color deepening, all peaks glorifying, all shadows purpling, all peril past."

Ah — Isabella Bird! That Victorian lady who traveled all over the world because she was sickly.

✦ Kathy

Kathy's feelings about backpacking have not changed a great deal over the 25 years she's been going, but as many of her miles are part of her job as the author of several trail guides, where she goes is often dictated by duty. Still, each trip brings a sense of exhilaration, freedom, and escape from the everyday world. "The landscapes, the experience is… inexpressible." "I've been where the dragons live," is voiced with a reverent tone.

✦ Marcy

Marcy's reasons for backpacking have been constant. "I love the mountains; above the trees, the higher I go, the more I like it." That is not to say she thinks it is easy. "It's never easy, but the first day is awful. The other days are less awful, but I go one step at a time." On her 1999 trip her hip bothered her, but she was carrying a lot of weight — 56 pounds at the start. She knew her large notebook was a luxury, but even without bulky items she was lugging a lot of weight that made every step an effort. Others they passed on the Pacific Crest Trail had 30-35 pounds, but the others were using food drops, which of course cut the average weight. She and Dottie did some fishing, but not enough to supplement their freeze-dried fare. "Thinking about how I keep going when it gets tough, one thing comes to mind: I write poetry in my head. Then, when it has been rattling around and feels complete, we have to stop so I can write it down. The composing makes the time go and the stopping is welcome."

✦ Irene

In 1985, when Irene Cline was 64, she toured with a group to Isle Royale National Park in Michigan, where they stayed at the lodge. "Each day as I hiked about five miles, then had to turn and hike back to the lodge, I was jealous of those people with backpacks who could continue hiking and camp at night. My decision was made to do that, too. In 1987, 1988, and 1990, I did. Isle Royale remains one of my favorite places. I hope to go there again."

I always feel a sense of power as well as a sense of humility in the wilderness. Backpacking allows me to feel connected to the universe. I love being able to get myself to granite peaks, to meadows filled with wildflowers, and to creeks and streams gurgling down mountainsides. The beauty of the outdoors — from the kaleidoscope of flowers to the breathtakingly beautiful craggy mountains — rewards me. I have time to experience wonder: "How extraordinary that such a delicate plant can survive the harsh nine months of winter." "What an amazing thing that the pika, with his cute round rodent ears, is up here at 12,000 feet surviving on the seeds of the scant vegetation." Much of what I experience while traveling through these alpine regions is unattainable by any other means. Nature is always changing; miracles occur on every side.

Even though I worry about bears, fording rivers, and impending rain, I find backpacking the time I am closest to being self-reliant. The world of backpacking is primitive, elemental, and real. Life in the city is good too, but being part of a community fosters inter-dependence. We have roles; we compartmentalize and specialize. In the wilderness, Ralph and I have to make our own way.

In addition, it's a tremendous relief to get away from the news for a week or so. Most of what we hear from the media is bad news. And because the bad is presented all out of proportion to the good, it's a constant challenge to sort through what's presented and keep one's perspective. In the wilderness I have few distractions. I am aware of my moods and my body, and my husband's. I have to solve the challenges of the trip — be they weather, bugs, bigger creatures, or trail conditions.

Epiphany: "an intuitive grasp of reality through something (as an event) usually simple and striking." One of my life-changing moments came as I was walking along a dirt road in Alaska's Denali National Park. At 45, I was a re-entry student getting my teaching credential. Because I had the summer off, I was able to work in the park. It was all for the adventure since the pay was minimal. And as I walked alone up the dirt road through the forest of sky-high conifers, the thought hit me, "I can do this, I can go anywhere in the world I want if I'm willing to travel on the cheap." I felt empowered; weight was lifted…

That is how I feel when backpacking is going well. It is nothing short of awesome to stand on a ridge and look back at what your own two feet — and a lot of sweat and labor — have gained you. You'll see a forest far below you in the valley where you began your day. You'll see the creek you struggled to cross and re-cross. Ahead, you'll see a pass and anticipate that lunch will be soon, if only you can catch your breath. There's an exhilaration that comes — usually after a couple of days of altitude and pack adjustment — when you and the trail are well matched, when you're taking long strides and feel like you could walk forever.

2
We Are Ready to Go:
First Trips

"A thousand mile journey begins with one step."
Chinese philosopher Lao Tse

My first backpacking trip was in 1989, just four months after Ralph and I were married. I was 48. I had met Ralph two winters before — on a car camping trip to Baja California with the Sierra Club. As we got to know each other, I discovered that he had been a backpacker and had climbed Mt. Whitney. Immediately I knew what I wanted to do — climb that mountain. Though I had never backpacked, I had hiked a great deal, so I was convinced I was capable. It helped that we knew that Whitney in the summer is a "walk-up," not a mountain climbing expedition.

We got together our supplies. I borrowed my sister-in-law Joyce's backpack. At home, we loaded the pack and I awkwardly struggled to get it on my shoulders. I straightened up; I had never lifted anything so heavy. It was so stiff and unyielding I could hardly move. I was supposed to carry this, walk with this, and go up mountains with it? I couldn't believe it.

It was a seven-hour drive from our home in the San Francisco Bay Area to Independence, California. We stopped in town so we could get "take-out" for eating when we reached the campground. Neither of us had eaten Kentucky Fried Chicken for years, but it seemed important to have a last taste of civilization.

At Onion Valley's trailhead, we set up camp among the quaking aspen. Ralph walked down bright and early the next morning to the ranger's outpost because there was a quota system in place; it was first come, first served for unreserved permits. We were lucky in two respects: we were setting out for Whitney on a Sunday whereas the "kids" who came up to do Whitney from Whitney Portal (the east side approach) on the weekend were already enroute. Secondly, we were starting north of Whitney and would reach the mountain from the west side several days later. Still and all, if getting a permit had been up to me (not a morning person), it's hard to know if we would have gotten the requisite pass.

We fixed our breakfast, locked the car, and shouldered our packs. And all I could think was, "Everything around me is higher than I am now." The trail went up, up, and up some more, headed towards Kearsarge Pass. It was August and the weather was good — clear, with neither rain nor wind.

We found a comfortable enough campsite. We were above timberline, which in this case meant that there were only a few trees, none much taller than we were. Certainly there was no place to hang our food that wasn't a joke to any self-respecting bear. But Ralph, who grew up in national parks because his father had been a ranger in Yellowstone and Sequoia, didn't see the lack of trees as a problem. "Bears don't come above timberline," he assured me. We made camp, ate dinner, leaned our packs against a nearby granite slab, and went to bed.

It was the middle of the night when we were awakened by the sounds of something large moving just outside our shelter. We heard the sounds of a pack being dragged away. We didn't have to actually see it to know that a bear was out there. We tried to spot it, but the amount that we could see with our penlights was minimal.

My pack was missing. Ralph's pack was now leaning against a nearby log; in disarray. Obviously we had interrupted the bear taking it. The rustling sounds continued. We banged cups against pans.

It was quiet, but we knew the bear was nearby. I lay in my sleeping bag terrified — my body rigid and quivering with tension, my jaw clenched so hard I could hardly speak. Ralph, after trying to calm me by telling me (once again, I might add) that black bears weren't going to hurt us, that it was only our food the bear was after, settled back into his bag.

Occasional scrapping and thumping sounds reminded us that our buddy was not far away. Gradually the sounds of the bear diminished and all was still. We looked around. We could see that my pack was some 20 feet away, but we knew that retrieving it in the darkness, with the bear in the vicinity, was not a wise choice. Ralph announced that we would survey the damage in the morning, rolled over, and went to sleep.

For what seemed like hours, I couldn't go to sleep. I heard the bear return and then its rustling and scratching sounds off and on throughout the night. When daylight came, we inspected my torn pack and inventoried our remaining food. Gone was the Chunky chocolate bar and the salami and cheese, which I had thought would be great treats for exhausted hikers at the end of the first challenging days. Tooth and nail marks indicated where the bear had ripped into the packets of dry milk, cereal, and soup mix.

However, Ralph's pack was intact and with it, most of our freeze-dried foods. We decided that we had enough left to continue our trip. As the day progressed and we hiked along, we passed a few people who were coming off the trail. After we traded stories, they gave us some of their leftover food. One of the men offered us canned food that his wife had packed for him. We declined; we didn't want the heavy weight either.

We continued slogging along. Ralph (as was to be repeated on several subsequent trips) suffered from sinus headaches from the altitude. Even with that, I could hardly keep up with him. Our methods for going uphill were very different — sort of like the tortoise and the hare. It drove me crazy that he could move much faster than I could. He'd get farther and farther ahead of me, then sit down on what seemed to be the only level perch in the shade and wait for me. When I finally managed to catch up to where he was, he would be rested and ready to go. Luckily for both of us, my husband can listen to a lot of complaining and remain unperturbed.

Our goal for the third trail night was to get over Forester Pass — at 13,180 feet, the highest point of the Pacific Crest Trail — and into the valley beyond. But as afternoon wore on, the clouds gathered, it began to howl and rain, and it became clear we could not get over the pass, much less down the lengthy switchback trail on the other side. Soon we were in the midst of the storm, with great flashes of lightning, crashes of thunder. There were absolutely no trees to provide shelter. We were the tallest things in the immediate area — and we were carrying metal packs. I considered lying down on the trail, but how long would we need to lie there in the rain? We decided to make camp alongside the trail.

I watched as Ralph tried to fasten down the tarp (which we carried instead of a tent). With the wind trying to whip the cover out of his hands and the rain pelting us, it seemed to take forever for him to untie the knots in the rope.

Then we discussed the food and bears. Clearly we no longer believed that bears didn't come above timberline. Now Ralph had another plan. He was going to put all the food in a bag and sleep on it. I told him he was crazy. He tried to assure me that his plan would work because bears didn't really want to tangle with people.

It was cold and windy. This was an impossible situation. I walked a few feet away, turned my back on him and our camp, and muttered, "Divorce, divorce, divorce!" I was certain I had read somewhere that saying the words three times was sufficient to make it happen.

We finally compromised; Ralph put the food in a cache of rocks. I still wasn't completely satisfied with the plan; it seemed to me that a bear was at least as strong as Ralph was. "What was to keep the bear from digging our food out of the cache?" I wondered. But we set our pots and pans inside the shelter to use as noisemakers, made a mound of rocks to throw at any predator, and tried to go to sleep.

We had no more bear problems that night, or any other, for that matter. The next morning we climbed to the pass and looked down with amazement at the descending trail. What lay ahead was a couple of miles of narrow switchbacks, totally exposed to the elements, with no easy place of shelter. Even though I look back now and think that we were lucky to have escaped hypothermia and lightning, we were actually safer where we holed up than if we had pushed on another quarter mile and gained the pass.

The trip continued free of any further calamities and improved day by day. After the first couple of days, my backpack began to feel like part of me — a somewhat awkward me, but we had become as one. I had gained in confidence, in that my feared knee problems had not materialized — and the mountains were beautiful. Ralph seemed to love nothing more than jumping out of his sleeping bag when it was freezing cold to make coffee for himself and to bring tea to me as I huddled in my warm bag until the last minute.

After nearly a week of seeing only a couple of people a day, we approached the final spur trail that would take us to the summit of Mt. Whitney. It was a busy crossroads. Long distance trekkers from the west (such as us) met up with the weekend climbers coming up from the east. We took a break and chatted with people. We were advised to leave our heavy packs at the crossroads while we made the round-trip to the top of Whitney. We heard about marmots; several people had stories about them chewing holes in backpacks to find food. The most sobering tale was of a marmot chewing through a car's emergency brake cable while the car was parked at the trailhead.

The desire to lighten our loads won out over our concern that we would return to find holes in our packs. We left them behind, grabbed our water bottles and lunches, and finished our climb. When we reached the peak, we encountered a couple of dozen people already there. Since it was a relatively warm day, people were sitting and lying on the rocks to pick up the rays. Others were taking a lunch break or using the outhouse — which sat off to one side of the rather broad summit and was completely open on one side, affording grand vistas to the west as one did one's business.

We ran into one fellow backpacker who was digging in his pack for lunch and came up with a giant roll of twine — about 12 inches in diameter. We asked why he would have packed anything that heavy and useless in his pack. It turned out to be part of a long-running joke. Through the years, he and a friend had managed to stick each other with this burden numerous times. The requirement was to bring it back and then catch the other with it. In this case, she had planted it in the crotch of a tree near the beginning of his trek, and he was obligated by their unwritten rules to pick it up and carry it with him. One time she had unwound the roll through rooms, hallways, and floors of the office building where he worked.

After our half-hour stay on the summit, we descended the east side of the mountain. This was my first experience with such a lengthy and rapid descent — from Whitney's almost 14,500 feet to Whitney Portal's 8,500 feet. The first 1,900 feet had more than 100 switchbacks. Long stretches of the trail consisted of loose, large rocks blasted apart by dynamite when the trail was built. I found that last downhill never-ending, probably because it seemed anti-climatic, and because it was just the kind of trail where I had to watch every single step lest I twist my ankle or fall.

The lower portion of the trail became less steep. Its surface was dirt; it was a relief to be able to walk normally. We descended into groves of pines and firs and passed a small stream. Almost to the parking lot, we encountered my in-laws, both then in their late 70's, who were waiting with fresh fruit, juice, and hugs and kisses. My mother-in-law appeared totally unconcerned about Ralph. It was me she wanted to be sure had survived unscathed.

My first stop in town had to be at a novelty shop to buy an "I climbed Mt. Whitney, 14,496'" tee shirt. Then my in-laws treated us to hamburgers in nearby Lone Pine before shuttling us north to our car at Onion Valley's trailhead.

Looking back, I see that I was somewhat of an unknown, if not a liability. I had injured my knees skiing the previous year, and every time we went for a hike with any steep downhill, I experienced a great deal of pain. I don't know why Ralph took me. Perhaps he knew I wouldn't have taken "no" for an answer. I was determined to crawl up that mountain if that's what it took. Since that time we have managed to go on at least a one-week trip in the Sierra every year but one.

✦ Emma

In 1954 Emma Gatewood, at the age of 67, started out to hike the entire Appalachian Trail. She had recently read a 1949 National Geographic article that intrigued her. She set out with the vision of a quiet, lovely hike through the deciduous woods of the Appalachians.

Her first attempt was highly amateurish and everything went wrong. She started in northern Maine one July morning and climbed Mt. Katahdin that same day. Within 20 miles she got lost. She searched for the trail the next day, and, not finding it, lit a fire to signal for help. A search plane missed the signal. The next day she bathed in a pond. While getting out she managed to step on, and break, her glasses. The day after that, she ran out of food. Late that day, she stumbled onto another lake, Rainbow, and found the search plane pilots playing horseshoes. They had given up on her but were glad to drive her to the town of Millinocket. She took the bus back to her hometown in southern Ohio.

The next year Emma decided to go from south to north to take advantage of the seasons. Also, she hoped the blackflies of Maine that had plagued her on the first trip would be gone by the time she got there; she figured it would be so cold "their tails would freeze off." On May 3, 1955, Emma set out from the southern end of the trail, Mt. Oglethorpe, Georgia.

During the 1955 trip and subsequent Appalachian trips, Emma usually avoided shelters and camped out. She found that the huts were generally in disrepair — burned down, blown over, or dirty. She chose to sleep outdoors and also thought that it might be safer for a woman traveling alone. She was inventive: when it was cold she heated rocks to warm her bedding, when the ground was uncomfortably hard she stuffed her denim bag with leaves. Sometimes she took shelter under or on top of picnic tables.

At that time the trail crossed a lot of private property. She became friends with many along the way — farmers, vacationers, and rangers. They enjoyed her company and found her accomplishments inspiring. She often relied on their generosity and appreciated invitations for a meal or an overnight stay.

On her first thru hike, she wore out four pairs of canvas-topped shoes and three pairs of sneakers. At that time equipment was not designed for women. She found that hiking boots bothered her bunions and gave her blisters.

By the time she reached Virginia she had become something of a celebrity. Her venture was widely followed by the press — which sometimes surprised Emma as she saw herself as an ordinary farm woman. "But," she told reporters, "I will finish the trail unless I break something." She promised to sing "America, the Beautiful" when she reached the northern terminus, Mt. Katahdin, and she did.

When she finished the hike in Maine, she appeared on the *Today Show* and *The Jack Smith Show* (NBC). An outspoken woman, she vehemently expressed her complaints about the trail: it went straight up and over the top of the highest mountains, it was littered with fallen trees never removed, it had burnt areas where the signs were not replaced, and it had washed out areas never reconstructed. "This is a nightmare," she concluded. She commented that she never would have begun the hike if she'd known how difficult it was. But once she had started, she said, she had been determined to finish.

✦ Irene

It's common that initial backpacking trips are filled with mishaps. Irene Cline describes her first backpack trip as a disaster. "At that time I lived in Indiana. I recruited a friend, Betty, who said she'd backpack with me. We had chosen the 30-mile Adventure Trail in Wyandotte Woods. All winter we researched, read, and shopped to get ready. After several day hikes with packs we thought we were ready. We thought we'd avoided the mistakes the books said new backpackers usually made. Of course, we made them all, adding a few of our own.

"We hiked in six miles to our first campsite. Because we were using the wrong section map we got there late. Darkness was approaching and we had all these new chores. We were frantic. Finally we got to bed and we decided to make the next day a layover day.

"The next day we did a day hike, and we discovered we were only a quarter-mile from the road, which was only a mile from my van. Clearly our map reading skills needed improving. The next morning we awakened to experience our first rainy morning. We made the decision to leave our gear, hike to the van, and come back for our belongings. End of first backpack — and the conclusion, 'We needed help.'"

✦ Carol

Carol and Al's first backpacking stint was on the Appalachian Trail in 1987; she was 49. They got off to an uncertain start. "We needed a sport we could share, so we decided to try backpacking. We went to an outfitter who sold us many dollars worth of equipment and gave us more valuable advice than we could pay for. The only trail book that our outfitter had in stock was one starting at Damascus, Virginia, so that's where we started after maybe two miles total practice here in flat Ohio.

"We almost died the first few days. We had never drunk water from springs, rivers, or ponds. In Cleveland one never drinks any water except from a faucet — and then you can't be sure! At our first spring, water was running over some rocks. Al exclaimed that our friends drink water 'on the rocks,' not 'off the rocks!' But by the end of the first ten days, we were pretty much hooked."

✦ Marching Mothers

The Marching Mothers group of Orinda, California, dates back to 1969 — and enjoys a successful and interesting history. While on a walk one day, four friends who played tennis, Marilyn (Manny) Marquis, Lu Dettmer, Pat Gerdsen, and Carmen Borrmann, decided that going backpacking together would be fun. On the first trip they took two daughters and a daughter's friend.

Carmen, who has backpacked since college, is an accomplished backpacker and has done most of the trails in the Sierra. She reflects on the group's first venture, "We were unprepared for the trip, but our problems were minor. We didn't have tents and had to scramble to rig up a plastic cover when rain began. There weren't sunscreens available, so [we ended up with] reddened skins, and the scarcity of fallen wood made a handful of twigs [our] 'firewood.'"

It was a good trip but when they noticed that two groups were forming — with the daughters going off on their own with the best food — they decided that next time they would go on their own.

The following year three of the original mothers, Manny, Lu, and Carmen, were joined by five other women for a Sierra trip over Kearsarge Pass and into Kings Canyon. They spent more than a week exploring, hiking, fishing, and swimming. Then two of the group hiked back out the more arduous Kearsarge route, returned to the cars, and drove several hours to the west side of the mountains to pick up the remainder of the group. This allowed the six others to pack out downstream and see more new territory.

✦ Kathy

"After a half mile of uphill, I thought I would die," says Kathy of her first backpacking experience. "In retrospect, I carried little and had lots of help. But when we reached a clearing and viewed the blue sky, the stands of trees, and the mountains around me, I had an epiphany — my life was changed." She joined a ski club, started to organize hikes, and, as she wanted to stay out longer, often went alone.

✦ Kathryn

On her Human Potential trip in 1969, Kathryn had maps but, nevertheless, managed to miss a turnoff at 9,000 feet. She studied her map more closely. "If I climb up these rocks, I should get back where I want to be," she thought. She proceeded to scramble up the exposed rock, but it wasn't where she "wanted to be." She reached the point where she was so panicky about being lost that the sudden appearance of a buck frightened her. Fatigue magnified her fears. Finally, she managed to calm herself down, take stock and continue. She came to Rock Island which, though still not where she was supposed to be, was at least indicated on her map. From that point, she was able to complete her hike in safety.

When Kathryn got back to work, she posted a sign: "FOR SALE, BACKPACK." There weren't any takers. Kathryn had second thoughts; in spite of that problematical start, she resumed backpacking and continued taking week-long trips almost every year for another 30 years.

✦ Valerie

After Valerie became involved with the UCLA hiking and rock-climbing club, she went with them on her first backpacking trip. That trip to Havasu in the Grand Canyon remains one of her favorites because it was her first, and because she was with the man who was to become her husband. Valerie added, "It was also a difficult trip in some ways because my equipment was horrible by today's standards."

✦ Jenny

Finally, there are those whose accomplishments make them legends in their own time. Jenny and Ray Jardine were experienced outdoor adventurers when they embarked on their first major backpacking trip together. They had just finished sailing around the world.

"Ray and I returned to San Diego aboard the sailboat in 1985. This was after our three-plus year circumnavigation. We really felt a need to spend a length of time on terra firma, to reconnect to the land and to spend some quality time in the mountains. It was about that same time when we happened upon Peter Green's book, A Pacific Crest Odyssey, and immediately knew this was what we wanted and needed to do. Ten months later, in 1987, we started the hike."

This was their first hike of the Pacific Crest Trail (PCT) — traveling the most popular direction — south to north.

JoAnne Dupper, Doris Klein, Doris Wiskerson
Jerrye Wharton and Roni Dodson
The Jane Muirs at Seven Gables in the Sierra Nevada, 1990

3
Maybe This Will Work Out after All:
The Adventures Continue

"Well done is better than well said."

Benjamin Franklin

✦ Debbie

Debbie had a frightening experience that gave her an even greater respect for natural forces. She and Bill were camped on the Havasupi Reservation near the Grand Canyon. It was a beautiful site with clear blue skies. They set up their tent near the crystal clear water and dozed off.

Debbie stirred when it began to sprinkle. "I hear water," she said to Bill.

But he didn't take it too seriously because the day was so pleasantly warm. Soon, the river was gray and swollen, and people's camping gear from upstream was floating by. Debbie and Bill grabbed their tent and moved to high ground.

It was four days before the water again ran clear. They had nine miles further to travel in the canyon, and it was not until the end of the trail that they were able to go up and out.

✦ Kathryn

Even though Kathryn's first trip had been frightening enough to make her consider giving up backpacking and selling her pack, the intrigue of backpacking remained. That's not to say that subsequent trips were without challenges.

One year it was a sandstorm severe enough to cause many campers to flee the winds. Another time it was an unseasonably cold Labor Day when her sleeping bag zipper broke, and it was only her dog's warmth that kept her warm enough in her bag. Still another time, it was a severe and frightening lightning storm which was accompanied by a heavy downpour that started to leak into their untreated tent.

✦ Betty and Sandra

Those who have backpacked in the Sierra know many of its delights — glaciated mountains and alpine flowers — but also its risks — summer thunderstorms and ice-cold stream crossings. Betty has backpacked in the Sierras many times. In fact years ago, she would regularly cover 40-mile segments of the Pacific Crest Trail. The first trips were with her son and other family members or friends and started near the border between California and Mexico.

"I continued year after year doing trips, snagging others to accompany me, until we got to the point where the Mojave Desert was coming up, which we didn't want to hike," said Betty. So they moved the trips to the north and started doing hikes in Yosemite and Desolation Valley, where they continue today.

But it was on an early trip — on the beautiful, remote, hidden north coast of California — that Betty and her frequent hiking partner, Sandra, had perhaps their most thrilling adventure. "The trail was along the beach. We had checked the tide books and knew when to expect high tide. What we didn't know was that a Tsunami wave would hit the beach that evening — sending us running from scallop to scallop of foam to get to dry land and safety."

✦ Elizabeth

Elizabeth's backpacking adventures began in the 1930s with her family. She enjoys reminiscing about those times. "My father, Jimmy, was fording a river on a large log carrying two packs, my brother's and his own. He slipped, fell into the branches, and was soon flailing about and yelling for help. The rest of the family broke into laughter about his predicament, which only made him angrier, and in turn, made us laugh harder. Finally a compromise was reached. We'd help him out of the tangle, if he'd promise he wouldn't get even.

"When I was 11, I was told to stay in camp and watch my sister, who was then three, while my parents set off to fish with my two brothers. Late in the day it started to rain. I moved the fire because I was afraid one of the cows we had seen earlier would stumble into it and then into our tent.

"It got later and later and I was worried that I'd have to take my sister back to the car. That was eight miles back and I hadn't paid much attention to how we'd come. Eventually, we went to sleep.

"The next morning I decided to make pancakes, because 'Surely my parents would be hungry when they came back.' And sure enough, they made it back just in time for breakfast.

"My mother was quite excited about our adventure and hardships — being one who liked some drama in her life. They'd spent the night huddled on a ledge they'd stumbled upon when coming back to camp. At that time there weren't contour maps, so my brother's route took them straight to the ledge, where they couldn't get down but had to backtrack in the morning when it became light."

✦ Carol

Carol and Al completed the Appalachian Trail. As a teacher, Carol was able to use her summers for backpacking but Al was not yet retired, so their trips the following years were two or three week ones, with an additional one week trip in North Carolina and another week in Maryland during Easter vacations. They found that hiking the trail and hitchhiking into town to get supplies led to novel experiences. "It's pretty funny to have to wait until you're a grandma to hitchhike for the first time," laughed Carol. In Vermont, smelly and muddy after being out ten days, Carol and Al came off the trail and put out their thumbs for a ride into the nearby "uppity little town" of Manchester Center. A Phyllis Diller look-alike, a woman of about 55 with hair sticking out, with a younger man in tow, stopped for them. "Phyllis" resumed her conversation with her companion — dropping the names of Ralph Lauren and Liz Claiborne, and reminiscing about parties with martinis with olives. Carol was amazed and amused to have run into this woman who obviously socialized with stars and celebrities. The woman dropped them off at Manchester Center — which turned out to be a discount-shopping outlet for brand names such as Lauren and Claiborne.

In the process of getting out of the car at the hostel, Carol forgot her map. Since there was nothing she could do about it she went to take a shower and get ready to go to dinner. "Phyllis" came barreling up the road. "I knew you'd need your map," she said. Then, she gave Carol a once over, noted Carol's freshly shampooed hair, and added, "You sure clean up nice, honey!"

Carol and Al made friends wherever they traveled. "We were just ready to go to bed one night at Gentian Pond Shelter when we heard footsteps. A young man rounded the corner and the usual greetings were exchanged. We somehow got to discussing our parents. He told us that he had a wonderful relationship with his folks except for one thing —   they wanted him to go out and get a job. As parents, we found this extremely funny. Years later we went to a large gathering in West Virginia. Late that evening, a little truck pulled up. Out jumped the same young man. He didn't have a job yet, he said, but he was thinking about maybe going into the ministry."

One of the interesting things about backpacking is that everyone is pretty much on equal footing. Initially most conversations are about the trail — where you're going, where you've been, the weather, the condition of the trail, animals spotted, places to get water or supplies, and other trips you've taken. Most people want to leave city life behind for a while, so unless you specifically ask, you don't know what kind of job someone has, how full their social calendar is, how much money they have, or what their other interests are. In that respect, it's a classless society.

So when Carol and Al met Adrian off and on during the Vermont segment of the trail, they were equals. He invited them to his home in England, but then the next year he arrived on their doorstep en route to Isle Royale. After an enjoyable visit, Adrian insisted they let him return their hospitality. That is how it came to pass that Carol and Al went to England in 1996 and walked coast to coast across that country. When Adrian met them at Gatwick Airport and drove them up north to his home, they discovered that he was a wealthy man. At his stately, expensive mansion in the Lake District, they were treated royally. Then Adrian drove them to the start of their hike at Wainwright on the west coast, picked them up at the end on the east coast at Robinshood Bay, and returned them to Gatwick.

They found that hiking in England was completely different from the U.S. For one thing, they had to rely on maps, as most trails were not blazed. And when directions were "turn at the red barn," and the barn had been repainted yellow, wrong turns were inevitable. In addition, what looked like a hiking path frequently turned out to be a sheep trail.

But their accommodations were more comfortable. As it was too cool to sleep out in October, they stayed in what Carol called, "A wonderful assortment of lodgings" — bed and breakfast inns, hunting lodges, churches, and youth hostels — all with "real" people instead of fellow tourists. The youth hostels turned out to be delightful; they provided private rooms, all meals, and drying rooms for drying out rain or dew-soaked clothing overnight.

Their zest for backpacking and hiking undiminished, Carol and Al have completed forty-four of the "Fifty in Ohio," the Laurel Highlands Trail — a seventy mile hike in Pennsylvania — and a sojourn along the Buffalo River in Arkansas, where ticks were a considerable problem. In fall 1999, Carol went to Hawaii, accomplishing another lifetime goal — to visit all 50 states in the Union. "That leaves two goals to go," she said, "to visit the pyramids in Egypt, and to perform at Carnegie Hall."

✦ Frandee

In 1982 Frandee and a woman friend went on a hike into the Grand Canyon. Park regulations required that backpackers carry a large amount of water. That 15 pounds of added weight caused a great deal of pain to Frandee's knees. En route they met a man and his son who insisted she needed a stick. Over her protest (she didn't want the encumbrance) the man took his son's stick away from him and gave it Frandee. Further down in the canyon she ended up tossing the stick away. They continued on but at Thunder River they found they could not get across, so they had to join the Grand Canyon Dories' boating party and go out with them by boat.

It's inevitable that if you backpack, eventually there will be frightening events. Frandee shares two. "There was a rockfall when we were in the Grand Canyon and a woman in the party was hit. There was blood but we were able to find a way to radio out and the injury was not serious.

"Another time, my husband and I were in Alaska in our tent when a snowstorm began. The tent and bags became soaked. My husband said that if we didn't create a vapor barrier for our feet, ford a river and get to safety, we'd be in serious trouble. We tore a plastic bag into pieces to create a plastic sock as protective footwear — and we made it out okay."

✦ Sylvelin

Sylvelin found out about toughness on a 12 day, 50-mile trip on the West Coast Trail of Vancouver Island, ending at Port Renfrew. "It was a organized trip led by a husband/wife team from Arizona. We were a group of strangers at the beginning who became friends by the end. The trip itself was primarily flat — in and out of beautiful Northwest forest terrain. Then the forest would end and the shale beach would begin. The weather, which can be quite wild on that exposed Pacific coastline, was not a problem; it was mostly mild with occasional drizzles. The challenge was where the rivers met the ocean. The canyons would be perhaps 300 feet deep: the way to cross was the climb down a series of rickety wooden ladders to a bridge, then up the other side of the canyon on another connected series of rickety wooden ladders. All this while I was carrying my 40-pound backpack. In theory, the ladders were connected to something at the bottom of the canyon, and clearly they were connected at the top of the ladders to the rim of the canyon, but the challenge of climbing into mid-air with my pack was frightening."

✦ Valerie

In subsequent years Valerie has packed in Southern California's San Gabriel and San Bernardino mountains and the Sierra. Her son's first trip was when he was five. She selected a trip she thought would be an easy one for him with no more than a 500-foot elevation change. She pointed out to him that another family they met along the way had young children who were carrying most of their own equipment. Her son, however, was only interested in carrying what he saw as the essentials — his sweatshirt and his candy supply.

Valerie loves Mineral King. "It's a beautiful bowl, like my image of Switzerland." She enjoys telling the story of how Walt Disney wanted to develop the area for skiing and sent a team to check out the area. Opposition to the plan launched a gigantic fight. Valerie paraphrased the Disney team's subsequent report, "Yes, it is a gorgeous area, but it would be a terrible liability because the whole area is loaded with crevasses and prone to avalanches, and is quite unsafe." The project never came off.

✦ Emma

After her comments about her first experiences on the Appalachian Trail, one would probably not have expected Emma to want to repeat the experience — but she did. In 1957, shortly before her 70th birthday, she finished her second thru-hike. This trip took her 142 days, an average of 14 miles per day. Over the next few years she made several shorter Appalachian Trail hikes. And by 1964, she had completed a third hike of the entire Appalachian Trail — this time in sections.

In between the second hike and the completion of the third Appalachian hike, Emma accomplished other impressive feats. In 1959, the 100th anniversary of the Oregon Trail, she hiked its 2,000 mile route from Independence, Missouri, to Portland, Oregon. She carried an umbrella to ward off the sun. Keds supplied her with the hi-tops she preferred. She was 71.

Her last lengthy hike was from Harrisburg, Kentucky to Springfield, Illinois — when she was 81. Most sources attribute much of Emma's success at long-distance hiking to her attitude. She believed success followed determination and was a firm believer in exercise. She ridiculed people who said they were too old to hike — saying it took more head than heels. "Most people are pantywaists," she maintained [*Ohio Camerica*, 1963}. Sometimes people took offense at her comments, but to most Emma was a beloved figure. People with whom she stayed while hiking the Appalachian Trail are proud that she stayed overnight in their homes. All of us can be inspired by her example of an older woman accomplishing remarkable hikes.

✦ Irene

Irene relates her entry into the annals of backpacking records as the oldest woman to backpack the Appalachian Trail. "My next trip was a women's hike in New Hampshire, then the Isle Royale Women's hike, both with guides. After a Sierra Club hike in the foothills in South Carolina, we decided 'We can do it.' All these hikes as well as the first hikes on the Appalachian Trail had been with her friend, Betty. "In 1990, I did my first backpack on the Appalachian Trail — 50 miles in Georgia and all of New Jersey.

"After that, I called my sister, Sharon Bloodgood, who had only been at Isle Royale and Porcupine Mountain along Lake Superior with me, and told her I had decided to do the whole trail, and that she must do it with me. She did. In 1991, we started in New York and finished in Kent, Connecticut.

"My friends in Indiana gave me the trail name, 'Go-Go Girl.' When my sister and I started hiking alone on the AT, we decided that was not an appropriate name to be recording in the registers. After she tripped one day Sharon said, 'I should be Trip Along.' And I said, 'Then I'm Tag Along,' because you always have to wait for me when going uphill. We're known as the 'Along Sisters — Trip and Tag.'"

The amount of time they were out each day and of each trip, varied, but in general their Appalachian hikes were two weeks long. "We usually hiked a southern section in the spring, then a northern part in the summer," said Irene. "The longest trip was the last one — 28 days out. I really wanted to finish that year, and so we determinedly kept going." It took them eight years to complete the AT. Irene finished first in Hot Springs, North Carolina on April 18, 1998. She added, "My sister still had to do New Jersey, which she finished in August 1998."

Irene says it never gets easy but after you stay out for two or three weeks you feel different. "You can do more, it gets easier, and you've become 'trail tough.'" (Unfortunately if you are hiking a long distance in segments, you have to become conditioned all over again for the next segment.) What kept her going was her sister — and vice versa. When one was up, the other was down. There were moments that were frustrating: Sharon hiked quicker, and Irene would just as soon have been able to keep up.

When Irene, Sharon, and a friend walked across England — the "Coast to Coast" — they treated themselves. They had a "Sherpa" van carrying their gear and only had to carry their daypacks. They slept in B & B's or small hotels at night.

"This past June we day-hiked Coast to Coast, from the Irish Sea to the North Sea, in England. Earlier this month we were at the Grand Canyon's North Rim. In October, we plan a short backpack on a section of the Ice Age Trail in Wisconsin. We've also hiked on the Pacific Crest Trail in San Diego County and most of Riverside County. Hope to do more next year, but doubt that I'll get to finish all of it [the PCT]."

Irene's hiked about 200 miles of the Pacific Crest Trail in the San Diego area. A couple of backpacking trips considered for 2000 were to the Cotswolds — the fairy tale region of England — during the summer, and to Lake Tahoe, California, in August.

✦ Fran

Though Fran found her backpacking trip with her husband and daughter to Mt. Whitney difficult, there were many good times too. Pleasant days found them following the Kern River downhill, fording the numerous streams, enjoying the waterfall. "We happily soaked off the trail dirt at Hot Springs in Kern Meadow. The concrete tub is filled from an artesian well. Users plug up the far side of the tub and let it fill, and then plug the incoming hole. [When they climbed out and changed to dry clothes], Vic wasn't too upset when he discovered some varmint had gnawed a hole in his T-shirt, but Melanie didn't appreciate the hole she found in a strategic place in her underpants."

✦ Della

When Della started on the Appalachian Trail, it must have been with a tremendous leap of faith. "I started the hike in terrible shape, and while others had their maps and itineraries and knew just where they were going to stop each night, I just walked until I couldn't take another step. Then I'd stop for the night, cook a pot of rice, and go to sleep." So she was soon nicknamed "No Agenda."

Della hiked the Appalachian Trail in what is called a flip-flop. She started at the southern end hiking from Georgia to Pennsylvania. She took a mid-route vacation, and then hitched a ride to the northern end, Maine, and headed south to end at Bolling Springs, Pennsylvania. This method makes a lot of sense when you consider the various climates. Maine's parks close for the season October 15; as a result help isn't easily found. Doing the flip-flop let her complete the northernmost portions before that mid-October cutoff, and also allowed her to enjoy the Indian summer as she traveled south again. Her hike ended November 7, 1997.

Della had a data book — a trail guide that tells how far it is to food, water, and shelter. And there are a lot of places, especially in the southern portion of the trail, where one can get provisions. Nearby residents were eager to help: they enjoyed hearing and swapping stories. Additionally, there are small communities that are pretty much supported by supplying food and shelter to AT hikers. Even so, Della was nervous about certain aspects of the trail. So she made several rules for herself before she even started her backpacking trip. Water was a concern at first, so she made it a rule to never pass up any water source where she could top up her containers. She also had toilet paper anxiety — "How much would she need?" she wondered.

And she hated hitchhiking. The first time she needed to get a ride, she was not very happy about it; she felt uneasy about people. But it was pouring rain and she decided, "I'd rather take my chances on getting murdered than get 12 miles wetter." A car passed her going the other direction, came to a stop, turned around, and came back. It turned out that the occupants were people who lived nearby and were backpackers too. Della was happy to get a safe ride into town.

Along the AT, Della found that it usually wasn't difficult to get a ride to the nearest town, but she observed that young women and boys were picked up first, then men, and then older women. "They assume an older woman with a backpack is crazy. I know I would," she added.

✦ Kathy

Kathy noted that while others are retiring from backpacking at her age — tired of the hardships — she is not only continuing to backpack but also expanding her interests by getting into desktop publishing. She is a friend of Grace, the Llama Mama, and has gone on several llama trips. She likes adding the assisted trips to her repertoire and enjoys the luxuries.

Though she doesn't weigh her pack, she estimates she is typically carrying 50-60 pounds. It's heavy enough so that, "When I trip and fall, I have to unfasten my backpack, drag it around to prop it up, and roll onto my hands and knees to get moving again," she says.

✦ Laurie

Laurie tells, "Bill had always had the philosophy that normal retirement was all wrong. You should do active things when you were young enough and go back to work later if needed." They had decided to hike the AT, so Laurie quit her part-time job (which didn't feel like much of a loss) and Bill took a leave of absence. With those responsibilities taken care of, they turned their attention to preparatory hikes and overnight camping, and because the AT is practically in their backyard, that was relatively easy to accomplish.

Still, setting out on an almost 2,200 mile journey was a "leap of faith." Though they had both always been active people who kept in shape playing lots of racquetball, the experience of hiking this big-league trail made a "major impact" on their lives. It was meeting the physical challenges, accomplishing things you thought you couldn't do, and the peacefulness that Laurie loved. And, Laurie added "the camaraderie of the trail." As she explained, "It's different than socializing with people at home. On the trail everyone is on equal footing. You are meeting people of all economic levels, all ages, a real variety of people, with a shared interest." Laurie and Bill gained and maintained many friendships formed while hiking.

Laurie and Bill always had it in the backs of their minds that they wanted to make another long distance trip after they completed the AT. They liked the trail and the added bonus of the people they encountered. They contemplated doing the Continental Divide or the Pacific Crest Trail, but the appeal of seeing people on the American Discovery Trail made it their choice. As it turned out, however, it didn't provide the same opportunities. Because the ADT is so new and not well known or traveled, it is logistically much more difficult to travel than the AT.

Laurie and Bill spent months preparing before they set out on their bicycling/hiking trip on the ADT. For some sections, they arranged mail drops of dehydrated food. Putting together a data book was a major effort; using a series of maps, they tried to plan how far they could travel each day, and where they might stay. But these estimates could not foresee weather or always accurately predict how far they could go. The bicycle portion was definitely an unknown since they hadn't ridden to any extent since they were kids.

They wondered about the possibility of being harassed during the trip. After all, we have all read in the newspaper from time to time about motorists throwing cans at bicyclists or trying to run them off the road. But as it turned out, Laurie and Bill had no problems with people or animals on either the Appalachian or American Discovery trails.

In fact, on their trips Laurie and Bill experienced many acts of kindness; they began to call them "trail magic." While on the American Discovery Trail hike they found it delightful that strangers were both intrigued by what they were doing and also very helpful. One Saturday in March of 1997, the two hikers arrived in Londonderry, Ohio, where they were to pick up their supplies for the next six days. They found the post office closed, but when they called the postmaster, Connie, she came down, opened the office, and gave them their mail drop. Then she invited them over to her place. Laurie and Bill ended up staying two nights with Connie and her husband, Mike. It was a welcome break from the road; Laurie and Bill were also able to get showers, a place to do laundry, great food, a tour of nearby Chillicothe, go to the movies as a foursome, and catch up with their e-mails.

The ADT trip was, however, psychologically challenging. The trail is varied. It goes into cities (though it generally keeps off the highways) with lots of people doing city things, through countryside with more land than people, and into wilderness with few tourist accommodations or people. So one of the anticipated rewards of the trail — the oft mentioned camaraderie of the AT — was lacking. People were interested, and Laurie and Bill could "educate" them about the trail, but that did not create the same bond that sharing the trail and its experience with other hikers did.

Nevertheless, Laurie found traveling the ADT an incredible experience. She has maintained her connection with ADT in various ways — including serving as the organization's coordinator.

✦ Marilyn

Fortunately, most backpacking trips do not involve either mishap or trauma, but they often do require ingenuity and flexibility. Marilyn was blunt in her assessment of the difficulties of backpacking. She has been on a couple of California backpacking trips and thinks the difficulties are overrated. "There's too much mystique about backpacking in general. It isn't all that hard. It's do-able. My most recent trip was a three-and-a-half to five-mile trip over a long weekend with a friend to Echo Lake and Fallen Leaf Lake in Desolation Wilderness. It was a good trip except for one difficulty — one of my boots decided to fall apart. So I just had to wrap it with string to keep going."

✦ Marcy

Of her July 2000 trip into the Sierra Nevada, Marcy wrote, "Our first trip was VERY STRENUOUS!!! The snow covered the trails from Donahue Pass, south of Tuolumne, all the way to Shadow Lake, where we threw in the towel and hiked out eight miles to Agnew Meadows and took the shuttle to my car at Red's Meadow — 10 miles further. It was very difficult trying to decide where the trail was or where it would go. We got very tired and every day turned up new challenges. We got caught in a hailstorm and lightning was very close. We got wet and cold, had to put up the tent in the rain and take off all our wet clothes and get in our bags and huddle close to get warm. Luckily, I had one last emergency hand warmer and that not only warmed up my feet but also dried the whole bottom end of the bag."

4
And *Whose* Idea Was This?
Partners & Support

"The world is so empty if one thinks only of mountains, rivers and cities; but to know someone here and there who thinks and feels with us, and who, though distant, is close to us in spirit, this makes the earth for us an inhabited garden."

Goethe

Being with a partner or group has the advantages of shared experiences and camaraderie, as well as shared chores and backpack loads. However, one person who complains constantly or shirks responsibilities, can dampen the spirits of everyone else. Some of the women that I interviewed have been backpacking both solo and with others, and some women have always backpacked with at least one companion.

✦ Debbie

For Debbie, backpacking is best with her husband Bill, or Bill and another friend or two. She likes sharing the pools they seek out, the sunsets, the quiet, and she likes the sensuous smell of Bill. And she's not ashamed of the fact that she feels safer having someone knowledgeable and physically strong around when she's in the wilderness. "I don't want to go alone because I would be hearing things, and worrying about creatures and strangers," she added.

✦ Laurie

Laurie and Bill had different styles of hiking, which had predictable results: "numerous discussions," she added jokingly. Their paces were similar, but she was usually better going uphill, and he, downhill. When they did the ADT with their combination of bike and hike, Bill's greater strength would have allowed him to really take off but morale would have suffered. Instead, they chose to keep within eyesight of each other 24 hours a day for the six months of the AT and of the ADT. Though some couples who have dissimilar paces will hike separately and meet up periodically and at the end of the day, this didn't appeal to Laurie and Bill. "Frankly," she noted, "those who didn't hike together were less successful."

There is an advantage, she commented, to being part of a couple. They found that when one was down, the other was up. "When I wanted to quit or Bill did, the other would carry more of the load. While we never talked seriously about quitting, that's not to say that we didn't complain! 'Why are we doing this! We must be crazy.' You accept soreness but don't dwell on it. In addition, having told family, friends, and everyone you know that you are doing this is a big motivating factor."

After completing the Appalachian and American Discovery trails, Laurie and Bill backpacked at Isle Royale. In 1998, they hiked in Nepal. Laurie and Bill's trips were always either as a couple or with a group. Laurie has never been solo but with Bill gone, she is toying with the idea. It would be a significant change, since operating as a team streamlines setting up camp and provides companionship and added security. After so many months and miles of traveling together, they had established camp roles: they would pull into camp and she'd immediately start setting up the tent and unrolling bags, and Bill would start the food, which he normally prepared. Of course, going solo also means no one is sharing the weight of shelter, stove, fuel, first aid kit, and so forth.

✦ Fran

"Melanie hasn't said this, but I think she figured that three of us was a good number. If one of us got hurt, she could get help with the other," quipped Fran.

✦ Sharon

When Sharon led a group of backpackers on a trip to northeastern California a few years back, she was somewhat nervous. No one else in the group had backpacked before. And, although she had previously taught friends individually or as a couple how to backpack, she had never led a group before. "I had talked to other people who'd had a miserable experience and thought it was so important that my group have a good time. I felt very responsible." But, for Sharon, the opportunity to share the out-of-doors was more important than her uncertainties.

The group backpacked a couple of miles in. It was a weekend trip — hardly time to work the bugs out and reach their stride. Predictably, the first day was difficult and uncomfortable with typical complaints of mosquitoes and sore muscles. "I did have to field two million questions: 'Where do I go to the bathroom?' and 'Where do I put up my tent?' being typical. Everyone had to buy, borrow, or rent equipment, and some found out the hard way that not all packs are created alike." But the evening around the campfire and the sharing of tents and camp-chores led to the pleasures of bonding, letting your hair down, and a sense of having proved something.

✦ Sylvelin

Like most of the women I have talked to, Sylvelin has found it necessary to slow down. She has come to terms with not being able to keep up with every hiker. And luckily, she Sylvelin has been able to find people to travel with who are not "peak-baggers." She doesn't describe herself as a competitive hiker and has companions who are younger, her age, and older with whom she can hike comfortably. Although she has had problems with an Achilles tendon, her philosophy has become to just accept minor aches and pains.

✦ Valerie

Valerie learned the wisdom of going at her own pace the hard way. She was at Mineral King and she wanted to climb Florence Peak. Along the way she met a very attractive man. He had no particular interest in climbing the peak but they started hiking together. Valerie was conscious of the fact that his pace was a little faster than hers was, maybe just a step a minute faster, but enough so that she was conscious of having to make an extra effort. She didn't ask him to slow down. She figured if she didn't keep up he'd go without her, so she just quietly made the effort. As a result, when they reached the lake she had a tremendous headache and was too exhausted to climb the peak. He was doing fine and went on to climb the peak; she never saw him again.

✦ Marcy

Marcy says, "How do I keep going when it gets really rough? It is never easy. The only thing to do is keep putting one foot in front of the other. Dottie and I have different rhythms. She goes really fast uphill. I go really, really slowly. I don't have a competitive nature, so it doesn't bother me that Dottie hikes faster. She waits for me somewhere. Her motto is never to be so far away from your hiking buddy that you can't see or hear them. But voice is lost quickly in the wilderness. Seeing Dottie way up ahead is a consolation and I know she will eventually wait. I have learned to be at peace with myself when I hike alone, for a time. I know we will meet up again before too long. Dottie has to deal with agoraphobia, and she battles that by getting moving but waits at the forks in the trail. I can go downhill pretty fast, so we sometimes lap each other, or hike together."

When Marcy was in her twenties she had an unsettling hiking experience. While she was hiking with her husband, he got far ahead of her. She called to him, but he couldn't hear her and she started crying. From that experience of the isolation and loneliness of being left behind came Marcy's sensitivity to not leaving hiking partners behind. Marcy and Dottie make a good team because, although they hike at different speeds, they make accommodations for each other.

✦ Kathryn

Kathryn also has learned the importance of choosing her companions carefully from personal experience. One trip was to the Minarets with an older friend. The friend brought not only a load of heavy clothes, but also came equipped with a Pacemaker. They went to Shadow Lake — a moderate climb from 8,700 feet to 9,600 feet in four miles. The friend did not ask to go again.

✦ The Marching Mothers

Sis and Carmen's group, The Marching Mothers, may sound militaristic, but this backpacking group is anything but. In fact, they describe themselves as non-competitive. "We don't think we can tell others how to form a similar group," agreed both women, "we were just lucky. We never had a leader; jobs like cooking and cleaning up were done by whoever was around camp at dinnertime. Events that could have become crises were taken in stride, with no one pointing fingers to blame someone." Both feel lucky to have participated in a group that has continued, with enthusiasm, since that first trip in 1969. Carmen is an original member; Sis joined in 1973.

Thirty years provides lots of time for exploration, and the group has been to the Sierras many times, to the Sawtooth Mountains in Idaho, to the Cascades in Washington twice, and to the Ruby Mountains in Nevada.

The annual trips have been laced with funny and sweet incidents. On the 1970 trip, the group was informed by the ranger that no wood fires were allowed in the area. They tried to comply — and managed to burn up their alcohol stove. Then they went back to build a campfire and sat around it discussing "all the alibi's, excuses, legal angles, or use of tears, if necessary, should the ranger return," as group member Sharon Winburn recorded in her journal. Another time, just after bedtime, one of the women yelled out, "Hey, girls, porcupine." Its heavy footsteps had awakened her to find it grunting at her face-to-face.

Then there was the time that Carmen screamed in the middle of the night because she thought she was being strangled by a murderer who had recently been in the news; it turned out to be a strap that had gotten tangled around her neck. Once a troop of Boy Scouts came upon group member Patsy while she was bathing; the leaders wanted to make camp nearby hoping to catch more than a glimpse. Another time a hiker happened upon Lu while she was bathing; both remained unruffled and were able to carry on a brief conversation. After that the man would whistle in advance of his walking by their campsite. Other incidents included Aleisha deciding that "spirits" would make a good fire-starter for their damp firewood and the time that Sis washed her teeth with first aid cream.

There are also many anecdotes of warmth and compassion, like the time everyone donated food to the honeymoon couple at Hamilton Lake who had lost all their food to a bear their first night out. Or the time at Tom's Pass on the way to Edison Lake where a shortcut lead to an ice-covered trail beside a sea of snow that dropped to the lake. Some of the participants stomped out footholds, and Patsy carried many packs across for those afraid to carry their own bulky gear. Or the time when Laurie, who had just laboriously pumped clean water, gave some of the water away to a dehydrated hiker who came upon her. He was so grateful that he told them to stop by his store in Bear Paw Meadow when they were in the vicinity and he'd return the favor. When they arrived at the meadow, hot and sweaty, he had six ice-cold beers ready for them.

One time a problem arose before the group had even begun their hike. They were at the trailhead, on the east side of the Sierras, camped out and discussing their plans to meet their packer the next morning. Someone asked, "Where's the food?" Sis said, "Surely you're joking?" Unfortunately, it wasn't a joke. One of the members, who had taken the entire supply of the freeze-dried food home to supplement with fresh food, had left it behind. She called back home. Her husband agreed to leave in the wee hours and meet them on the west side of the mountains, so that he'd still be able to get back in time to go to work. She and Carmen drove out, picked up the food, and returned the next morning in time to meet the packers.

As the years have passed, the planning, participants, and types of trips have changed and evolved. Their trips in the '70s involved arranging for the care of many children; thirty years later, their trips increasingly include adult children. Now, children and grandchildren are discussed as the women hike. Trips must be planned between weddings and other vacations. Some trips have been non-backpacking ones — a letdown to Sis who prefers the more rugged country, although she still looks forward to the camaraderie.

Sis and Carmen offer advice both simple and complex, "Choose your companions carefully." It's obvious that this group's greatest strength has been its ability to enjoy, support, and complement each other. They agreed, "On occasion after occasion, things have been settled by amicable discussion. Whoever was able, did what was needed. And that includes everything from where they would go the next year, to who would start dinner, to what time to hit the trail — 9: 00 a.m. invariably."

✦ Carol

"I do all of my hiking with my husband. Hiking and backpacking are the only sports that we have found to be enjoyable for both of us. We have shared many thoughts along the way. We have had highs and lows during our travels, which have served to strengthen our relationship. We've had funny things happen and scary ones too."

Carol thinks that being part of a couple is what kept her going on the Appalachian Trail. Towards the end of the hike, when she was in pain from shin splints, it was especially difficult to continue. That's when they would sit down and talk about it. Throughout the several years and segments of the AT, they would lean on each for both physical and emotional support. Sometimes one or the other would carry extra to lessen the other's burden.

✦ Jan

Although Jan considers backpacking alone safe enough, she prefers to go with others because she enjoys the sense of community. "I love the mountains. Backpacking is different from hiking because it's more intimate," she said. It was an important refuge when the kids were young; now it is also important for the exercise and for being with friends.

Memorable trips have included one to the north and another to the south slope of the Alaskan Brooks Range in two different years. The north slope is particularly remote

— accessible only by small plane or on foot. Jan, her husband, and another couple were dropped off by a bush pilot with a fourteen day food supply. The plan was for the plane to pick them all up 10 days later.

When the 10 days were up, things got dicey. The weather was turning bad. The pilot did not show up as scheduled. The device they had planned to use to contact the plane if necessary, didn't work. They were truly isolated.

After a couple of anxious days as the weather continued to disintegrate, the pilot was able to get through and pick them up. As a postscript, Jan added, "There's no substitute for good companions."

✦ Doris and the Jane Muirs

"I began hiking with Nancy Skinner who had a group in Marin; I made every Tuesday I could. I wanted to go backpacking and I didn't have anyone to go with, so one day as we were hiking I said, 'I wonder if women could possibly go by themselves?' She said, 'Oh course they can; women are just as good as men.' And I said, 'Well, do you think we could do stoves and put up tents? Are we strong enough?' 'Well, certainly we are,' she said. 'Well, where would you start?' She had it all planned. We went to Trinity Alps that June and Kennedy Meadows that July. From Nancy, I learned about latrines, trowels, bagging food, and packing light. We went five times. Then we had a disastrous trip."

Nancy organized the trip. The group was Doris and Nancy, who were then in their 50s, and three others in their 30s. Doris was the only one Nancy had hiked with before. The three younger members took over — leaving Nancy highly stressed. Doris continued, "By the end of the trip, Nancy's neck just killed her. She went to the doctor upon her return and ended up with a neck brace. She never led another hike."

"So here I was all primed, I'd had 35 miles of the John Muir Trail, and I thought 'Darn!' So with the John Muir Trail in mind, I started inviting my friends. We went first to Mammoth area: start at Agnew Meadows, up to Shadow Lake, a layover day to do Lake Ediza and see Cecile and Iceberg, then go north on the John Muir Trail to 1000 Island Lake, and then back on the high trail of the Pacific Crest Trail (on the other crest). It's about 25 miles, and two lay-days.

"I got pretty good as a hiker. About the same time there was a gas crunch, and I felt so negligent driving across three counties to go for a walk, and I'd say, 'Well, I'll walk at home,' but I don't walk at home; I don't like to walk around the block. It's boring. People said, 'You can't find anyone to walk with in Vallejo; it's not a walking town.' I said, 'I can too!' I marched down to the YMCA and proposed a hiking club. All we did was carpool over to Mt. Tam and Pt. Reyes and go on the trails I'd learned with Nancy. That was in 1981."

1981 was also the year Doris started leading the backpacking trips with the group that she soon named the Jane Muirs. "When I went with Nancy we were all middle-aged ladies, and she called us the 'Hot Flashers;' I didn't want that name to stick. They let me do all the planning; I can take them wherever I want to.

"Our first trip on the John Muir Trail took five days and everyone got hooked. We finished the trail in 1987. We did it in concentric circles all along, not in order, sometimes from the east, sometimes from the west."

Annual trips have continued. Days routinely begin with an early start and end early afternoon. Distances vary; cross-country hikes may be only four [difficult] miles, whereas hikes on trails can vary from six to as many as seventeen. Doris said, "We do a lot of cross-country; trails, we can go a long way on trails. We stop at 3:00 p.m. at the latest and everyone does their laundry, fishes, reads a book, climbs a mountain — if they're not tired."

As we were studying photos of their group's visit to Duzy Basin in the Sierra, Doris remarked, "Ronnie is our fly-fisherman. She doesn't sign up for chores when we arrive, but does breakfast so that she can fish immediately. [Here is where] she came back and she had a fishhook in the fleshy part of her thumb. The problem was the only tools we had were Swiss Army knives. We ruined one, tried another — it just wasn't working. So we decided to tape it up, and go out in the morning; it was twilight at this point.

"I sent up my prayer, 'God, you put me here, take over.'" Doris and her companions were in an isolated area — where few people ventured. "I looked up and there were two men walking around. They were scout leaders from a camp about a mile away who had come down to see if there were any fish jumping — 'cause it was twilight. I ran down with my 'Lady in distress! Please, kind sirs.' Sure enough, being fisherman, they had tools on their belts — with pliers. [We] were able to cut off the barb and back it right out. We cleaned and bandaged it and it was fine. We always talk about Boy Scouts being helpful; this was really providential."

One time Doris and two friends took their husbands backpacking. "It was a great trip. We went in south of Whitney and camped at the road end at 11,000 feet. We picked up the trail and went on over to Crabtree Meadows on a beautiful cross-country route. And the darn husbands, they were all taking over. We got to a spot — I'm tottling along with my share — I didn't make it easier on myself [when hiking] than I did when packing, and so I had the fishing pole. My husband suggested that I should hand him the fishing pole. And he said, 'Gee, put the tent over there,' and 'Honey, would you wash this tee-shirt?' 'Cause that's what I did at home for him all the time,' I thought."

"So I did as I was told. After dinner, we went over to pack up the remaining food. The other Doris and I were trying to show the men what to do. They just [acted like], 'Go away little girls, we're men and we know everything.' Then they tied a certain kind of knot and we said, 'That's no good, you should let us show you a knot that works really well. In the morning, when the rope is frozen...'

"Go away, we know knots," was their attitude. The next morning the other Doris and I just chuckled; the knot was frozen and they were trying to undo it — not swearing, but quite frustrated."

✦ Barbara and her women's group

Barbara's first backpacking trip was in 1975 during the time when she was helping to organize field trips for the Oakland Museum's Natural Science docent training program. Within that community there were backpackers and wildflower enthusiasts. She and a college friend were taken with the idea of backpacking and so they went with a group out of Rubicon on the California side of Lake Tahoe on a five-night trip. Barbara remembers, "Though my buddy and I were ill equipped, we loved the experience, and came home inspired to go with contemporaries."

A group of eight women friends was formed, all within a five-year age span. Generally they were acquainted — neighbors or tennis partners — though Barbara invited two college friends whom only she knew. Their first group trip was into Desolation Valley in the Sierra.

They were a fairly homogenous group, their lifestyles similar; all were mothers and the primary caretakers for their families. The conversations around the campfire and on trail revolved around how they had provided for their families' care while they were gone. (Barbara had prepared and frozen casseroles for the week.) They worried about how husbands and children would cope, and discussed feelings of guilt for taking this time for themselves. They were on the cusp of traditional roles evolving into an era of shared responsibilities.

"I had never asked much of my husband before this," said Barbara. Generally in that era, husbands were the breadwinners and women cared for the families' needs — with little expectation of time for themselves. Some of the husbands saw this all female excursion as a threat, "What would happen with this taste of freedom?" some wondered. But, even with their concerns, from the first trip, the women were hooked.

The topics of conversation changed through the years — from those early ones that centered on making sure they'd left their family well provided for, to later questions such as, "Should I put contraceptives in my daughter's orange juice?" There were also worrisome conversations about family problems and divorces (they experienced a bit less than the California average), health issues, and current events.

Seven of the original eight still go together (one in spirit, as her health has weakened her). Not everyone has been able to go every year, but when the group meets early in the year to plan the summer's trip, they try to schedule around upcoming weddings, graduations and such, so that most can go. Some years a new person has gone. Sometimes there's a misfit — like the time a newcomer brought a complete make-up kit with her.

The group has been outside of California on some trips — including the Tetons of Wyoming and the Sawtooth Mountains in Utah — but most trips have been in the Sierra Nevada. At this point, Barbara figures they have essentially covered the whole of the John Muir Trail.

Though the group has essentially remained constant over the last quarter century, that is not to say that there has been no conflict. Indeed, many years back there was a problem that briefly threatened the group's cohesion. As with any hikers (two or more), there are adjustments to be made. In this case, there was a Group A, who generally wanted to go faster or further, and a Group B, who preferred to go at a more leisurely pace, take breaks and eat lunch sooner, and cover less distance.

There had been several agreements made. They would stick together — not walk in each other's footprints, but stop at any forks in the road and wait for the others. Those wanting to have more of a challenge would take day hikes on layover days, and would plan an additional trip that year of their own. For many years there were no problems — but one time their luck ran out.

Two of the women were ahead; five were following in a second group. The two in the lead were so engrossed in conversation that they did not notice a fork in the road and kept on going. When they realized they had gone on the wrong trail, they decided to cut cross-country and intersect the other trail where the second group should be. Unfortunately, when the second group came to the fork in the road, they did not proceed; they decided to wait at the "Y." After some hours they decided they should return to the car, several miles back, because they assumed that something was wrong — that someone had been hurt.

The pair who had hiked cross country realized, belatedly, that the other five were behind them, not ahead. The two had enough food and shelter, so they set up camp. The following morning the group that had returned to the cars hiked in and all were reunited.

"By that time," Barbara said, "everyone was exhausted and irritable…" "There was quite an uproar with wounded feelings on both sides. Everyone who had been worried was now angry. Then a day passed with little talking. Finally, the feelings were sorted out, and compromises were reached."

Barbara continued, "We value our friendship most of all and we were moved to all have a truthful discussion to sort out hurt feelings and misunderstandings. We have maintained honest communication ever since."

The group has made some modifications to their trips over the years. The trips are a bit shorter; there are more layover days. Some trips have used packhorses. In 2000, for example, they had horses carry the equipment in, and two members rode. Another member, however, remained adamant about carrying her own pack. They used to joke that it proved they were strong because they could carry their packs; now they joke that they are strong because they can still sleep on the ground.

Barbara's suggestions for groups included the importance of limiting the group's size. Not only can too large a group have too much impact on the trail and campsite, it can also interfere with the bonding she assumes is one of the goals of the trip. Group members should be comfortable with each other and with the environment. Though they spend time together and share chores, the women also value aloneness. They have a like-minded attitude that it's okay to pursue individual interests. Some prefer to read; others like to paint or fish. Occasionally someone will want to spend a solo night — and that is accepted.

✦ Judy

Judy considers herself to be quite fortunate to belong to a large network of women friends. From this group, several backpacking trips have been arranged over the years. Five or six years ago a woman friend suggested a backpacking trip to Lake Ediza in the Eastern Sierra, so the group of four women hired a guide and his assistant and pack mules to carry the heavy equipment. It was a late thaw, so even though it was July, there was lots of snow, in some places up to their hips. Judy loved the experience. She found that as they hiked they would be walking along with one person and then later, another. As they hiked and shared confidences, a wonderful intimacy formed.

✦ Betty and Sandra

Betty is the trip planner and trailboss. "We're up at 6:00 a.m. or when the sun comes up, and hike for an hour, 8:00 a.m. breakfast and wash-up, 12:00 lunch, 5:00 cook dinner, hike to campsite." They usually do seven or eight miles a day. They sleep in a depression in the granite — preferably where Betty can see the stars.

✦ ✦ ✦ ✦ ✦

Ralph and I have our own work division:

Ralph	Susan
plans routes	provides feedback
collects water	keeps journal
pumps drinking water	does dishes
sets up tent	lays out sleeping bags and pads
cooks meals	eats meals
builds fires	helps collect firewood
stores food	re-sorts food as needed
carries 45 pounds if necessary	carries 35 pounds max

does morning packing of backpacks	locates sunscreen and sunscreen & lip balm
packs lunch	folds up tent in morning

Clearly, our division of chores is more work for Ralph than it is for me. Although this hasn't bothered Ralph, it has been somewhat difficult for me to accept because I want to be an equal partner. I don't want to be overly dependent or a burden on him. But the truth of the matter is that Ralph is stronger than I am and has few of the physical problems that I regularly deal with (bunions, blisters, lower back problems, etc.) If I insisted on carrying the amount of weight that he carries, for example, because I wanted everything equal, I would be so miserable that we would never be able to go again. Partners need to find a division that works — and not worry about what is politically correct.

Sharing camp chores and helping one another are at least as important as being able to tell funny stories at the campfire. To be successful, hiking partnerships, whether a couple's or a larger group's, have to recognize, support, and value the unique contributions of each member of the team.

Marcy Clements and Dottie Shamah
John Muir Hut, Sierra Nevada

5
What's That Strange Sound I Hear?
Going Solo

"It was a high counsel that I once heard given to a young person, 'Always do what you are afraid to do.'"

Ralph Waldo Emerson

There are advantages and disadvantages to going alone on a backpacking trip. When you go by yourself, you will likely have more time for self-reflection, independence, and creative pursuits. Going it alone also adds more risk, requires carrying more equipment, and may provide more isolation than you anticipated. No matter which route you choose and whatever degree of independence, quiet, and privacy you seek, *always* leave a detailed itinerary of your trip with someone back home and sign any backcountry registers provided.

Trails vary in foot traffic. On the Appalachian Trail it is likely that a solo hiker will meet other hikers traveling at the same rate and that they will encounter each other repeatedly. Often hikers meet up and hike together for a time. On the more rugged and remote Pacific Crest Trail, there may be days of solitude interspersed with days (especially on the sections that join with the John Muir Trail) when you will see a dozen other backpackers.

✦ Sharon

For Sharon, her first solo backpacking trip was at a turning point in her life; she was ending her second marriage. One area where she and her husband had been successful was backpacking. Now she needed to do it herself. She set out for Emigrant Wilderness for a two-week trip. A horsepacker took her 17 miles in. She was to stay at a lake a couple of days, eat up some of the heavy food, then go on.

When the packer dropped her off late in the day, reality set in; Sharon had never gone through the whole process of setting up camp alone. She had two weeks' worth of food, and since she was in bear country, she knew she needed to hang the food. It had looked so simple when she had watched her husband do it; you just needed to counter-balance the bags. She tied a rock to one end of her rope and tried throwing it over a high branch. No luck. Her husband had a good arm; he'd been a baseball player in college, but Sharon couldn't throw very far. She knew her trip would be over if the food got eaten. She tried putting together some bungee cords and rigging up a slingshot arrangement. Those attempts failed too.

She didn't know what to do. She knew she wouldn't starve and that she could walk out, but she didn't want to end her trip. She did what she would do a lot in the days to come — she sat down and cried, and ate some food.

Then she looked at her pack again and noticed her backpacking fishing pole. She had never been fishing, but she *had* brought instructions and was planning to learn how. Maybe she could cast the line over the limb. She figured out how to assemble the pole. Her brother had been with her when she bought the pole and he had insisted she bring some practice plugs. She tried them and it finally worked. And that is how she hung her bear bags the remainder of the trip.

Sharon had had visions of setting up a cozy campsite with her comfy hammock, spending quiet moments meditating, sitting by the campfire watching the stars. The second day she fell while gathering wood and gashed her leg. It wasn't a serious injury but it was enough to make her consider what could happen if she broke her leg. She realized that she was on her own; she had to pay attention constantly to where to put her feet when on the trail and when gathering wood or doing other camp chores.

It was disconcerting; she could never feel as relaxed as she had when camping with other people. She got lost a couple of times, always when daydreaming, but never seriously and never for more than a couple of hours. She was amazed at how little time there was to do the reading she had thought she would do.

There was lots of self-chatter: "Need to get the fire started. It's getting dark." When she was lonely, she cried. The feelings of loneliness would pass, and she found that the feelings were usually related to being cold, hungry, or tired — comfort issues. She traveled about five miles a day. Her biggest comfort concern was that her period had started, unexpectedly. [This is not an uncommon occurrence when traveling]. This added to her worry about bears. [That bears are attracted by women's menstrual blood does not seem to be born out by scientific evidence]. She sacrificed a couple of T-shirts and washed them out as needed, much as she assumed her grandmother would have done in her time.

One day she decided to go on a dayhike. She left her pack in camp because she didn't expect to be gone long. She got lost.

"The forest draws you in. The trail runs out. You follow what you think is the trail, but it isn't. You stop. 'Where am I?' you ask yourself. Clouds of mosquitoes surround you, adding to your confusion.

"'If I push on, I'll get there,' I told myself. But I forced myself to stop, and took stock. I am a determined person, but this was a dangerous situation. It was late, I had no pack, and I wasn't sure how far my destination was. I knew I had better figure out how to get back, but it was so hard to turn around. Finally, I climbed out of the valley, and found shelter.

"From a ledge, I watched an unusual feast of lightning and wind as a storm passed through. I really had succeeded. I experienced an intense feeling of androgyny. I was not woman or man; I was a human being. I felt 'solid' — that I had taken care of myself. It was an intense moment, a highlight of my life.

[But] "As the trip continued, I got lonelier and lonelier. At first I had hidden from people. I resented them for being on my trails, interrupting my thoughts. Soon I was stopping everyone I passed with the usual, 'How're you doing? Where've you been? Do you want a cup of tea?'

"Friends were going to meet me later on. They had been worried that I wouldn't know what day it was and wouldn't show up on time. I kept my journal religiously, partly so I could keep track of the days. I decided to hike out a day early so I wouldn't have to worry about the meeting time, and they wouldn't panic. It was the most liberating day of the whole trip, no worries. I was three miles from civilization and yet I could spend the whole day naked, doing laundry, being 'Little Miss Hostess' getting ready for company. The day they were due in, I set up the hammock, and the hour they were due, I lay down in it and waited for them, positioned so they could see me, utterly comfortable, perfectly safe, as they trudged into camp. We devoured a two-pound bag of Oreos by nightfall — and they did remark that I seemed a little 'chatty.'"

✦ Joyce

Joyce had a rather exotic trip to Peru where she backpacked solo for a week. I thought this sounded rather hazardous, such a big unknown, but Joyce responded, "I chose a route where I would probably see others, and I had arranged to meet my son and a friend to continue my trip and climb mountains with them. Actually, I don't mind going alone; I feel safer in the wilderness than in cities."

✦ Valerie

Valerie has also gone alone. After she divorced, she was "inspired" by a story a friend told her. Her friend wanted to go backpacking and didn't want to go alone. The only person available at the time was Lou. He was a rather anti-social type; he would sit at parties with a jacket over his head. But the friend decided that it didn't matter a great deal, because they could just hike at their own speed, and she didn't have any special expectations of him. What Lou did, however, was recite epic poems on the trail and at the campsite. There was no stillness. The friend decided there were worse things than being alone. And so Valerie has gone alone a number of times, and other than having a deer startle her by bounding through the trees, she has never felt uneasy or unsafe.

✦ Della

"It was hard to keep going the last weeks of October and into November," said Della. Going north on the Appalachian Trail, she had often been hiking in tandem with various groups of people. "You pass people during the day, they pass you at lunch or dinner time, you pass them again at night time or the next morning. You have a chance to strike up conversations, compare notes, share stories. You help each other from time to time." But when Della did her "flip-flop" (hiked portions going south against the general flow of people), she lost that fragile, but real, community. "I was alone, and lonely," she said.

✦ Kathy

Kathy loves backpacking and mostly goes on her own or with a friend. She believes there are advantages and disadvantages to both. Being an introverted person, she likes the freedom of being by herself. She can go at her own pace and pee whenever she wants to. But she thinks it may be safer with a friend and she enjoys the camaraderie.

✦ Jeannine

Jeannine went to Kings Canyon on her first solo backpacking trip. "I found myself asking which appealed more — being in the mountains I love, or escaping what seemed to be an increasingly unhappy marriage. I was tentless, sleeping out in my bag. Everything was fine until the night when I was jolted out of my sleep by nearby screams. At first I thought it was a woman — then I realized it was a coyote."

✦ Marcy

Marcy's first experience of going solo was short but exciting. It left her anxious to do it again but longer. "Your worst enemy is your brain," she said. Following are excerpts from her journal entries of her Big Pine Lakes backpack of August 7-13, 2000:

"**August 8**, 6:00 a.m.: to Black Lake (Marcy nicknamed it 'The Chalet'), 10,650'. Last night I heard a scratching — a heartbeat not my own. I sprang up — but there was nothing." The next morning she found "there's a squashed cricket in my bivy." By mid-afternoon, she was experiencing foot problems: "excessive weight in my pack — 55 pounds is too much."

"Here on my little chalet above the lake, on the bluffs — high up — I thought I'd escape the mosquitoes! Thought!

"The lake is a deep blue-green color. Having a Sierra cup bath. Across the lake, a man is bathing in the willows —

buck-naked. Went fishing from 6 to 7 p.m. What's it like to backpack alone? Don't have much time to play harmonica — too busy taking care of myself.

"**August 9**, 6:44 a.m.: to Fifth Lake, 10,787'. What a terrible night — slept a few hours, now and then — tossed and thrashed, bivy full of feathers from my bag. Heard a noise — what was that? Bear? The rangers told me the bears were not active in this drainage. A rhythmic scritching. A mouse? Oh, it's me, when I breathe the down bag rises, scratches on the bivy bag. Saw a huge fireball heading east, with tiny stars falling off it. Legs hurt, back hurts, hips hurt. My heel at least is better, after two soakings in glacial melt streams and flyfishing by wading in sandals.

"7:26 a.m.: It's 45 degrees F. Last night, I woke up feeling very nauseous. 'How am I to get out of here, if I'm sick?' I worried. This morning, I'm OK. I'll make it!

"12:35 p.m. 5th Lake. I call my camp, on the south side of Fifth Lake, 'Penta-house.' The lake looks very deep; the sides against it are steep. The color is a clear turquoise. A hummingbird just came to investigate my Army baseball cap — its red and green camouflage colors must look natural.

"**August 10**, 6:37 a.m.: from Fifth Lake to Palisades Glacier and back. Finally, a good night's sleep. 'Course I had to drug myself with Motrin — still in a shadow of the headache. Thank you Lord, there are no bears, got too cold for mosquitoes, I feel pretty good, and I'm here!

"Perseid [meteor shower] is beginning to be more active. Also saw those flashes of light in the sky again — like I noticed at Piute Lake last year — once right from Milky Way to the ground — like a Jacob's Ladder. Saw one shooting star that must have come directly at us — a bright wink and then gone. Time to shine, there's a glacier to climb today.

"10:21 a.m.: Sam Mack Meadow. Discovered one of life's great secrets this morning: Always go the last steps to what seems to be the end of the trail and the way will be opened up to you. The trail zigzagged so much to get up here; I'd look up and say 'I've lost the trail! Where'd it go?' Then two more steps — to the end of the zig — and there was the zag — sharp right.

"There are two smallish glaciers at the head. I'm totally disappointed — but without crampons, ice axe and a strong, young guide — I cannot climb out of this steep bowl to get to the main glacier. I can't even see how to get to Sam Mack Lake.

"11:09 a.m.: Found a man and his young son, Michael and Jason, with backpacks. In an hour they are going to climb to the glacier. They don't mind if I go along with them. I'm so stoked — maybe I'll get to see it after all — not this little baby, pretend one.

"3:07 p.m.: Palisades Glacier Overlook, 12,200.' Decided not to wait for Michael and Jason, they were taking so long. At 12:30, I started up. At 12:35, I saw them; Jason was looking at the Yellow-legged frogs. I waited long enough to wave and holler that I'd go slowly — thinking they'd catch up to me quickly. I did go very slowly — took pictures of flowers, identified them in the flower book, ambled along.

"First I was on a good trail — then one amply marked with 'ducks,' finally up great slabs of boulders. Twice I saw them and waved — but after an hour of not seeing them, figured they turned back. Some kids coming down told me where to go on the ridgeline to see the overlook — so I kept climbing. Almost to the top, I saw Michael and Jason again — but as I write this I've been up here twenty minutes. I'm getting cold — where are they? I'm taking pictures of the glacier, of 5th & 6th Lake, Summit & 4th, Black & 1st & 2nd Lakes.

Spectacular views! Spectacular glacier! I'm so glad I made it! P.T.L.!! [Praise the Lord!].

"3:11 p.m.: Oh, great! I see Michael and Jason. Now we can have a good photo op.

"8:00 p.m.: 5th Lake. I'm cozy in my bivy with two hand-warmers on my feet. My Olbas [oil used for easing aches and pains] on legs and neck. Light failing fast — so much to write. A little over two hours to get up from Sam Mack Meadow, same down, and another hour back to camp — wanting so badly to do my friend Doug's "Astro travel" [*will yourself somewhere*]; I'm fantasizing a mule train picks me up.

"**August 11**, 1:49 p.m.: Fished from 11 to noon — caught a 9" Brookie. He was delicious with Neapolitan ice cream. Going to 6th Lake now.

"9:22 p.m. My last night on 5th Lake. Climbed back down to 5th Lake, fished 2 ½ hours, caught five. How come these fish are all the same size? Gave all of the Brookies to the painters [whom she had met previously]. We had an art show and poetry reading — I had written one at midnight during insomnia.

"**August 12**, 7:31 a.m. 'Penta-house' to 'The Bluffs.' Slept really well until midnight, then woke as usual and watched the falling stars for a long time. They were intermittent, but sometimes three at once. Don't want to leave here — this, the most beautiful lake.

"5:34 p.m.: 'The Bluffs'. Last camp, marvelous view of the cascade out of 1st Lake. Reluctantly, I headed down the trail about 10:30 this morning. Pack still heavy, but livable. Talked to folks along the way. That's one of the drawbacks of being alone – you pester everyone with questions, but that's how you find out the best place to camp and other stuff.

"I do so love my solitude. I call this camp, 'The Bluffs Apartments,' although it is more like a giant rock slide, with soft D. G. [decomposed granite] in between — and best of all — unobstructed views of the heavens! Tonight is supposed to be the peak for the Perseid.

"6:55 p.m.: The sun dips out behind Temple Craig — out come the zip-on legs, the shirt, down vest. Tonight — a little harmonica concert.

"**August 13**, 8:13 a.m.: 'The Bluffs Apartment'. Goodness — just woke up, again! Tossed until 11:30 p.m. last night — visited by a small furry creature. Saw only two falling stars — the Perseid a bust. Dreamt that Rick [her husband] cleared out his clothes from closet and drawers. 'Has he left me?' Gotta get this show on the road."

View from on top of Mt. Whitney, CA 2002

6
Don't Miss the Photo Op:
Congratulating and Rewarding Yourself

"Use what talents you possess, for the woods would be very silent if no birds sang except the best."

Henry Van Dyke

The trips that many of the interviewed women have attempted or completed are major coups. But, although we women backpackers may undergo weeks or months of training, and then set out for difficult hikes requiring strength, stamina, and mental discipline, we do not receive much notice. Even those who accomplish heroic feats or set records can't count on achieving media recognition. We do not get the fame and fortune heaped on major league sports figures.

Therefore, it's important to acknowledge your personal achievements. Consider how often we beat ourselves up about what we have not done, and how seldom we recognize, savor, and reward ourselves for what we have accomplished.

◆ Carol

Carol and Al take the time to celebrate their backpacking achievements. "We have a feeling of accomplishment when we're done, and we toast the trail. Then we spend hours reading about the section upcoming."

They celebrated the end of their Appalachian backpack in a memorable way. They planned an event in advance — giving them something to look forward to and an added incentive to complete their journey. So when Carol and Al stepped off the trail, a van met them and took them to the college where they were staying and a conference was being held. It was the opening of the 1995 Appalachian Trail Conference in the Shindoh Valley at Waynesboro, Virginia. It was also Carol's birthday. They celebrated their accomplishments and adventures at the pre-arranged Italian dinner for forty. All of the celebrants were people who had helped them one way or another on the trail — including a driver who had given them a ride on their very first hike, nine years previously. "At the beginning of the party people didn't know each other, but by the end it was *loud*."

Besides the sense of accomplishment from completing her many trips, and the satisfaction of discovering that there are in fact, a lot of woods out there in America, Carol expressed a sense of wonder that "a girl from Cleveland can go into the wilderness." "Awesome" was how she described her experience of watching the Perseid meteor shower [most years the peak of the Perseid shower is all night August 12th].

◆ Doris

Recording that you've "been there" dates back to prehistoric times. The fact that we like to write that we've made it to a major pass, climbed a mountain, or walked a lengthy trail doesn't seem much different than the cave-dwellers drawing pictures portraying their way of life. When Doris and her companions made it to Split Mountain in Kings

Canyon at 14,000 feet, "We were so disappointed, here we were, we opened the metal box to sign the register, and found that everybody had made such long signatures — poetry, and so forth — it was all used up!

"Other people were putting in note pads and such. All we had was a little piece of map and we wrote on that. Later, I looked in the Sierra Club schedule and saw that a fellow was going to climb the pass and so I telephoned him and he assured me that a new register would be put at Split Mountain. Not in time for us, but we were so triumphant. The core of our group is eight to fifteen years younger than I am. I'm not the fastest, and I'm the shortest and the oldest. But the others made sure I went ahead to the top. They all paused and said, 'You should be the first.' That was so thoughtful and dear of them.

"With that segment, our last segment of the John Muir Trail was completed. We all posed for pictures of the auspicious occasion. That night, the girls just treated me royally. JoAnne composed new lyrics about the John Muir Trail to "There's a John Muir Trail winding into the trail of your dreams" [instead of "long, long trail"]. Gerri had made the lyrics into a parchment certificate, and they all signed that I had done every inch of it. Then they treated me like a queen; they draped my sleeping bag around me — for my ermine robes. They carved sticks to spear smoked oysters, and didn't let me help with the meal. They are wonderful gals."

Doris had begun her backpacking career doing the John Muir Trail — a little bit at a time. "It took 13 trips. Sometimes I did only five miles, sometimes 35, but in seven years I had the 210 miles completed. There's a publication, a freebie, called the *Mammoth Times*, in Mammoth Lakes, California. They published an article on my completing the John Muir Trail."

✦ Emma

Emma called her Oregon Trail hike the most difficult of her trips, yet the most satisfying. When she arrived in Portland, crowds swarmed to meet her: reporters rushed to interview her. When one photographer persisted after she asked to be left alone, she bopped him over the head with the umbrella. Immediately she apologized and went on to enjoy Portland's warm welcome. She received a key to the city and the mayor named the opening of Oregon's Centennial "Grandma Gatewood Day" in her honor. Appearances on *The Art Linkletter Show* and on Groucho Marx's *You Bet Your Life* followed. She returned to her Ohio home by bus via a trip through Canada.

✦ The Marching Mothers

Sis and Carmen's group has nothing but appreciative comments about the support that they have had from families through the years. In the decade when they started their trips, it was not the norm for women to go backpacking — particularly on their own. The few women they did see were almost always accompanied by men.

Often the men they encountered on the trail were surprised when they first met the group, "Where's the rest of your group?" they'd ask, meaning, "Where are the men?" "There were all kinds of comments," wrote Sharon Winburn of their 1970 trip. "'How can we get our wives into your group?' but more typical, 'Women — alone?' 'Your husbands let you?' 'What are they doing, babysitting?' At Kearsarge, one puzzled camper we passed wandered over to see what kind of camp eight women would make — and was surprised to find it ship-shape. The crowning event was when a man snapped our picture — to prove to his wife that women did pack into the Sierras."

They had their supporters. On five or six occasions, the "Lone Ranger" who was Lu's husband, Phil, started out on their trail ahead of time. He never let himself be seen, but would leave notes for them. At the end of the trail, he would meet them with all the things one misses while backpacking — fresh fruit and vegetables and salty snacks.

And, their families coped without them. [Not without incident, however. One time Babs carefully provisioned her husband with a supply of TV dinners for the week. He invited Carmen's husband over for dinner, and while they were sitting around talking, they finally noticed a horrible smell. It turned out the smell was the box burning — he had neglected to take the dinner out of its container. The following year, Babs put together a social calendar for her husband so that he could eat at friends' homes each night].

✦ Valerie

Valerie, like most of us, keeps going at difficult times, even if just plodding along. "I'm somewhat competitive. Occasionally I fall apart. When I climbed Mt. Whitney, there were places where the 'friction pitch' — the angle of the slope — was frightening. There was the possibility of sliding to your death." What worked was her boyfriend encouraging her, and after the fact, a little brandy in her coffee made it all better.

✦ Della

Della's Appalachian Trail hike was not without difficulties. She had wandered off the main trail and onto intersecting trails a lot, especially in the beginning. This wasn't exactly a surprise to her husband and son who knew she had "absolutely no sense of direction." Her husband taught her how to use a compass before the trip, but the number of trails were a source of confusion. Her son suggested she might want to wear a bear collar so they could send a helicopter in to rescue her if necessary. But of course her husband and son were also among her strongest supporters. Once they got over the initial astonishment that

Della was really determined to do this, they proudly watched her progress.

There were still low points for all concerned. When Della called home on her birthday, and was feeling cold and lonely, her son panicked and said, "It's okay to come home."

At first her mother worried too. "I'll have a stroke," she cried. But Della bluntly told her, "Go ahead and enjoy your stroke if you must, but I'm going to do this." Then she called her sister and asked her to talk with their mom. Della knew she had enough to deal with just making the trip — having to reassure her mom every time she checked in was more than she could handle. Her mother turned out to be the best contact person — she was usually close to home, and gave Della great support.

Della was one happy camper when she finished the Appalachian Trail. Her husband and family were able to drive up, as well as her best friend. They greeted her with champagne and roses. Della was thrilled: "It was the best day of my life."

◆ Barbara and her women's group

Barbara feels having enough time is important on a backpacking trip — since it takes time to let go of outside concerns and get into the moment. She finds that this process is helped along by survival needs. It was a refreshing change for her to break out of traditional male/female roles of who would get the firewood and who would fix dinner. Her group has decided, over the years, that they can *all* get wood, or *no one* can get wood. They find it's a relief to not have layers of responsibilities such as one has at home. There aren't assigned tasks, but each woman has different skills. From the outset, each member has brought her own breakfast and lunch. They used to have soup or an appetizer with dinner, but they have simplified meal preparation. Nowadays a different person provides dinner each evening and it's usually a one-dish meal, often vegetarian, based on freeze dried foods — either store bought or home prepared.

When they first starting backpacking as a group, their husbands would meet them for a big welcoming party. But in time, that event was dropped; for some, it was too hard to go from the wilderness into a social occasion so quickly. Barbara was one who found re-entry difficult. She probably wasn't the only one who needed time to phase back in — not to mention catch up with the laundry.

As it turned out, Barbara's husband, who initially was uncomfortable with this venture, became a genuine supporter. He learned he could fend for himself — and that Barbara came back nourished. Barbara is proud of providing a role model for her four daughters that includes being a capable and enthusiastic backpacker. And she is as enthusiastic about backpacking today as she was at the beginning. The group's trips have almost always been at least a week long: long enough to transition to a space where home and the outside world slip away, and where they can attend to important things, such as being in the moment, or dealing with basic needs — or survival. In many ways, Barbara finds backpacking close to meditation — and very rewarding.

✦ Doris

"In 1996, I turned 70; I was so paranoid about it. My parents died in their 70s and people get hip replacements at that age. I thought, 'Oh gosh!' I went on 10 trips during the calendar year, trying frantically to do everything.

"There I was on my 70th birthday chopping footsteps in the snow for some neophyte backpackers on Silver Pass. We always get an early start; I'd forgotten we were going to have icy conditions on the pass. As we were going up to Monte Lake, we passed a packer. He had us get out of the way of a couple of mules — 'grumble, grumble.'"

"We were about a mile from the lake, and I shooed a couple of our party ahead to get us a campsite because one of the other women was kind of slow. The packer came back. He'd off-loaded his people, and he said, 'If I'd known it was your 70th birthday, I'd have taken your pack up.' So I couldn't stay mad.

"I went on up and there was the man who'd had the packer-assist sitting on a rock. He nodded pleasantly and said, 'I'm waiting for Doris.'

"'I'm Doris,'

"'You're 70?!'

"Well, you know, that sort of makes your day. He sent wine over that evening; you can have wine when everything comes up by mule."

In 2001, Doris rated an article on the front page of her local newspaper. At 75, she had summitted a 12,340 foot pass in the Sierra Nevada with six other women.

✦ ✦ ✦ ✦ ✦

The rewards of backpacking are usually more internal than external. They will come more from your sense of accomplishment than from public acclaim. Because of the nature of the sport, there is plenty of time for introspection. I think it is important to consider the adjustment period at the start of and at the end of your backpacking trip. You have to cut yourself some slack. I sometimes have found it difficult to go from "normal" life to the wilderness experience. There is an adjustment period as my body gears up to the physical demands and my mind shifts into a more relaxed state. Likewise, when I return home from a backpacking trip there is a transition period. In the wilderness I have pared down to just the essentials, now my life becomes more complex.

Most of us are seeking *some* change to come from our backpacking experiences; some may simply want relaxation and a change of scene, others may be seeking answers to life's major questions. However significant a change is desired, it is wise to consider that returning to "civilization" will require some transition. The longer you have been away from home, the more likely you will come back in an "altered space." Most likely your work, your home, and your family will expect you to drop right back into the familiar routines. Anticipate this, but give yourself the gift of time to consider the wisdom you have gained on the trail. Instead of falling back into the same patterns, use the opportunity to think about how you can incorporate into your everyday life what you have learned in your wilderness experience.

Sometimes reading the poems or stories we have written or showing photos we have taken can be a way to share our experiences with friends and family. For me, a camera is an essential piece of equipment; it provides not only a way to remember the details of a trip — the dizzying number of passes climbed and miles of cross-country traversed — but also a way to slip back into the wonder of the adventures.

Tip: Use a highlighter pen to mark your route on your topo or trail map and then frame or otherwise mount your map on the wall when you return home to remind yourself of your adventures and accomplishments.

Grace Lohr with her llama, Bodie

7
Llama Beans:
Trekking with Llamas

"Like the body that is made up of different limbs and organs, all mortal creatures exist depending upon one another."

Hindu proverb

✦ Grace, the Llama Mama

Subject: Summer plans with llamas

May 3, 2000

Dear Susan:

Winter has gone and although I promised myself that I would contact you, I'm not sure where the time went. I'm the Bishop lady with llamas. I've been in the backcountry for 30 plus years and still marvel when I run into other women hiking without the "protections" of men.

One of my aims with the llamas was to reach out to other slightly beyond prime women to show them anything is possible and no place in our mountains is out of reach because we're "too old" or "just women." I've got many trips planned this summer — some alone, some with other women, and some with men. They're all going to be wonderful!

Sincerely,

Grace Lohr, llama mama

Grace has been a backpacker for more than 30 years. Her first trip was in 1972 when she was in the process of trying to get a job at Tuolumne Meadows in Yosemite. She got to know a naturalist and began backpacking. She became a seasonal employee in the Yosemite high country from 1974-1976, and then moved to Bishop where she hiked and backpacked the Eastern Sierra every chance she could. In addition, she's backpacked in Colorado, the Tetons of Wyoming, and in British Columbia.

"That was during the '70s, my peak-bagging phase, where the challenge was to do 25-milers day-after-day. I did lots of cross country hiking — and scary-silly stuff," she said.

The next phase, in the '80s, was backpacking trips Grace described as "more genteel." She was less interested in miles, and decided it was okay to use a stove instead of relying on salami, cheese, and crackers. She got a tent and ditched the poncho.

Then came the '90s — Grace was now in her 50s. She continued to backpack, but was often in pain. She decided she did not want to hurt anymore, and she was no longer interested in staggering home, pretending that backpacking had been fun. She came up with a plan — the seeds of which had been planted when she was a child.

Grace explained how she discovered llamas. "When I was nine years old, I went to the LA County Fair and saw llamas for the first time. Two were on exhibit. I thought they were 'awesome.' I read about how they were used as pack animals in the Andes."

Then years later, in the '80s, when her two kids were at U.C. Davis, she would visit the llama exhibit during the school's annual "Picnic Day." It got her thinking about their use in backpacking, but the price was out of reach — $2,500 each.

A couple of years later, however, Grace visited her hairdresser who just happened to show her a picture of her latest purchase — a llama — for which she had paid $500. In April of 1992, she drove up to a ranch in Garnerville, Nevada with a halter, and wrestled two of the six-month old "babies" into her car. She turned them loose on her property. (Luckily, her land is on the outskirts of town and bumps up against Bureau of Land Management land where she can walk them).

Then she asked herself, "What do I do next?" She read everything she could find about raising llamas and learned by trial and error. Mostly, she learned that training them requires much patience, but providing for them takes little more than a fence, shed, pasture, and hay.

At first, she didn't have any way to transport them, but eventually she acquired an old Dodge van and life became easier. Because they are only about four feet tall, she can carry two of them standing up.

Llamas have to be three years old before they can carry full loads, so there was a two and a half-year wait before Grace could fully utilize her animals. By 2000, she had five and she was finding that training the more recent arrivals was much easier than training the original ones because the older ones were helping teach the younger ones.

In October, 2000, she acquired a new, young llama. The breeders had one they described as "pretty wild," which they offered for $100. After thinking it over, Grace called to say she wanted it, and they said they would only charge the gelding fees. Then, when Grace went to pick it up, they gave it to her free.

"I named him 'Otis' because he is going all the way to the top," said Grace. At first he was picked on by all the older ones, as they settled on the pecking order, and Grace's first attempt to put a lead rope on him took a half hour of coaxing and chasing him around the pen. She expects he will learn from the others and settle down.

Grace has found that the llamas have allowed her to meet more people on the trail, and have been a wonderful way to continue her wilderness travel. She quickly explains the advantages to using them and clears up any misconceptions. She loves to preach about the advantages of these graceful, docile animals.

Llamas come from South America where they are commonplace in the Andes. Because they make less of an impact on sensitive areas, they are much more compatible with a wilderness experience than a horse or mule. Grace says, "They are so alert and curious; they are great at spotting wildlife. They are as easy to train as a Golden Retriever." Llama provide many additional benefits because they:

- can carry 60-80 pounds of gear.
- can be lead with a slack rope on the trail.
- don't run off, and spook less easily than a horse or mule.
- eat selectively, like deer, and can browse on willow, grass, and sage — or in sensitive areas can be feed alfalfa or "Llama Chow."
- don't tear up the trail. (They have cloven hooves: their foot is divided into two parts with a nail on

each half. And when they walk, they are putting their weight on the leathery padded sole of their foot. Therefore, they do much less damage to the backcountry than horses and arguably less damage than the hiker's boot.)
- don't draw flies and mess up the trail; their droppings look like deer pellets, rather than "horse apples."
- weigh 400 pounds to the horse's 1500.

There are also disadvantages to using llamas. They:

- are not permitted on as many trails or parks as horses or mules.
- are not available in all areas of the United States.
- entail new responsibilities. Like any animal, they can become ill or suffer injury.

Just as the unexpected can occur when one is backpacking, Grace has found that llama trekking can have its challenges too. The high Sierra can have deep snowfields as late as August and new snow as early as September, and Grace has encountered areas that couldn't be crossed. Once she had a llama get its leg caught in the rocks during a thunderstorm dumping hail and rain. Luckily, though he was lame for a while, he recovered. All things considered, Grace feels safer with the llamas than being alone on the trail, and certainly safer than in most cities.

Three Days of Llamas

When I finished interviewing Grace for this book, she invited me to go on a llama trip into the Sierra during the summer. What follows is my journal entries of the trip:

Thursday, June 29th (trip scheduled for July 1-4, 2000):

I am very excited about my upcoming llama trip in the Sierra high country. Grace and I have been trying to set a date for a while, and I wasn't sure if the trip would happen. But we have a date. It will just be three of us — Grace, Grace's friend Gaye, and me. I called this past Saturday to be sure it was on.

"Are you a tee-totaler?" she asked.

I hesitated a moment to process the question. "No, why?"

"Well, we usually bring wine or beer."

Wow! The advantages of having the llamas carry the gear was suddenly clear.

"And you don't need to worry about bringing a chair; we have an extra."

A chair? Taking a chair backpacking had never occurred to me. "How do you do the food? Do you take freeze-dried, or what?" I asked.

"Well, I just got back from visiting my son in Alaska, and I thought I'd bring some halibut for the first night." She added that everyone usually does their own breakfasts and lunches. I offered to do one of the dinners; now I have to figure out what to bring.

My thoughts are bouncing up and down. There's the exciting prospect of hiking with just a daypack in the high Sierra and having the freedom to go beyond what you can normally get to on a day hike. There's the anticipation of meeting a couple of women who obviously love being outdoors. But, that's also the rub. Will I measure up? Will I be able to keep up? Will my knees, or some other body part, give me grief? Will Grace and her friend be able to stand my griping — or alternatively — will I be able to spend four days without griping? I don't suppose they will serve me tea in my sleeping bag (as Ralph does). Will I be able to light the stove when it's my turn?

It's funny how other people look at these things. When I called to make a campground reservation for Friday night —-so I could have a jump on the Saturday drive to our rendezvous spot — I felt somewhat of a wimp for not just driving up and doing a "first come-first serve." And staying in a huge campground seems very tame compared to sleeping on a granite slab. My neighbor, Janet, who has a high-powered job in business, earned by her intelligence, hard-work, loyalty, and savvy, commented that she wished she was as "ball-sy" as me — because I can just "take off" on a long drive, or camping trip, or foreign trip. After we laughed about how "ball-sy" was not perhaps politically correct, I wondered again where I fit on the "wimp-brave" scale.

Friday, June 30th:

I loaded up the car and headed for the mountains. My hope was that by leaving mid-morning, I would avoid the holiday traffic. Still, it was late afternoon before I got to Yosemite's Crane Flat Campground because I had made several stops along the way to the park — to get gas, to pick up food for my overnight camp and the llama trek, and to eat lunch. No matter, I wasn't in any hurry anyway.

6:20 p.m.: Weather is mostly clear and in the high 80s. I'm sitting in relative comfort at a picnic table before a fire I finally got going. My back was somewhat achy for a couple of hours after I arrived — where I think my kidneys are — but after going for a walk and taking some Tums, I feel better.

Though this campground will be full tonight, this afternoon it's quiet. As soon as I arrived, I unpacked everything and put my food in the campsite bear box. Then I sat there worrying about bears. I think when you feel the least bit unwell, you worry about everything more. But my fears about bears were put to rest after I talked to the campground host — she said there hadn't been any problems with them.

There have been problems with coyotes, however, and she told me that three women sleeping out in their bags last week had been bitten. I'm still having a hard time believing her story — how could three people be bitten? After one person yelled out, or something, wouldn't the other two have gotten out of the way? But when I went for my walk, I took the precaution of carrying one of my hiking poles. Sure enough, I soon spotted a coyote trotting alongside me about twenty feet away; fortunately, he kept at that distance.

I'm sitting here enjoying my beer and hoping my plan for heating my Dinty Moore stew in a pan of water atop the fireplace grate will work — sort of a double boiler arrangement. If it does, I'll have a warm dinner and no clean up.

Evening: I called home and everything is okay with Ralph. Later I went to the evening's ranger talk, and he gave an informed presentation on Yosemite's frogs and other amphibians. He presented many of the theories being considered to explain the decline of frogs; we learned that many lakes in the alpine regions are no longer being stocked with fish because the fish eat the tadpoles.

Saturday, July 1st. The trip begins:

I got an early start for the long drive ahead. Shortly after I arrived at the trailhead, Grace arrived in her van for our initial meeting. After our brief conversation, she began the process of unloading her llamas and gear. Soon came Gaye and her husband, Milt, with their car and llama trailer. After further introductions, both Grace and Gaye launched into loading the panniers the llamas would carry with our sleeping bags, tents, food and so forth. While they were working, I was mostly standing around wondering if I should somehow be helping, but also keeping my distance because I didn't want to be spit at or kicked. (Later Grace told me that in the six years she'd had llamas, she'd only been spit at three times.)

All four llamas are male. Grace's Bodie, named for the eastern California ghost town, is a tall, handsome, brown and white animal. Her Chewbacca is reddish-brown and is named after the popular Star Wars character. Gaye's Macho is a white llama with a very sweet disposition. He has a "sweet spot" on his back where he loves to be rubbed. When Gaye rubs him there, he opens his lips and shows his teeth in a big smile. Gaye's second llama is Redman. He is named after Redman chewing tobacco — which people spit. I didn't see him spit, and I found this short and stocky llama to be quite lovable.

About 10:30, Kathy, another friend of Grace's from Bishop, arrived. She was just going to dayhike in with us. The trailhead was approximately 8,600 feet. The trail was fairly level at the first leading through the forest of red fir and lodgepole pine. About two miles in, we stopped to eat a leisurely lunch creekside. Then we began gradually ascending through granite areas of juniper and Jeffrey pine. The wildflowers were wonderful along the way — the nodding asters, the delicate looking, yet hardy, shooting stars, the cool blue lupine, the brilliant red Indian paintbrush, the mountain penstemon, the hug-the-ground pussypaws. Spring has only recently come to this area.

As the trail continued, we traveled through the forested areas with their duff trails and the granite areas where stone ducks lined the pathway. We started our climb in earnest through a series of switchbacks. Luckily, we were mostly in the shade of trees.

I stopped often to catch my breath and slow my heartbeat. I was definitely the slowest — even the llamas were faster. At the top of the climb, we stopped to rest. We had reached the junction where our trail left the main one. We hadn't seen many people, and had decided if we encountered too many, we'd move tomorrow. After we crossed the ridgetop, with its wide-swept, stunted growth, picturesque hemlock and pine, we came to an awesome view of the mountain ranges to the north. After taking some photos, Kathy had to turn back. We began to descend steeply by switchbacks, through granite and scrub, to the lake area and our campsite-to-be.

That was when the llama problem began. As usual, I was at the end of the pack — thankful for every occasion when the llama train stopped to drink, browse, pee, or "squeeze out some beans," as Gaye put it. But Grace's second llama, Chewbacca, really began to give her grief. Several times, he just lay down and would not budge. For all the yelling and tugging Grace would do, Chewy wasn't going anywhere. Grace decided to stay with the llama until he was ready to move. They connected Grace's first llama, Bodie, to Gaye's two — Macho and Redman, and Gaye took all three the rest of the way down the mountainside.

I was afraid to lead any of the llamas because I was pretty tired, and I was really depending on my walking poles to keep my balance on the steep downhill. After Gaye and I reached the campsite area, we dumped our daypacks and tethered the llamas. Gaye went back up to help Grace. Finally everybody made it down the hill, and we were able to set up camp.

Our campsite is just at the base of the switchbacks in a little clearing. There is a small stand of hemlock and pines separating us from a small meadow — and the llamas can be moved between the two open areas to browse and rest. On the other side of the meadow, other groups have set up their tents, but as best I can tell, we have the choice site. No mosquitoes.

After we set up tents, we sat out in the sun with our paperback books in our cushion chairs — what a great invention these folding chairs are! Gaye handed me a chilled Sierra Nevada Ale. What a treat! Backpacking does not allow for this kind of luxury. Late afternoon, Grace and Gaye fired up their stoves and prepared a fine dinner of Alaskan halibut (which Grace caught while in Kenai two weeks ago), Caesar salad with croutons and parmesan (from the bag), and a respectable Loach Valley Chardonnay.

As it grew darker, we started trading stories and watched with fascination as a deer wandered into camp and stood seemingly mesmerized by the strange herbivores we had brought with us.

Sunday, July 2nd:

Last night, as usual, I worried about a bear coming into the camp. Not everything would fit into the bear canisters. As I lay there, I tried to convince myself that all would be okay, but I went through several episodes of teeth-chattering fear. Finally I managed to calm myself down and go to sleep. This is something I always seem to go through — I know what the facts are — bears are interested in our food, not us, and additionally I know that the llamas probably keep them away, but my fears are not based on the rational. I guess I will just have to continue to struggle to overcome my irrational feelings.

I also have to get used to the llama noises; apparently all the animal noises I heard during the night were from them. As they moved around to eat, plants would rustle and small rocks would roll down the hill. Our camp equipment, including the bear canisters, was untouched.

We got up slowly, since we were in no hurry. We each prepared our own breakfast.. When I was choosing my food to bring, I was still thinking "backpacking food" and so I brought pre-packaged oatmeal. I watched Grace eat a delicious-looking bagel. My oatmeal — even with raisins and nuts on it — tasted like wallpaper paste. I am envious of their "real" food.

We took Grace's Chewbacca and Gaye's Redman with us today for hiking. We did a fairly steep trail which switchbacks up to see some of the nearby lakes. In addition to the lake near our campsite, we saw, or explored, another three. We followed the trail along its edge until we came to a shallow area where zillions of tadpoles were zipping around — a very good sign for the health of the lake. We could also hear the frogs. Maybe this is one of the lakes that has been fished out and no longer is being stocked — I hope so. The far side of the lake was inaccessible because of the steep slope of the granite meeting it. The patches of snow in the shady crevices added to the picturesque scene. No one was camped nearby; we only saw a couple of other people during the time we were there.

It was a beautiful day — clear blue sky, no clouds, and temperature in the 60-70s, but as evening approached, it became increasingly chilly. When we returned to our campsite, we had another chance to read and nap. Our dinner was again wonderful — I presented a salmon pate with crackers which went over well, and Gaye fixed a succulent chicken dish — large chunks of tender chicken with yellow and green zucchini squash sautéed in Oriental sauce. We were not suffering from lack of food.

After we returned, Grace wanted to know if either of us wanted to take a "PTA bath." When I looked at her quizzically and asked what she meant, she looked at me like she wasn't sure she wanted to answer. I shot a look at Gaye, and she didn't say a word.

"What's that?" I asked again.

"I have Baby Wipes for a PTA bath — pits, tits, and ass," Grace replied.

Monday, July 3, 2000, 10:30 a.m.:

Last night was significantly colder, but I slept much better. I was reassured about the bears, and maybe the llamas do keep them away. Whereas yesterday we were sitting in the sun at this time, today is much colder. Lots of clouds are being blown rapidly by and piling up on the mountains to the North. We are going to hike today back up the trail that leads out — probably take the spur trail that we passed when we came in. A different Kathy, Kathy Morey from Bishop, is supposed to walk in today to meet up with us — then she will hike back out.

4:15 p.m.: Well, I wouldn't have bet a dollar that it would stay clear today — but it did. We took Macho and Bodie, and they were both good. I have learned (not first hand, thank goodness) that llamas do most of their spitting at each other — sort of a dominance thing. And there are three kinds of spitting — first type is saliva from the mouth (not too bad), second is with color (sounds yucky), and, finally, a green sticky gob (gross). I have tried to stay out of their way — and especially to avoid getting between them.

By the time we got to the turnoff to the spur trail, we still had not encountered Kathy. So we made a "K" and a large arrow with rocks, pointing the way for her to find us. Then we went over to a lake we hadn't yet explored. It was as beautiful as the others, with lots of buttercups, heather/heath, and bluebells. There was a small waterfall, which was the inlet to the lake. This lake also offered limited campsites, but with more mosquitoes than the others.

When we returned to the fork in the road, the rock markers were still in place — no Kathy. But when we got back to camp, there was Kathy waiting for us — she had not seen any of the messages. After all that effort, she was only able to stay about half an hour, since she had a four hour hike ahead of her back to her car.

It was my turn to make dinner. I served Japanese crackers and a nice Merlot. We fired up both stoves; I made fettuccine with clam sauce containing mixed mushrooms and added clams. The freeze-dried green beans were quite good. And for dessert, we had rice pudding. We gathered firewood for our first campfire of the weekend and enjoyed the intimacy that gathering around a fire seems to bring.

Tuesday, July 4th:

We were to be out at 2:00 to meet Gaye's husband, Milt, so we got ourselves going earlier than usual. We weren't sure whether Chewbacca would stage a sit-down strike or not, so there was some concern that we allow extra time for hiking out in case he did. I was very proud of myself for being able to climb out much faster than I had been able to the day before. It took about 35 minutes to ascend the mountainside — compared with probably twice that long previously. I enjoyed the freedom of going at my own speed — at times going ahead and then trailing behind. The trail is well marked, but it would be easy to lose it for a bit if you didn't pay attention. We only had one incident with Chewbacca trying to lie down. That attempt was swiftly handled by Grace's yanking on his rope. Grace explained, "If he learned he could get away with it, he'd be taking control all the time."

We had our leisurely lunch at the same area where we had eaten coming in and got back to our cars on schedule. This was the end of memorable trip, and it was made even more special by the fact that Grace invited me to go again. I felt so empowered — not only for having experienced this beautiful area in such company, but also for being physically capable of doing it.

Llamas and Bears, Oh My!

In August 2001, I had my second experience with llamas, which was much more sobering than my previous one. Ralph and I were on the last leg of our fourth portion of the John Muir Trail on a long northern climb to Donahue Pass (11,056′). We began to see llama footprints on the trail and wondered if we would be lucky enough to run into Grace. A man approached and asked if we had seen a llama along the trail. We hadn't. "The group up ahead rented three llamas from a llama ranch and one got away. A large bear came into their camp last night and spooked it," he said.

We came to the camp — two women and a young girl (who was on her first backpack trip). The people who had rented them the llamas had told them they wouldn't need bear canisters above timberline. Ralph and I looked at each other, remembering that we had made the same mistake many years ago on our first trip into the Sierra.

One of the women explained what had happened. "Two bears, a large one and a smaller one, came into camp after we had gone to bed and started knocking the food packsacks around. We tried to yell and make noise to frighten them away. But Bud broke loose from his tether and took off up the mountainside," she said.

Their plan was to continue searching for Bud and to stay there one more night. They knew that llamas are herd animals and hoped that the two remaining llamas would draw him back. "Unless we find him, we're going to have to abandon our trip. We can't carry all the supplies Bud did."

We suggested that they do the rest of their cooking away from their tents, so that food odors near the tent would be reduced. There were no trees over eight feet high, so attempts to hang food out of the way were doomed. "The bear might return tonight, so try to wedge your food across the way in a rock crevice," suggested Ralph. "Bears' arms are shorter than ours."

We continued on our uphill journey — eyes scouring the landscape for a brown and white ruminant. It seemed that a llama, or anything out of the ordinary, would show up clearly on that gray, rock strewn terrain, but we saw no sign of Bud. We wondered about the irresponsibility of renting out animals to people who aren't experienced at traveling with them, and why the hikers hadn't been told that bears might be encountered anywhere along the John Muir Trail.

Information on llamas and their rental is available on the internet. Before you decide to use llamas (or any other animals) for a trip, be sure that you will either have a packer accompany you, or that you have adequate experience handling them. Certainly, it would be prudent to ask for references from previous customers.

Grace summarizes the advantage of using llamas, "I want to get the message out about llamas to women who have never gone into the high Sierra, and to those who are 40 or 45+ and are thinking about giving up on the whole idea of backpacking because they think it's too hard, or they're afraid — they *can* do it, if they can walk."

8
Beauty and the Bugs:
Exploring Sequoia National Park

"Success seems to be largely a matter of hanging on after others have let go."

Unknown

Backpack to Sequoia

What follows are my journal entries of a 12-day backpack trip that Ralph and I took into Sequoia National Park — Lodgepole to Bearpaw Meadow via Deadman's Canyon, Elizabeth Pass, and Hamilton Lakes:

Day 1: August 10, 1998: The weather was perfect — clear blue skies, temperature in the 60s & 70s. The trail was mostly dirt and duff as we were primarily in fir and spruce forest. The waterfall we passed along the way was a wonderful cascading one. Our campsite is nothing special, but the surrounding area is quite beautiful. There are lots of wildflowers — shooting star, aster, leopard lily, fireweed, lupine, and many delicate ones.

I did fine for the first four miles, then quickly began to tire. The last couple of miles had me in tears. Initially, I didn't even want dinner because I was so exhausted, but after a few minutes rest, I changed my mind and even helped Ralph with the stroganoff. He always has more energy at the start, but also stops to rest at least as often as I do.

I'm carrying 35 pounds, and he has 55, partly because of the weight of the three bear canisters. I find my lack of stamina very upsetting. We've been waiting forever to go on a trip — we missed going at all last year — and now I'm wondering why I'm doing this. That's what I get for bragging about how into this I am; right now I feel like a complete phony.

We saw seven deer today. Clearly, it's mating season since we saw mostly pairs.

Day 2: Tuesday, August 11th: Twin Lakes to Ranger Lake (3 miles, over Silliman Pass (10,165'). While we were on the trail today, Ralph managed to trade our excess gorp for a half can of bug spray. We had brought a combination sunscreen and bug repellent because we thought it would save weight to have a two-in-one. The problem is we need sunscreen during the day and the bug repellant mostly in the evening. The combination has been going alarmingly fast, and the mosquitoes are pretty bad.

While Ralph was negotiating that transaction, I had to dash on ahead because I was hit with an attack of diarrhea. We were descending steeply on switchbacks, and it was very hard to find a private, suitable place on such exposed terrain, especially one so well traveled. This is the sort of thing I dread.

The view from Silliman Pass was spectacular, and the verdant meadows and beautiful wildflowers continued. It was pretty steep going up and over, but luckily not too hot. Some warm afternoon sprinkles provided a welcome relief. Ranger Lake is pretty, and warm enough to swim in, but there's too much thunderstorm activity this afternoon for it to be safe. I took some photos of the marmots on the rocks behind our tent.

Because today's distance was short, we arrived early afternoon at our campsite. Ralph seems to be feeling the altitude. He needed to rest, and felt light-headed and dizzy when he stood up too fast.

My shoulders felt better today, but my neck really hurt because I absolutely had to look down with each step so I wouldn't stumble on the granite. In general I feel better today, but this intestinal upset makes me a nervous wreck. I hope tomorrow is better body-wise.

Day 3: Wednesday, August 12th, 7:30 a.m.: Ralph is up and preparing breakfast as usual. While he's getting scrambled eggs with bacon and added jerky, tea, and coffee ready, I'm doing my usual morning inventory of aches and pains.

About 1:30 this morning I awoke feeling nauseous. Eventually the feeling passed, but not until after I had contemplated the merits of airlift, ditching packs, and giving good food away. Then, because I still couldn't sleep, I made a mental list of all the places I want to go yet in my lifetime. I need time to go to Africa — to see the wildlife, to Machu Picchu and the surrounding area, to see Spain and Portugal, Paris and the countryside, and New York City. I want to revisit Mexico, Alaska, and the Southwest. I wasn't feeling any real enthusiasm for any of them, but I guess I was looking for something to feel good about, to look forward to, and to get my mind off of my self-recriminations.

This morning I actually felt pretty good, though lazy. I need to watch what I eat until my intestines settle down. My right foot is only a little sore, just in the mornings. As I lie here, concluding I feel moderately well, it's hard to understand the intense emotions the trail brings forth. It annoys me when Ralph is far ahead and then seats himself on a rock to wait for me. Then, when I take the lead, I get annoyed because it feels like he is right on my heels.

It's not that I don't want him anywhere around me; it's that I'm feeling irritable and don't want anyone witnessing it. When I'm uncomfortable or feeling exhausted, I misplace my emotions. It's scary to have so little reserve energy and I come up with frightening scenarios: 'What if a bear charges us? What if all the campsites are full and we have to hike on several miles?'

7:30 p.m. We did seven miles today — and the day was better in many ways. We're about one and a half miles past Comanche Meadow — probably about a quarter mile to Sugarloaf Meadow. We're between two pretty peaks and alongside the stream that runs through the valley. All the water that we've seen on this trip comes at a price — the surrounding areas have been thick with mosquitoes. But not here, so I'm thankful.

Luckily, we've had no rain today, and we were able to wash clothes and ourselves — including hair — which was very nice.

We get to have a campfire. We've now left the security of the bear lockers. Ralph hung our excess food, which is mostly freeze-dried dinners. The food's been pretty good, but unfortunately it still goes through me too quickly. My left toes are sore from the downhill and by the end of the day I was hobbling a bit, but that's not bad considering the mileage.

We saw a few lizards today and a tree frog. Moments ago two beautiful bucks walked through our camp about two and a half feet from the tent. Just saw a bat.

Day 4: Thursday, August 13th: (5 miles) to Roaring River Ranger Station (Scaffold Meadows) Kind of up and down, not very steep today. Most of the trail was dusty from pack trains and general overuse. We had two good fords (river crossings), neither dangerous, but my Tevas were invaluable because Ralph and I could take turns using them and keep our boots dry. Luckily for me, he's been carrying both packs over the more difficult crossings.

We had another good mid-afternoon thunderstorm, but it didn't last long. We're enjoying a campsite with lots of benefits; we have few mosquitoes and a bear box locker (which makes food storage easier), and campfires are permitted (which they won't be in upcoming areas). We are camped so close to the river that we can hear it roaring at a tremendous volume. We are surrounded by Jeffrey pines, firs (good Christmas trees!), and ponderosa. The camp bird is the junco — one of my favorite birds because of its neat black hood.

And there's a "Powder Room." A sign directs you to an outdoor "can." The toilet is pretty fancy; it is surrounded on three sides by boards and even has a coffee can with a roll of toilet paper. It's amazing what a luxury this seems.

On today's hike we saw fewer wildflowers, but many chipmunks, golden mantled ground squirrels, striped lizards, and a marmot. The trail paralleled the river for several miles but although we could hear the river, we couldn't see it because of the surrounding vegetation. It was frustrating to be so close, and to be walking in two-inch deep dust, and yet not be able to get to the water. But every so often we would have a glimpse of the cool, rushing water — and that view would revive me.

Last night Ralph gave me NoDoz because I had a headache. We thought it would provide the caffeine I was missing since I wasn't having my usual two cans of soda daily. I didn't think that the pill would keep me awake; I often drink tea and soda late at night and have no problem. Well, I couldn't sleep for hours. Fortunately I didn't panic at the prospect of a sleepless night, and found it to be a peaceful meditative time.

Day 5: Friday, August 14th: I felt good yesterday. And this morning, after being lulled into a good sleep by the river, I feel great. I couldn't worry about bears, because we wouldn't have been able to hear them over the sound of the creek. My body feels (mostly) good and strong.

Gads, it's only 7:15 in the morning, and it's already heavily overcast.

7:00 p.m. Upper Deadman Canyon (7 miles). We're above the very beautiful Deadman Canyon (named after a sheepherder whose grave is along the route). It's another two or three miles to the base of Elizabeth Pass and the mountains that surround it. There's plenty of snow up there. We're camped in a little grove of Jeffrey pines. The valley was quite long, and we spent much of our time following the deep, narrow trail through knee-high wildflowers. We had two pretty good fords — deep enough so the bottom of my shorts got wet. But even I, chicken maximus, didn't feel at risk. The hike was extraordinarily beautiful — such an awe-inspiring place where the unknown shepherd got to spend much of his life.

I had some adrenaline rushes when the lightning came, but it wasn't right on top of us, and the rain was light.

The huge fly in the ointment was the awful mosquitoes. They couldn't be batted away; they were trying to go up my nose and I know I swallowed at least three (they are dry going down). I was just about frantic by the time I managed to put on my wet bandanna — outlaw style. On top of that,

I managed to lose my new hat, which is a real loss as it provides relief when the sun is beating down.

Tonight's highlight was lovely alpine glow up and down the valley. We met only two people today — brothers. One of them said the hike over Elizabeth Pass, coming from the other direction, was the hardest trip he'd encountered in thirty years of backpacking.

Day 6: Saturday, August 15th, 7:20 p.m. Last night Ralph spotted a forest fire on the top of the western ridge of Deadman Canyon. Of course, I was spooked about it, but he explained that it wouldn't be a problem because there wasn't enough vegetation to provide fuel. Then we heard a tremendous scraping and scouring sound, and looked out and watched a rock-slide across the valley.

Now, we're camped about 1,000 feet below Elizabeth Pass. Today's hike through the upper meadow and over a few patches of ice was beautiful. The path often became a watercourse, but luckily the flowing water was not often over the tops of our boots. At this elevation there is lots of heather — and its perfume fills the air. It's cold, but beautiful. I can't believe where we've had to stop. The rain started early, about 1:00 this afternoon, and we had to find a place below the summit. Ralph found a big, fairly flat granite slab to pitch our tent on; I guess you'd call it a boulder field. There's a small cascading stream about fifteen feet away.

We had hardly gotten settled when rain, lightning, and hail started in earnest. A rivulet next to us became a wider rivulet. It was frightening — strikes three seconds away — which means the lightning is less than a mile away. The sound was tremendous, amplified by the high canyon walls. I was terrified; Ralph was in seventh heaven.

He managed to calm me somewhat by pointing out that the waterfalls appearing across the valley and on our side of the valley were following the stains from all the previous times. Looking at it objectively, and realizing that the watercourses were predictable, made it less mysterious and scary.

Then I felt the bottom of the tent; it felt like I was pushing down on a waterbed. The water was under us. I had visions of us floating away. Ralph put on his rain gear and got out to take a look. I pulled all the sleeping bags and dry clothes around me in the middle of the tent so I could keep everything dry. I sat there shaking, worrying about hypothermia setting in when we got wet.

After what seemed like hours, but was actually 15 minutes, he returned. "That was great, I felt just like a kid playing in the rain," he reported. He'd been making little dams, diverting the watercourse, and having a good time — totally unfazed by the downpour. He explained that the water above us would go under the boulder field we were on, and the small amount of water that had been collecting under the tent was now re-routed.

I hope tomorrow morning is clear so we can go on over the pass. I don't want to go through this emotional wringer again.

The rain stopped about 4:30, and we've been able to dry everything and cook a hot meal. For the last hour we've been watching a couple of marmots and a pika. Pikas may be rodents, but I think they are really cute with their big, round ears.

I think I'll stop writing, since my hand is freezing. If I drop the pen here, it will fall below us in the rocks and I'll never see it again. We lost my hat yesterday, and a Teva and the dental floss today.

Day 7: Sunday, August 16th: Junction of Hamilton Lake/Elizabeth Pass trails. Today was a highlight day of highlight days. We went over Elizabeth Pass which is 11,000 feet. Getting up so high yesterday and sleeping on a slab of granite — which actually was very comfortable — and getting up at 6:15 and leaving at 7:00 after eating a cold breakfast — really paid off.

We had a beautiful, clear blue sky. It took almost three hours to reach the pass and here we are at this lovely crossroads.

For all my fears, nothing I had imagined materialized. When we initially got to the snow areas, the snow was more like ice. It was too hard to cut into, but as it warmed and melted, Ralph was able to kick into it and stomp a path — which made my crossing easy. We moved across the snowfields from one rocky area to the next.

Only once did he sink in up to his knees, and that was right next to a rock, which we were trying to reach to sit on. Apparently the sun had warmed the rock enough times so that the underlying layer of snow had been melted away.

Otherwise it went beautifully, though very slowly. We concluded that the brothers we had talked to earlier who had had such problems probably came to the snow late in the day and found the snow so soft that they were constantly sinking deep into it. We didn't get wet at all.

The views from Elizabeth Pass were magnificent in every direction. The descent was tedious, but my feet and all else are doing well. The major obstacle ahead now is fording a river on the trail to Hamilton Lakes.

Usually water flow is lighter in the morning than in the afternoon because the sun melts the snow and ice upstream during the day. We've made our camp on the only flat area near the crossing — a sandbar. Though the sandbar is dry now, I've been watching the snowmelt from today slowly work its way down the gully that is next to our tent. Ralph's theory is that it would take a storm even worse than yesterday's to deliver enough water for us to get wet here.

I wish I wasn't afraid of my own shadow. I'm pleased that the register on top of Elizabeth Pass tells that we were the only people to come over in two days, and the comments attest to its difficulty. I'm also happy that we seem to have left the mosquitoes on the other side of the pass.

Day 8: Monday, August 17th, 10:25 a.m.: We're on the trail to Bearpaw Meadow — which represents my caution winning out. Ralph was convinced it was safe to ford the stream next to where we had camped, but I wasn't. Going downhill will add a couple of miles to our hike, but we will be able to cross the river safely on a bridge. Also, by going in this direction we will be able to pick up needed sunscreen at Bearpaw Meadow.

Since the trail is called "Over the Hill," I assumed it would be an easy stroll. It wasn't. The first part of the hike was discouraging — uphill, dry and hot. But then we entered a beautiful stretch with firs and fern grottoes. There was lots of evidence of lightening strikes on lone trees at the top of the gorge. Then came a 1,000 foot descent into Bearpaw through pockets of blue lupine (knee high), "quaking" aspen, bracken fern, thimbleberry, currant, leopard lilies (which I called tiger lilies until I realized they had spots instead of tiger lilies' stripes), and the tiniest of violet and yellow snapdragons. About 11:00 we arrived at Bearpaw; it was much more inviting than we had thought it would be. We were momentarily tempted, but it was early, and even though its $125 per-person-per-night would have included all-you-can-eat and showers, it seemed pretty steep for a tent cabin. We decided it might be a nice splurge as a way to start or end a lengthier trip some other time. It requires a 11-mile hike from Crescent Meadows — but that's along a well-maintained trail and not terribly strenuous.

The staff was very nice to us. We were in luck; they had one tube of sunscreen left. They gave me a large, delicious brownie and notepaper (I was almost to the point of having to write in the margins of my book). The views from the lodge were awesome.

The hike from Bearpaw Lodge and campground was terrific. This side of the pass (southern) is very different from the other side. Deadman's (northern), which we just came up from, is surrounded by mountains that are more jagged. Here the rock faces are more rounded and massive. Whereas it felt like spring on the other side, here it is drier and feels like summer. I guess we're dealing with differences in elevation as well as orientation towards the sun and weather. We passed huge waterfalls, and one of the creeks had to be forded. But the trail was much easier and better maintained than any we have found thus far.

Evening: We are at Upper Hamilton Lake (8,400′). It would be a nice place to stay a couple of days, but the plan is, if my blisters stay under control, to go on to Kaweah Pass and back down.

Day 9: Tuesday, August 18th, 2:15 p.m.: We had an argument last night — probably due to tiredness and lack of sex. Ralph insisted on a layover day here at Upper Hamilton Lake. It is a beautiful lake, but we had expected to go on to Kaweah Gap. I was so disappointed that I couldn't stop arguing for us to go. Luckily, Ralph prevailed. Going today would really have been too soon for me. All we've done is lie around, cook, eat, and cleanup, and stare at nothing and everything. We had the lake to ourselves for a few hours and were able to wash our bodies and clothes. How much easier it is to contemplate sex when you feel clean and rested.

We're in the "overflow" camp area, but though we can't see the lake from here, and have to climb over a little rise, we're alone nestled in a grove of pines. There are two kinds or pines — one has small, scaly bark (lodgepole), and the other has large, scaly chunky bark (white pine). It's sad to observe that a lot of the large scaly-barked ones are dead or dying — probably from some kind of blight.

We didn't see the bear, but others did. This makes the third day of sunshine, no storms.

3:00 p.m. I wonder when I last lay on my back watching the clouds drift, distracted only by a hummingbird, the coo of some band-tailed pigeons, or having to move my foam pad back into the sunshine. Stirred long enough to walk to lakeside and soak my feet. Amazing — I thought the day would be boring, but it's been just fine.

Day 10: Wednesday, August 19th: We did a fairly leisurely hike out from Hamilton Lake, past Bearpaw 1 mile, to a tiny "campground" at Buck Creek. The creek is full, but the surrounding area is dry, and has a more "used" feeling. Still pretty. We had the creek to ourselves for a couple of hours which we put to good use bathing, rinsing out clothes, and "fooling around" — no fooling!

About 5:30 this afternoon, another couple came stumbling in — their first day. It's 6:50 and another hiker just came by. This feels too cozy. The other couple's tent is less than 12 feet from us.

Day 11: Thursday, August 20th: From Buck Creek to Merton Meadow. The first part of the hike was fairly easy — and I teased about "baby steps." But upon leaving the High Sierra Trail, well-maintained for heavy usage, we started climbing and went up about 1,200 feet in a mile or so. It's a beautiful campsite nestled in the pines, with gurgling water (for once not threatening us), and the adjacent meadow is filled with shooting stars. The lower elevation had some pretty spots, but in general, it was manzanita and scrub.

We finally saw a bear today. We were just finishing our beef jerky at lunch when I spotted him about 40 yards away. He was across the ravine, working himself up the mountainside. We packed up our things and continued down the trail. I nervously kept glancing back at him, but he didn't show any sign that he was aware of us. The campsite we're in now doesn't have a bearbox, but we have plenty of room in our canister.

My body feels good now — firmer. Maybe I've lost weight, but I'm still not running up hills with my pack. We may not have company tonight, but if we do, I hope they're not duds like the couple near us last night. Ralph — always generous to a fault when judging others — thought the woman who was part of the couple was just shy, but I thought she was unfriendly. I also didn't like the fact she was wearing a loosely buttoned top that showed her uplift bra and her tattoo whenever she bent over. Am I just jealous?

The skies are still blue. Butterflies everywhere. Blue-bellied lizard. The lupine — here in the higher elevations — has dark leaves. Ralph is whittling a new walking stick because his old one broke in the snow.

Day 12: Friday, August 21. It was an easy hiking day as we continued the gradual downhill towards Crescent Meadow and then over to our car at Lodgepole. It was easy to know we were getting closer and closer to what is called civilization — the trails were increasingly dusty from overuse; the plant life less varied because of its fragility. We passed Lodgepole campground with its vehicles packed like sardines in a can, its campsites littered with toys, tools, and towels. (It's always such a shock to see what so many other people feel necessary to guarantee themselves a good time while camping.)

After we got back to our car and dumped our backpacks into the back, I went to pick up the extra toiletries I had left in the parking lot's bear box. The only bag I could find in the container was one with empty pizza boxes; our things were gone. A naturalist, Jay Snow, approached me. He had found the bear box open the night before; he was interested in determining if we had lost anything. I explained that we'd had a few items —aspirin and the like — but nothing of great value. We were delighted to learn more about Jay. It turned out that he was working for the season on bear management. Sequoia was his last stop before he reached the San Francisco Bay Area, which would complete his backpacking trip across the United States. We invited him to stay with us when he reached the west coast (which he later did.)

Hanging bear bags

Bearikade® bear canister

Part 2: It's Your Turn – *Getting Up and Out*

Grace, Susan, and Gaye
with llamas Chewbacca, Bodie, Redman, and Macho

Llamas browse quietly in the meadows.

9
Brain or Bruin?
Bears and Other Things that Go Bump in the Night

"The greatest griefs are those we cause ourselves."

Sophocles

The Bear Went Over the Mountain

The bear went over the mountain,
the bear went over the mountain,
the bear went over the mountain,
to see what she could see.
To see what she could see,
to see what she could see.
The other side of the mountain,
the other side of the mountain,
the other side of the mountain,
was all that she could see.
Was all that she could see,
was all that she could see.
The other side of the mountain,
was all that she could see.

author unknown/ "she" for "he" substituted by S. Alcorn

Most of us know this old song from our childhood. Along with *Teddy Bear's Picnic*, the stories of *Winnie the Pooh* and *The Three Bears*, and our own favorite teddy bears, our earliest days were sprinkled with images of bears — usually cuddly, sometimes grouchy (Pooh Bear really needed his sleep): these tales were more friendly than frightening.

Some of us, now in our 50s, 60s or beyond, remember when the National Park Service fostered bears' dependence on human food — primarily because of the bears' entertainment value to park visitors. Until the early 1940s, Yellowstone officials set up bleachers for visitors so they could watch the nighttime show of grizzlies feeding from the local garbage dump, where trash was dumped onto the open ground.

Traffic jams were common in the park because everyone wanted to leap out and take photos when a bear was spotted (actually, many visitors still want to do this, but stiff fines may be assessed). Some visitors tried to line their children up next to bears to add interest to their photos.

In the 1920s, Yosemite rangers were charging visitors 50 cents each to watch bears eat some of the 60 tons of table scraps they provided each year.

Bears responded to being in close proximity with humans by losing their natural fear and caution, and by becoming increasingly aggressive. They roamed campgrounds and broke into abandoned cabins, empty cars, and occupied tents. From the 1970s through the 1990s, we read of growing numbers of bear encounters.

Officials also noticed that the black bear populations were increasing. That, along with the fact that human populations were continuing to expand into bear habitats, meant that more and more encounters could be anticipated.

Clearly something had to change. Thus, increasingly over the last 20 years, the measures to reduce vandalism by bears have switched from an emphasis on blaming "bad" bears, and removing or destroying them, to educating people about appropriate food storage and garbage disposal, so that bears do not become habituated to human food.

In Yosemite National Park, a strong public awareness campaign, "Keep Bears Wild" was implemented in 1998. More storage lockers were installed for visitors to use, laws that require responsible food storage were enforced, and bears were "re-educated" by various hazing methods — everything from an acorn from a slingshot, to yelling, to using dogs — when they entered campgrounds.

For a couple of years, the incidence of property damage to visitor's property was significantly reduced. It went from 1,590 cases in 1998, to 654 in 2000, and to 220 in 2001— an 80% drop. The damage amounts also decreased significantly: from $659,000 in 1998 to $30,273 in 2001. Approximately 45% of the 2001 damage was sustained in wilderness areas. In all of Yosemite in that year, there was only one reported human injury. Then in 2002, the number of bear raids to find food climbed again. According to park management, it was likely a combination of two factors: less availability of the bears' natural food — berries, grasses, and insects — and more carelessness by people about proper food storage. By August 2002, there had been 329 bear damage reports.

To backpackers, the most noticeable aspect of the Yosemite program is the requirement that wilderness visitors store their food in campground storage containers, or carry and use portable bear-proof food storage containers. Wisely, the program has made these canisters available for rent at entrance stations and backcountry stores for nominal fees.

When we go into the wilderness, there is risk involved. The wise backpacker will check out the area she is going into and follow the regulations for preparing, cooking, cleaning up, and storing food. However, it's important to keep in mind that serious injuries from bears are infrequent. Though bears have killed people, it is rare. According to Stephen Herrero, author of *Bear Attacks — Their Causes and Avoidance*, who based his conclusions on records kept since 1906, in North America there has been an average of about one fatality per year.

The Great Smoky Mountains National Park, the most visited park in the east, had 17 people injured, none seriously, in 1989. Then in May 2000, it had what officials reported was the first of its kind in the Southeast: a 50-year-old woman was killed by a pair of black bears — a sow and her cub (both of which were subsequently destroyed).

Certainly it makes headlines when someone is killed by a bear, and no one would make light of any death, but it's also important to keep things in perspective. Glacier National Park, Montana, has recorded 16 million visitors since it was established in 1910. Yet Glacier did not have anyone killed by a grizzly bear until August 13, 1967 when two women were killed. Yellowstone, which became a park in 1872 and has both brown and black bears, has had more injuries by bears than any other National Park and only six deaths. None of this is told to frighten you. Herrero basically reminds hikers that we should have "concern…[and] be cautious," but not have much fear.

For your own safety it is important to know not only if bears are native to the area where you will be hiking, but also which kinds of bears.

Types of Bears

In the United States, we have two types of bears – the black and the brown (including the grizzly). The **black bear, ursus americanus,** is much more widespread in the lower

48 states than the brown bear and is the smaller and generally considered the less dangerous of the two. Black bears are found in the West, primarily in mountainous areas, and in the East, mostly in the swamps and forests. Their range extends from Alaska across most of Canada, dipping down into the areas around the Great Lakes. They are numerous throughout the West including Washington, Oregon, California, Montana, Idaho, Wyoming, Utah, Colorado, Arizona, New Mexico, and Texas. They are also found in areas of Louisiana and the Gulf states into Florida. The Great Smoky Mountains National Park (North Carolina and Tennessee) has the largest bear sanctuary (population estimated at 1,800) in the eastern United States, and the range of the black bear continues north along the Appalachian Trail and into the New England States.

The black bear is: five to six feet in length, three and one-half feet high at the shoulder and weighs 200 to 475+ pounds. Its color may be black, brown, honey, or cinnamon. It has a brown face and a sloped rump. It can run more than 30 mph for short bursts and climbs trees readily. Though it is primarily nocturnal, it is occasionally out at daytime, especially at dawn and dusk.

Though it may have its den on the ground in a downed tree, hollow log, or under roots, it may also, in the East at least, have its den above you in the large hollow of a tree. Because its sight is poor, and its hearing is only moderate, it relies heavily on its sense of smell, which can easily detect food in the backpacks of hikers and the trunks of cars.

The grizzly, ursus horribilis (which is a member of the brown bear family) is nearly extinct in the Pacific Northwest (the Game Department estimates there are approximately ten in Washington's most remote mountains). They wander widely within their home range. They are found in Alaska (south of Brooks Range), western Canada, and parts of Montana, Wyoming, Colorado, and New Mexico.

Their habitat is forested areas of oak and beech trees (and the tundra of Alaska). The grizzly is: four to six feet or more long, three to three and one-half feet at the shoulder, with claws on the forepaws that may be three to four inches long. Their color varies, but is often yellowish-brown with the hairs tipped with white, hence the name grizzly. The grizzly has a large shoulder hump and dish-shaped face. They swim well, and the cubs can climb trees.

What a Bear Does in the Woods

In light of the rising frequency of human/grizzly bear encounters, the Alaska Department of Fish and Game has issued the following advisory to hikers, hunters, and fishermen while in the field:

"It is strongly advised that outdoorsmen wear noisy little bells on their clothing so as not to startle grizzly bears that aren't expecting outdoorsmen to be walking in their habitat. It is also strongly advised that outdoorsmen carry non-lethal pepper spray with them in case of an encounter with a grizzly. The Department of Natural Resources for Alaska states it is a good idea to watch out for fresh signs of bear activity. Outdoorsmen should be able to recognize the difference between a black bear poop and grizzly bear poop:

Black bear poop is small, contains lot of berries, and, occasionally, squirrel's fur.

Grizzly bear poop is large, has little bells in it, and smells like pepper."

Author unknown

(When I was hiking in Alaska, I always wore the aforementioned "bear bell," but I often wondered if the bears would consider it the "dinner bell.")

Returning to our more serious discussion: Rangers have observed that the bears have special techniques for getting into different types of cars, and that they pass this knowledge on to their young. A favorite ploy is to insert their claws just above a rear side door and rip the doorframe out. Next, they claw through the backseat into the trunk, where food has been stored. Based on availability and ease of entry, bears prefer Hondas. Toyotas are a close second.

But though humans are seldom physically harmed, bears do not fare nearly as well. When a bear injures a human — whether while defending its young, or trying to keep food it has stolen — or when it repeatedly raids campers' food, the bear is either relocated or put to death.

The bears' loss of fear of humans and the association of food with them, has increased backpackers' difficulties as well. It used to be a lot easier to keep your food when you were backpacking. Ralph remembers using his as a pillow, or just keeping his pack nearby. Then it became necessary to hang it — counter-balanced — high up in the trees. Nowadays, in much of the Sierras, only approved portable storage canisters (or food lockers at some camping areas) are a guarantee you'll have your food in the morning. Some backcountry areas, including Yosemite, Kings Canyon/ Sequoia, and Inyo require hikers to use these canisters.

Until the unfortunate attack in The Smokies in May 2000, the region's black bears were not considered quite as "bad" (defined as breaking into cars and campsites for food) as their western relatives. Now, however, park personnel are trying to educate visitors so that the situation there will not worsen. The Smokies "pack snatchers" are so cunning that hikers are advised to hang their packs from the nearby cables anytime they walk away from camp to get water or use the toilets.

Precautions in Bear Country

Every article I read has a different slant on the relative danger of black vs. brown bears, and somewhat varied hints on surviving a bear's visit, charge, or attack, but there are several pieces of advice that are consistently offered to help you reduce your risk in bear country:

- In grizzly country, make noise (talk loudly, sing, wear bells, or bang cups and pans) when you travel in known bear habitat. This is especially true when you are on a blind curve, or there is heavy vegetation such as berry bushes and willows. When you see fresh scat or claw marks, be alert.
- In grizzly country, travel in groups, which inherently will provide more noise and less likelihood of surprising a bear.
- Don't bring strongly scented items into the wilderness: food, soap, lotions, toothpaste, etc.
- Prepare food, cook it, and clean up away from where you will sleep. Change from the clothes that you cooked in before you go to bed.
- Prepare, eat, and clean up early, before bears are more active.
- Stay off trails at dusk, dawn, and night.
- Know, and follow, the food storage methods recommended by the authorities of the local area.
- After you have removed the food and toiletries from your pack, leave the backpack pockets unzipped and open.
- If you carry spray for grizzlies, be sure it is the type for stopping bears, not muggers. Bear spray should contain at least 1% capsicum, be labeled "bear spray," and be approved by the EPA. (In their September 2000 issue, Backpacker Magazine tested the five approved sprays: Bear Guard, Bear Peppermace, Counter Assault, Guard Alaska, and UDAP Pepper Power. Check their website: www.backpacker.com for details.) You can find

these products at sporting good stories, by mail order, or by using search engines directing you to the manufacturers' websites. This stuff is not cheap — $40 and up for an 11-oz. container.

Remember that you can't take such sprays on an airplane, so if you are flying into an area, be certain you have a source where you are headed. Learn to fire the spray from your side or front, where it should be in a holster, since you will not have time to remove it from a pack.

If, after all this, you still encounter a bear, stay calm. Your brain is your most important weapon since each situation will be unique. Most charges are bluffs, but if you intend to spray, you have to do it before you can know whether it is a bluff or not!

Bear Tales

One of the pleasures of backpacking is swapping stories — so initial encounters with other hikers usually involve describing the upcoming trails and passes, the weather, and camp spots. "Any bear problems?" is probably tied with "Where're you headed?" for the most asked question on the trail.

✦ Sharon

The reality was that by dark, Sharon was afraid of everything. She was certain that sitting by the campfire would allow animals to sneak up behind her. Her night vision would be reduced by the fire's light. She thought her hammock would make her into a "hanging sausage for bears." She went to bed as soon as it became dark.

That first night she heard rustling sounds. She was certain something was rubbing against the tent. It became louder and louder, more and more persistent. Finally, she discovered that it was her carotid artery pounding against her sleeping bag.

✦ Kathryn

Kathryn never had losses to bears even though she found it difficult to throw the required ropes into place. She did hear them on occasion, but banging pans and yelling seemed to always work. A previous visitor had left a sign warning, "Bear was here, God saved me."

✦ Doris

Doris, after hundreds of miles of Sierra trekking, comments, "We've had more problems with mice than bears. Never lost any food to bears. We have bears come through maybe four out of nine nights. We avoid them by hanging our stuff, or tying it between rocks where bears can't reach. They are shyer away from the parks. The books say you don't find them above 9,200 feet. Well you do!"

✦ Valerie

When I interviewed Valerie, we traded bear stories and discussed how black bears have become both more aggressive and numerous in the Sierras. She remembers when it was adequate to store your food by hanging your food bags using the counter-balance method and knows that nowadays it is necessary to use plastic canisters in Yosemite and other heavily travelled parts of the Sierra Nevada.

Valerie remembered with some fondness the warning given her by a ranger in the Sierras several years back. "Here are the directions for hanging your food bags. Read them, memorize them, and then chew them up and swallow them. Bears can read."

✦ Elizabeth

Elizabeth and her companion planned to hike from Yosemite's Tenaya to Clouds Rest, about a ten-mile hike round-trip; they decided to stash their empty backpacks at their campsite. They left the backpacks unzipped and open so any visiting bear would be able to paw through and wouldn't need rip into them. They hung their food in a tree using the recommended counter-balanced method. Then they set off for their climb.

To their relief, when they returned they saw that their stuff had been gone through, but was undamaged. Suddenly, nearby, they heard the bear's snorting and snuffling. Mama and baby had food all over. They managed to chase the bears off with their banging of pot lids and yelling, then surveyed the damage. The freeze-dried foods were gone; the only exception was the Kraft Macaroni and Cheese. "The most interesting souvenir was a tin of clams — the bear had punched it open by sticking one claw all the way through and had drained the contents."

When they talked with the ranger later on, he said the bears often worked as teams. Both bears would climb the tree, the cub would reach out far enough to get the bag swinging, and when it swung close enough the tree to snare, mama would grab it.

✦ Betty

Betty has been lucky in that she has only had one bear visit, because she and Elizabeth don't usually hang their food-bags. She attributes their luck to the fact that they move on after cooking, leaving most of the food odors back at the dinner-site. When she had that one visit, she found her whistle worked to run the bear off.

Marcy's Kearsarge Bear

"The summer of '99, my friend Dottie and I (as we were each approaching our sixtieth year), wanted to do a 20-day backpack on the John Muir Trail. Several years before, we had gone from Cottonwood Pass to Whitney Portal, sleeping the night on Mt. Whitney, which was a memorable experience because of the Perseid Shower all night.

"This year, we had invited our friend Cliff. Although he is several years our senior, he had previously climbed White Mountain with us — the third highest peak in the lower 48 — and is a strong climber. We planned to hike from Onion Valley to Lake Mary at Mammoth. It was to be over seven passes, a total of 123 miles. But we made a couple of mistakes.

"The first day we stayed at Dottie's cabin in Whitney Portal to acclimate. We emptied our cars of all food, and I put the cover on my car. We had heard that the bears were very active. During the night, I had a nightmare that the bear got in the cabin, rummaged around the Great Room, then came to my little room and slammed his huge paw twice down on the bed by my feet. I woke up shouting, "Go away!" and kicking out.

"The next morning we found that a bear had shredded both the driver's side and the passenger side of my cover, trying to look in. I was thankful he had left before scratching the paint or breaking a window (I don't know if the teddy bears inside deterred the bear, or if he was satisfied that there wasn't any food or gum inside).

"After stashing Cliff's truck at the Lake Mary Trailhead in Mammoth, we returned to the beginning of our trek, in Onion Valley. The three of us started up the trail to Kearsarge Pass, much too heavily loaded. My pack was 66 pounds. Since I weighed in at 124 pounds, my pack was way too much, but we kept telling ourselves we would eat our way lighter.

"The three of us had all purchased the expensive plastic barrels that are bear-proof. They were strapped to the outside of our packs. I had divided the dehydrated dinners between Dottie and Cliff's bear cans, and all the desserts were in mine.

"At 4 p.m., we reached an overlook to Hear Lake — maybe four miles. We were too bushed to go any further. We unpacked and helped each other put up the two tents. I slept out on a flat ledge next to the tents, because it was the first night of the Perseid meteor showers, and I didn't want to miss the show.

"Cliff looked around and asked where his bear can was. It wasn't there. It must have slipped off somewhere between where we had lunch and here, I told him. Without his pack, we figured it wouldn't take him more than a half-hour to hike back down there. It had his name on it; I wrote it myself in gold nail polish. We were sure he'd find it. Dottie and I were too tired to go back with him; we decided to wait for him before fixing dinner.

"By 7 p.m., all thoughts of a meal had vanished. We gave up our futile attempts to hang our food bags in a tree; we were at timberline where the trees were all stunted anyway. Dottie was frantic with worry, 'Suppose he fell? Suppose he got hurt?' I thought that he might have gone all the way back to the parking lot.

"We gave up trying to throw a rope in a somewhat taller tree and started down after Cliff. It was 8:00 p.m. when we finally met him toiling slowly back up the trail — without the bear canister. He had hiked all the way back to the cars, asking people as he went. We were so glad to see him. We told him not to worry, he was safe, and that was all we cared about.

"We slipped into our bags and Cliff was instantly asleep. It was 9 p.m. and the meteor shower had begun. It was fantastic. Dottie and I watched the falling stars for over an hour.

"Sometime in the middle of the night, I woke to a different sound than the night wind. It was a plastic bag, flapping against the boulder. I started up, called to Dottie, and blew my whistle, but the bear had already silently gone with one of our stuff bags of food. We brought back what was left and spent the next hour and a half trying again to hang our food in a nearby tree. I finally managed to get a rope over a branch and hoisted the first sack; the rope broke. I tried again; again the rope broke. At last, I found a fresh rope and tossed it successfully into the tree. We hauled up two bags and stashed the other two in a tree behind us. Chilled, I shoehorned my way into Dottie's tent and tried to sleep.

"Within a half-hour, the bear was back. Dottie saw him on his hind legs, batting at the bags. He snagged one and pulled it lower. I saw him too; he was standing on all fours, above us on the boulder. He looked down at us. In the starlight I could see his round ears, his little black eyes. He was looking into mine. I wasn't afraid of him — knowing he preferred backpackers' food to backpackers — but at that moment he appeared to me quite fearsome.

"I exploded from the tent, yelling, and slammed my ski pole on the rock — sparks flew. I blew my whistle loud and long. The bear catapulted off the high boulder and disappeared into the blackness. He had never made a sound. We spent what was left of the night staring at the bags swinging in the tree, but the bear did not return.

"In the morning we assessed our situation. The bear had taken all of Cliff's breakfast and trail food. [Since the canister was lost], half of the dinners were gone. It was obvious we had to hike back out and start over. On the way back down, we looked for the missing bear can, but it didn't turn up. Dottie thought one of the frisky young men who passed us yesterday might have appropriated it.

"A wonderful couple let me hitch a ride all the way to the Portal for my car. Then the three of us retrieved Cliff's truck from Lake Mary, and we drove back to the cabin at the Portal. The second night of meteor showers was supposed to be good too, so we slept out on the terrace. Unfortunately, I was so tired, I fell asleep immediately and missed them.

"In the morning, Cliff returned home. It was the 14th of August; Dottie and I regrouped. We had enough dinners for a 12-day backpack. We picked a route that was only 60 miles and over only three passes. We reduced our packs to about 50 pounds. It was a much more sane arrangement for us. We never saw another bear, but when we got back to the Portal, Dottie's front windshield had been cracked by one. I had been told to take everything out of my car and leave the windows down. That way, the bear would be able to look inside, but would see nothing and would go on. That was exactly what happened. I had his muddy paw prints to show — but no busted window. At Whitney Portal, the bears are a real problem; at Kearsarge Pass, there is a bear waiting for you!

"At the end of our trip, we found out that on the 18th of August, Cliff's wife had a very serious accident that totaled their car. Luckily, Cliff was there when she needed him to take her to the doctor and to physical therapy. The American Indians believe that the bear is a messenger."

The Bear

The bear stood on the boulder
above us and looked
down at us in our little tent,
his black eyes — in the starshine
peering into mine — before I
blew the whistle,
slammed my walking stick
into the rock, making sparks fly.
And he plunged off the boulder
into the darkness.
It was only the night before
I had the dream, that the bear
broke into the cabin
rummaged around the Great Room
then sniffed his way
to my bed and
pounded down his paws,
twice, on my feet.
I woke up screaming, "GET OUT,"
and kicked.
And now as I lie
in my bag, on the edge
of a meadow, half way
along this 60-mile backpack,
I think of him,
the blood in my heel pounds,
the last of the half moon
slips below the clouded ridge,
the dry sticks cracking
in the wood
might be him,
returning.

by Marcy Clements, Nov. 1999

And Other Creatures:

✦ Betty and Sandra

Most people think of bears as being the major animals to concern them, but imagine having a skunk hanging around your campsite all night. That was the experience Betty and Sandra went through on one of their several trips to the Lost Coast — a remote area of the northern California coast. Betty finally tried her whistle to scare it away, which worked for the skunk, but not for the millions of mice. They finally decided to rebuild the fire, and that kept the hordes at bay.

Another time, they went to bed with their food by Sandra's head. This is not an area where bears are a problem, so it seemed a reasonable way to keep "critters" out of their supplies. Soon they saw a raccoon stick its hand out and grab the bag of food. As the raccoon withdrew, Sandra crawled through the nearby bushes in hot pursuit of their granola, gorp, and cheese.

She didn't have much success that night, so she returned to their camp. The next morning they recovered what they could from the raccoon's lair — and also found other food, as well as old clothing swiped from earlier campers.

✦ Sharon

Sharon reported animal problems of a different variety, "I left my car at the trailhead to Emigrant Wilderness, and returned to find the ranger had left a note on my windshield: 'Porcupines will chew brake cables,' and a second note, 'I think he's gotten to the second one.' So we had to drive down the mountain without brakes, using the hand brake."

✦ ✦ ✦ ✦ ✦

On most of the trips that Ralph and I take, we see evidence of bears — either scat (droppings) or swinging ropes that once were used to hang food — but we actually have seen the bears, or had them move our containers around, about half of the time.

Every night we go through our routine. First we put our food, toiletries, and bug dope away (either in the bear boxes, our canisters, or hang it) as prescribed. Then I put together my arsenal. I gather small rocks to throw (piled at the head of our sleeping bags), and set out our Sierra Club metal cups along with our walking sticks. Inside I have my whistle, my mini-Swiss Army knife, and my boots. I have decided the boots would be the most effective — I mentally rehearse twirling them like a lariat.

As night approaches, I become more nervous. I'm afraid of bears, but at the same time intrigued by them. I want to see them, but from a comfortable distance. So what happened the last night of our backpack trip on the John Muir Trail was a surprise to all concerned.

We had gone to bed just after dark. I had read for a while, written in my journal, and snuggled into my bag. We were under the tarp, but it was warm enough that I was wearing a short-sleeved blouse. Ralph had placed the bear containers about 20 feet away and had set his backpack at the front of the tarp to give us a little privacy in the campground.

Being in a campground, with dozens of other campers, was a huge change from the previous several nights of solitude. The four women camped behind us had told us they were going to finish their UNO game, but promised they'd be done and quiet by 9:00.

Shortly after that, we dropped off to sleep.

A faint sound woke me. I looked up. There, not four feet from us, was a bear nosing at Ralph's backpack. I was instantly incensed, "How dare she bother our pack!"

I yelled at the bear in my best teacher's voice, "Get out of here!"

The bear took off into the darkness.

"Where did that voice come from?" I wondered. After all the years I had spent anticipating and dreading this moment, how could it be *indignation*, not fear, that I felt?

When we were awakened later that night it was by other campers. People were shining flashlights up, down, and all around. I lay there wondering if they had spotted the bear and might hurt it. Did I need to yell out to leave it alone? The bear was just trying to find food. I wished her freedom and safety. I realized that, for the brief time that the bear and I had looked into each other's eyes, we had understood each other. I had sensed that she had not been trying to hurt us; she had wanted food. I wanted her to get out of my space.

Now, as I write this, I don't know if I've completely lost the irrational components of my fear of bears or not. I hope I have. Bears live in the wilderness, and when we venture into their territory, it is best to go with respect rather than be paralyzed with fear. My challenge will be to face the fears.

Irene Cline
Golden Canyon, Death Valley, CA 2001

10
Now Where Did I Pack the...?
Equipment

"Chance favors the prepared mind."

Louis Pasteur

"In those days the costumes were quite different from what they are now. The women all wore skirts, fairly long. Some very daring ones had bloomers. When they were actually on the climb of Mt. Lyell, they took off their skirts and went up in their bloomers." When he said this, Francis P. Farquhar, former Sierra Club president, was referring to a 1911 Sierra Club outing.

We really do have it much easier, equipment-wise, than the women of a century ago. We even have it easier than the women of the 1960s did — their faded blue jeans were heavy, hot and took forever to dry when washed, or when soaked by a sudden downpour. In addition, being of cotton, their jeans lost their insulative value when wet — a potentially hazardous situation. While today's backpacking clothing may contain such natural fibers as wool and silk, increasingly high-tech garments are of synthetic materials under such names as Goretex, Supplex, Spandex, and Intera — fabrics that are light-weight, moisture-wicking, water resistant or repellant, quick to dry, and that provide greater flexibility of movement.

Handling the logistics of what clothing, food, and other supplies to take on your backpack trip doesn't need to be a chore, but it must be done carefully if the trip is to be much fun, and even more importantly, safe. Most of the women of this book have it down to a science; they've developed a list through the years by trail and error. Beginners will have an easier time by going with more experienced people or by using a published checklist. *Backpacker Magazine*, for one, has a packing list on their website.

Sometimes it's a good idea to look for a regional list. My equipment (detailed in the Appendix) reflects not only my personal preferences, but also *where* and *when* we backpack — in the Sierra. Backpackers in the Sierra in the late summer and fall can generally expect to encounter daytime temperatures of 50 to 80 degrees, with nighttime temps in the 30 to 40's. Afternoon thunderstorms and rains are frequent during the summer; snow is possible. If I were going to the Pacific Northwest, the eastern U.S., or the Southwest, I'd use a guide to that area to make modifications to match those very different climates.

Lighten Up

There are a couple of other fundamental decisions to make before you start out. First, do you want to pack *heavy*, carrying luxuries to enjoy at day's end; or do you want to pack *light*, and hike with greater ease all day? Secondly, do you want to cover long distances, difficult terrain, and travel at a quick pace from camp to camp, or do you want to hike in a couple of miles from the trailhead and set up camp for two weeks. These decisions will guide how you pack.

Although Ralph and I have not carried the "go-light" philosophy to the extreme, our goal has been to carry less each time we go out. Over the last ten years, we have steadily decreased the amount we carry and increased the number of miles we undertake. These reductions have come from decreasing the weight of necessities and reducing the number of non-essentials carried.

In 2000, we lightened up considerably. I had about 30 and Ralph had 35 pounds. This was down from his 55 the prior year, but on that trip we were carrying two weeks' worth of food, and the 2000 trip was only one week. We eliminated our tent and carried a fancy GoLite® tarp that is about one and one half pounds, and Ralph got a GoLite® backpack that weighed the same.

The change from tent to tarp represented a savings of approximately three pounds. But initially I was not happy about giving up a tent. It provided a sense of security — to be able to dive into it and be insulated from the outdoors seemed very important. I was very skeptical when I first saw the tarp set up on our deck — propped up and tied down with numerous thin lines. But when we used it in the backcountry, I was won over. I no longer had to wonder what each little sound might be — magnified into an enormous creature by my overactive imagination. I could see what was around me — especially on moonlit nights.

Other changes we have made have been easy and practical — changing from jeans to pants with legs that zip off to become shorts, for example. In addition, I have found that improvising is one of the more enjoyable features of backpacking. It's fun to substitute, create, and "make-do." When you learn to be a part of nature, you are less inclined to view it as the enemy. This in turn helps you become more competent and confident of your ability to deal with whatever situations arise.

Most articles suggest that backpackers carry no more than 25% of their recommended body weight, which works out to 37.5 pounds for a 150-pound woman. But, being able to carry more weight is not the same as enjoying it. Nowadays, when I see people with 45 to 60 pound packs, I wonder how they carry such cumbersome packs and what they could possibly be carrying. Since it's very easy to have pack-weight creep up when you start adding notebooks, cameras, and extra food, and since most of us are creatures of habit who carry the same items trip after trip, even the most experienced backpackers might benefit from periodically reevaluating their lists of equipment.

When you are selecting new equipment, also consider that most manufacturers of backpacking gear produce sturdy, long-lasting, relatively heavy, and expensive gear. A manufacturer of lightweight gear may produce gear that is significantly less weight than standard gear. Sometimes the materials (such as titanium) command premium prices; sometimes the gear is of lighter materials and sells at lower prices. Don't assume that lightweight gear will last more than a few seasons. Ask questions, read labels.

It all goes back to what kind of experience you want and what kind of trip you are planning. For the trip of two or three miles from the trailhead to set up housekeeping for two weeks, carry more pack weight so that you can have a more comfortable bed and more exciting food. But for the challenging long-distance backpack trips as you pursue far-distant goals, you'd be wise to scrutinize every item you carry.

✦ Jenny

Advocates of lightweight backpacking believe carrying reduced loads leads to more pleasurable hiking experiences. They are able to hike farther, faster, and with greater mobility. But for Jenny and Ray, leading figures in the "go-light" movement, who have chosen to select gear, clothing, and food that reduce pack weight, physical benefits are only part of the picture. They also approach wilderness travel with a different mentality. Rather than entering the wilderness loaded with outdoor products to protect themselves from the hostile outdoors, they prefer to understand nature and work with what they have learned. To many, nature is not hostile; it just is. With that fundamental shift in perception, one sees that observation and improvisation provide more security than fancy, and often heavy, equipment.

✦ Jeannine

Jeannine started backpacking in the late 1960s. She'd heard others at work talk about it and managed to drag husband, Lou, along. Her mother, at age 65, was game, as were Lou's daughter from his previous marriage, and another couple. Their equipment was poor and heavy, by today's standards. Jeannine had a cotton sleeping bag, pointed tennis shoes, and no down jacket. They cooked over heavy Sterno containers, holding their "basic" food over the burning fuel with sticks. But Jeannine didn't mind; she loved being out-of-doors.

✦ Debbie

Debbie's backpacking "in earnest" began in the early 1990s with her husband, Bill. They, and another couple, went on a two-week trip — the longest she had ever been on. She set out with a 50-pound pack. When they moved into the 10,000-foot and higher Sierra elevations of the Golden Trout Wilderness area, she quickly succumbed to altitude sickness, complete with vomiting and exhaustion. Bill was able to take most of her pack until the load was lightened and Debbie was stronger.

✦ Grace

Some women have tried it both ways. When Grace started her backpacking trips, she was content with the more Spartan approach — no tent and just carrying an ensolite pad and basic food. Nowadays, she wants more comfort, so she goes on treks with her llamas. With llamas carrying the major part of her gear, Grace can have her own pillow, inflatable sleeping pad, and multiple changes of clothing. She can have gourmet meals, wine, and carry an oven for baking brownies and muffins.

✦ Emma

Emma's equipment was minimal. Backpacks in the 1950's were heavy, did not have a hip belt, and were designed for men. She figured if she had to carry all that weight, she'd never start. So, she fashioned a duffel bag out of old jeans. This drawstring bag was easily tossed across streams, crevices, and rocks. In it she had a light blanket and an old shower curtain for bedding, a plastic rain cape, a sweater, a change of clothes, and a few utensils. She also carried a 15-foot rope which she used to pull or lower her pack through overgrown vegetation. Most often she carried food that provided quick energy and could be eaten cold — raisins, nuts, crackers, canned meats, cheese, and candy mints. Her pack usually weighed 14-17 pounds.

✦ Marcy

Marcy knows first-hand the difficulty of carrying a pack that is too heavy, but seems to end up staggering under the weight of 50 and more pounds. Nevertheless, she advises, "Go light!! Our packs were always too heavy. I have always taken too much. I can't seem to get rid of things that seem essential. Dottie even comes over and we go through every last item. This last time she cut 10 pounds out of my pack. But when I got ready to leave, at the second weigh-in, it was still 54 pounds. I need to work on getting lighter."

Others they passed on the PCT had 30-35 pounds, but the others were using food drops, which of course cuts the average weight. Marcy and Dottie do some fishing but not enough to supplement their freeze-dried fare.

"Yes, I would like to get my pack's weight down to 35 pounds — how blessed that would be! The tarp is one of the things suggested by Ray Jardine in his book, *Beyond Backpacking,* but I like to see the stars when I wake up. The big problem was my fear of going alone and thinking I needed all this STUFF to survive. One thing I will leave home from now on is the altimeter. It is never accurate due to the atmospheric adjustments needed.

"I have never been lost in the wilderness. The trails and the topography are really clear to me. We may be off the mark just a little, but we usually find where we need to go. A compass is a must, along with the topo map. Knowing how to use same is helpful too."

Marcy swears by a product called Crystal Energy. "It is negatively charged hydrogen ions in a water base. I put just one drop in my orange juice before we set out and I notice a boost from it. The going never is easy, but I do think the Energy stuff really helps a lot. It is expensive, but worth every golden drop."

"We're still using 20-year old packs. I must say I love my new Whisper Lite stove. Dottie's water pump is faster than mine, it's called PUR. Mine is a MSR Waterworks (ceramic). It is supposed to filter out microorganisms better than any other model. I researched them. But it is heavy and slow. I've heard that there may be new technology out now where you will not ever have to pump again. There are new pads now, but I'm satisfied with my ThermaRest. I'm very happy with my new down sleeping bag from LL Bean, that keeps me warm down to zero, it says on the label. I froze before I got that. I wish they made a pop-up tent that would be ultra lite weight and fit on the pack. Dottie got a new tent that's supposed to sleep two, but I'm very claustrophobic in it. I slept out every night.

Food

Carrying freeze-dried food saves weight and space, and the meals are filling. It's often recommended that you take one and one-half to two pounds of food, per-person-per-day, but we have found that one pound a day each (approximately 1,600 calories) is more than enough for our trips (typically up to three weeks). Some people jokingly talk about the JMT (John Muir Trail) Diet — a combination of weeks of strenuous exercise and limited access to food. As a welcome bonus, we generally lose five to eight pounds during our one or two week trips.

We also consider the amount of fuel required for cooking, and the ease of preparation and clean-up. Given the choice between two equally flavorful items, one that needs to be cooked several minutes over the stove and one that is cooked by pouring boiling water into the pouch, we'll go with the pouch item. We find it an advantage to repackage these freeze-dried dinners at home: then put them in our cooking pot and pour the boiling water over them.

Our breakfasts are either prepackaged oatmeal with raisins and Milkman, or freeze-dried scrambled eggs with bacon. Some require no cooking — just add boiling water. We drink coffee, tea, and Tang. Lunches are our heaviest meals — jerky and dried beef, thick crackers, snack bars, dried fruit, and trail mix. When we have dinner, we carefully check the number of ounces of our freeze-dried meals and use up the heaviest ones first. Since we want our packs as light as possible, we do not take desserts. Though some people don't like freeze-dried foods, most agree that there has been substantial improvement in the quality and variety of these products over the last twenty years. When I'm ravenously hungry from exertion and the outdoors, I think such meals as "Santa Fe Chicken with Beans" and "Teriyaki Beef" are quite good. I enjoy trying various kinds and keep track of favorites (I like almost everything Alpine Aire offers, and we also take Mountain House and Natural High). Freeze-dried green beans are a welcome addition. Even so, after a couple of weeks, we lust after fresh fruit, vegetables, meat, and "junk food." Since most of our backpacking trips are relatively short, we are generally not too concerned about the ratios of fat to carbohydrates to protein. When we are going to be out for longer trips, we look at the nutritional values of our foods more carefully.

While we are hiking, we snack on trail mix — some variation of "g.o.r.p." (good old raisins and peanuts) — and water or lemonade mix. Experiment with your trail mix: both the ingredients and the proportions of ingredients. We have found that we prefer more nuts and less "M & M's." We made the mistake on our last trip of taking some popular energy bars that we had not tried beforehand. We found them too sweet for our taste, and we were stuck carrying a two-week supply. Hence, my recommendation that you try in advance any item you are planning to take in quantity.

✦ Irene

Irene takes some commercially prepared freeze-dried foods on their backpacking trips, but cooks and dehydrates most of the food using her own recipes. On the Appalachian Trail, she and Sharon would typically carry enough food for a week, then stop for packages they had mailed to themselves or to buy needed provisions. Occasionally they would have a craving for ice cream and hamburgers (the younger hikers wanted pizza, Irene added), and they could satisfy that in town. One day they pushed themselves to go 17½ miles — instead of the planned 14 — because there were hamburgers at the end of the trail.

✦ Della

At the beginning of her AT hike Della would have to stop and rest every 30 minutes or so, and have frequent snacks. After 1,000 miles, she found she didn't need to snack;

she ate her three meals a day. Basically, breakfast was dry cereal or Pop Tarts, lunch was from a jar of chunky peanut butter, Ritz Crackers (she found they don't break like soda crackers), and cheese, and dinner was Lipton dinners of various sauces on rice or noodles (which she never tired of). She didn't have a food drop (food mailed ahead), but went out to the hiker towns along the way.

✦ Marcy

Marcy likes freeze-dried Neapolitan ice cream. "It's very tasty — tastes just like ice cream, only dry, like a chalky cookie," she assured me. [I have seen this item in sporting goods stores many times, but have never tried it. It is also sold at our regional science center because it has been carried into space by our astronauts. After hearing Marcy's opinion, I watched one of my students with interest when she purchased it during one of our field trips. She was not quite so crazy about it. "Ooooo!" she grimaced. Then she hurried to the nearest trash container to spit it out. "It tastes like bubble-gum flavored cardboard," she said. I guess it all goes to prove that even shoe leather would taste pretty good when you are starving after a day of backpacking.]

In 2000, Marcy went on her first lengthy solo trip. As she recorded in her journal, "I was a bit nervous. I will tell you outright, there was too much food!!! Psychologically, I thought, I'm going to be all alone — better take some more food. How crazy is that!!! Those dried fruits are so heavy and I hardly ate any!"

✦ Kathryn

Kathryn's backpack starts at 25 pounds, ends at about 20. Her food is mostly freeze-dried, and she carries lots of water. She has oatmeal at breakfast, soups at noon. She has never treated her drinking water except when she took her granddaughter with her.

✦ Marching Mothers

The Orinda women take about 35-45 pounds each, with most carrying tube tents. They share a big cooking pot — which is a determining factor in their eight-person limit; sharing such gear reduces the weight that each person has to carry. They mix their freeze-dried food in interesting combinations with spices to liven it up. Fish is always a welcome addition, and they have invariably had someone who was a talented fisherwoman as part of the group.

✦ Frandee

Frandee and her companions usually take 35 pound packs for a two-week summer trip. "It's hard to keep the food weight down because we don't care for commercial dehydrated foods, so we have to do our own dehydrating. I consider the process a chore," said Frandee.

✦ Elizabeth

Though Elizabeth no longer backpacks, she lends a wonderful perspective to today's backpacking by reminiscing about how it was to backpack in the Depression years, when she was a child. Her family: mother, father, and the four children were headed for Devil's Bathtub in California. The adults and children carried old-style packs loaded with flour and bacon, and with the eggs carefully tucked in the bedding so they wouldn't break.

The family counted on catching fish as the mainstay of their diet. "Fishing was good, up until the end of the trip." Then dinner became flour and water pancakes with flour and water gravy — not their idea of delicious. "That made it the end of the trip," she added.

Food Preparation and Storage

Stove: Your decision will be based on the kind of camping you will do, and the availability of fuel where you are going. As we prefer the higher elevations, we have a MSR

WhisperLite, which uses kerosene or white gas. The WhisperLite puts out greater heat at high altitude than bottled gas stoves. For our two-week trips, we carry two or three aluminum quart containers of fuel. We're also experimenting with a homemade alcohol stove.

Cookware: You probably won't want to pack a cast iron skillet unless you have a llama carrying your gear, so you'll basically have aluminum, stainless, and titanium from which to choose. Aluminum has been the standard for years, and the lightweight mess kits are inexpensive, lightweight, and easily obtainable. It is also easier to dent, and the lightest gauges tend to heat unevenly. Suggestion: Unless you enjoy KP, look for non-stick coatings. Stainless steel is stronger and heats more evenly than basic aluminum pans, but it is also heavier and more expensive. Titanium is very lightweight and strong. It is also quite expensive and, being relatively new on the market, is only available in limited sizes.

You will probably want two cooking pots (almost all sets nest) with tight-fitting lids. We use one for heating water to add to coffee, tea, and the entree, and for the subsequent wash-up, and the second for actually preparing the dinner. Depending on what you choose, you may need a pot lifter. If you want to add fried fish, pancakes, etc. to your menu, you'll want a coated frying pan also. **Hint:** Try the pots you are considering buying on your backpacking stove; you don't want your pot of stew falling off the stove into the dirt at your campsite because the stove is too small for your pot. It's also a bonus if your stove will nest inside your pots.

By using our titanium cups for beverages and hot meals, we've eliminated the need for carrying plates and bowls. We bring two Lexan spoons for cooking and eating.

Bear Canisters: I first saw bear canisters being used in Alaska (20 years ago) to keep campers' food from grizzlies. Now the containers are a common sight in the Sierra —

mandatory in a few areas — as protection against black bears. We have *almost* learned to love them. Weighing up to two and a half pounds, these canisters add significantly to your pack weight. However, since having your food taken is quite likely to spoil your trip — to say nothing about adding to the problem of bear dependence on "people food" — they're well worth it. We use the canisters in camp in several additional ways. After taking the stored food out (someone must guard the unpacked food during this process), we haul our water from a nearby lake or stream to wash ourselves and our clothes. We also use the empty canister to haul water to the campsite, and then pump it into our water bottles. After the containers are repacked, we turn them upside down (with some models, rain will run in if they are right side up), and use them as campstools. Before you set out for a backpack trip in bear habitat, check for the latest developments in products.

Types of Canisters: Garcia's Backpackers' Cache® containers are widely available at outdoor sports stores. They are approved for use in the central Sierra and may be purchased and rented at various sites within Yosemite and Sequoia/Kings Canyon National Parks. Easy to use. Disadvantages: mainly weight, but also access to food is somewhat awkward because of the wide outer rim. More info: (559) 732-3785. BearVault® canisters are also widely available. They are slightly lighter, have somewhat greater capacity, and cost a bit more than the Garcia. (866) 301-3442 or (858) 204-6164.

The Ursack® is a collapsible food storage bag made from bullet proof fabric. Its capacity is about 650 cubic inches, weight only five ounces, and its cost $49.95. Unfortunately, at present (2005) it's not approved for use in various parts of the Sierra, and not in stock because the U.S. military has all the bullet-proof fabric. The website promises a new model will be available in July, 2005. More info: www.ursack.com.

The Bearikade® is the brainchild of three engineers and backpackers who, being involved in the aerospace industry, have first-hand knowledge of the lightest and strongest materials. Their Bearikade® has some advantages over the Garcia® — much lighter weight and a bigger opening, and over the Ursack® because it has conditional National Park Service approval. We used the Bearikade® on our last Sierra trip. The main disadvantage is its price ($195-245). But then, losing one's food in the middle of a trip is an expensive proposition, too. The units are available for purchase or rental. More info: www.wild-ideas.net.

Cool, Clear Water

You will need a lot of water when backpacking — as much as a quart an hour if you are working hard. Because a quart of water weighs two pounds, you will be generally be depending on streams and other natural sources of water to replenish your supply.

Water filter and purification systems: Water-born protozoa, bacteria, and viruses can be found in our water sources, even the most pristine looking mountain streams. Water *filters* can eliminate protozoa and bacteria, but not the smallest contaminates — viruses. *Purification* systems (requiring approval by the EPA) can eliminate all three water-born pathogens. The following lists the advantages and disadvantages of several methods of water treatment. Before making a final decision, talk with a knowledgeable salesperson at an outdoor supply store. It's a good idea to have a back-up system for your main one. You can purify water by boiling it (7-15 minutes at higher elevations), but it requires extra fuel and tastes flat.

Iodine tablets: Advantages: lightweight and non-bulky, easy to use, inexpensive. Good backup in case of problems with filter systems. Disadvantages: 20-30 minute wait after treatment, not for pregnant women, taste, does not kill cryptosporidium (an important consideration because this protozoa is prevalent in our water sources). Additionally, though ingesting iodine may not be a health concern if used on a short trip, it is not recommended for extended trips.

Chlorine dioxide: Aqua Mira (drops), Katadyn MicroPur, or MSR Miox. Advantages: kills bacteria, lightweight and non-bulky, little aftertaste. Disadvantages: 20-30 minute wait after treatment, *drops* require accurate measurement. We use the MicroPur.

Water filter: Advantages: no wait to drink water, kills protozoa and bacteria, removes dirt and other sediment, the carbon in the filter makes the water taste good. Disadvantages: does not kill viruses, weight, requires routine maintenance, eventually clogs, moderately expensive (Katadyn Hiker Filter $60).

Combination filter/drops: Advantages: *purifies* by the combination of filtration and virus-eliminating drops (chlorine). Disadvantages: weight, wait time: five minutes. (SweetWater Guardian Purification System 14 oz., includes water container $69.95).

Ultraviolet Light: Advantages: *purifies*, kills bacteria, parasites, and viruses in less than a minute, lightweight, suitable for use of small amounts of water for individual use. More suitable for travel than backpacking. Disadvantages: requires AA batteries, impractical for treating large amounts of water. Expensive (SteriPEN Water Filter $149).

Although some people don't filter their drinking water, I'm not willing to take that risk even though there may be times when it isn't necessary. We take either our Katadyn Hiker Filter or MicroPur tablets. We feel that the benefits far outweigh the inconvenience.

Water bottles and bladder-type systems: How many bottles you want to carry will, in part, be determined by the availability of water along your route, and the weather you expect to encounter on your trip. For our Sierra trips, we carry Lexan wide mouth bottles: one 1-quart bottle, and two 1&1/2-quart bottles. Wide mouth bottles are easier to pour drink mixes into and to filter water into.

Many people like the convenience of bladder-type water-systems; some backpacks are fitted with a pocket for holding these containers. The backpacker can sip from the long tube as she moves along rather than stopping to get out a bottle. Clearly, this is advantageous since keeping well-hydrated when you are active is important. However, since the bladders are more complex than bottles, they are less versatile and more likely to leak.

Backpacks

Selecting gear and packing up is a lot more difficult than when John Muir was hiking. He wrote of setting off with a loaf of bread and a hunk of cheese, bedding down in piles of pine needles, and building roaring campfires. As with any other purchases you make, read the catalogs, scan the Internet, and visit outdoor supply stores and talk with salespeople.

I have an old Kelty backpack that I acquired at a garage sale for $25. It's worked well for me for many years and I love the way it feels on my body. Though its capacity isn't great, it's enough for our trips where heavy items are divided between us. But because the Kelty weighs 4.9 pounds, I've decided to replace it with a lighter pack. You may initially find the variety of packs bewildering but the number from which to choose can quickly be reduced by avoiding those that offer lots of "bells and whistles" that mainly add weight. Consider borrowing or renting before you buy.

✦ Valerie

On Valerie's first trip, she carried an ancient Trapper Nelson backpack that her cousin had loaned her. "It's a wooden and canvas pack that hangs from your shoulders, has no hip belt, and manages to gouge you in numerous places," she explained. Along with a well-fitting backpack, she recommends that hikers bring good socks, moleskin, plenty of toilet paper, and water.

Backpack cover or sturdy garbage bag: We have always carried a second groundcloth for putting over our backpacks at night, and to use during sudden downpours, as well as a large plastic bag or trash compactor bag that fits over our packs. Some people appear to favor ready-made pack covers for their sturdiness and convenience.

Shelter

Sleeping bag: My choice is a *down* mummy bag. It is the warmest material for its weight. If, however, you are traveling where moisture could be a problem choose a synthetic fill because once down gets wet, it loses its insulative value and can take days to dry. Some people sleep warmer than others, so the amount of fill you need may be different from a friend's.

Sleeping pad: You have three basic choices: ensolite, foam, and inflatable. Ensolite has the advantages of being "closed cell" (won't absorb water), inexpensive, and lightweight. I use a thin foam pad covered with a waterproof covering; it's heavier, but is somewhat more comfortable. Most expensive, most comfortable, but also heaviest, are inflatable types. However, they are subject to puncture and leaks.

Tent or tarp: As stated earlier, we have used both tarps and tents. There are advantages and disadvantages to both. Modern tents have the advantage of being quick and easy to erect, but they are heavier than tarps, and definitely more expensive. Tents will keep out mosquitoes and other insects, but most will also prevent stargazing. In general, a tent will keep you warmer than a tarp — handy on freezing nights, but enough to drive you out on sunny afternoons. Tarps are now available (Internet) that have both netting and a floor. Properly cared for — by packing loosely, storing dry, and reapplying waterproofing at recommended intervals — either should keep you dry during rainy periods.

✦ Grace

When Grace went into the sporting goods store, the salesman remembered her from the year before when her son had purchased a tent for her. "The tent's defective," she stated. "What do you mean? It doesn't work?" he asked. "Well, it said it was a two man tent and there weren't any in it."

✦ Betty and Sandra

Betty prefers no tent, though she uses a tube tent sometimes. Sandra likes her "Pocket Hotel" made of Goretex; it covers her head and lets the lower part of her sleeping bag stick out.

Groundcloth: We use a piece of Tyvek® building wrap that is just slightly larger than the "footprint" of our tent. Being fairly sturdy, it can also cover you, or your gear, quickly in case of a sudden downpour.

Additional Necessities

For me, two hiking poles are a necessity; for some they are optional. Read the advantages discussed later in Chapter Eleven, "Staying Healthy."

Swiss Army knife, compass, maps, whistle, light-weight flashlight/LED headlamp, extra batteries and bulb, first-aid kit, needle and thread, rope, and lots of matches. We prefer book matches, plus a few of the waterproofed, "emergency" ones. Keep matches in more than one place because they easily get damp.

If you regularly drink caffeinated beverages (including soda), withdrawing from them suddenly may cause headaches. Over-the-counter sinus medications may relieve pressure; ibuprofen may relieve aches and pains.

If you depend on eyeglasses, bring an extra pair, kept well packed in the bottom of the pack.

Boots and Clothing

Prioritize your spending. Wearing a well-fitting pair of boots is much more important than wearing a pair of shorts with a trendy logo.

✦ Doris

"My favorite way to cross streams is to wear my boots. I put Snowseal on them. I feel as though I have good stability crossing the slippery rocks, and on the other side I pour the water out, and wipe it out with my ever-present bandanna. I put my wool socks back on. The socks do absorb water, so if I need to put on a pair of dry socks later on, I stop and do so. I also carry canvas shoes for wearing around camp. Sometimes I use them for crossing little streams, then put them on my pack to dry.

Most people now carry sandals. They're good for crossing water, they don't get wet, and with socks, they're warm enough. I even ran into a man who'd come across difficult terrain wearing thick wool socks and sandals. He'd gotten a blister and couldn't bear boots. I've read that a lot of the new books are saying you don't need Vibram soles, but I believe in heavy, leather boots."

✦ Della

Della quickly found that her equipment was all wrong on the Appalachian Trail. "My shoes were so tight that I had blisters for the first part of the trip. My toes were black; the boots fell apart. My knees became swollen almost immediately. I realized that I was in terrible condition for such an undertaking, but I couldn't go home like that." With the determination that carried her the entire trip, she got kneepads, new shoes, socks, more suitable clothing. At one point her husband picked her up and drove her to town to replace her backpack, which was too large for her. He told her, "You can't let the wrong equipment be the cause of not succeeding."

Gradually, her strength increased — and so did her sense of pride. But it was not until the 45th day that Della wrote in her journal that she enjoyed the whole day. The trip became easier.

✦ Marcy

After Marcy went on an overnighter on the Mountaineer's Route to Mt. Russell, she wrote, "Right away my heels begin to hurt and I know now that my darling new boots, with the purple Gore-Tex inserts, that were fine in the store and walking the dog on city streets, are too small. Why didn't I bring moleskin? I brought everything else. My pack weighed in at 33 pounds. Too much for just an overnighter. I think I have way too many Power Bars. I like these loose shorts, the legs wide enough to pull aside and pee standing up. Very convenient."

"Didn't take a pump, used iodine and boiling and had the filtered bottle for sipping on the move. Very refreshing.

✦ Carolyn

Because of her personal experiences with rapidly declining weather, Carolyn urges beginners to carefully select fabrics and clothing for backpacking — for example, use Coolmax instead of cotton. She recommends fleece and Goretex (or other adequate raingear that wicks moisture away from the body), Smartwool socks, and dressing in layers. "Women should have a flashlight and whistle, too."

✦ Doris

Doris responded vehemently when I recommended Ray Jardine's books on traveling light, and then went into detail about his elaborate plans of how to do the PCT in one season, and how to travel light with lightweight shoes, not hiking boots, and how he mails food ahead. "I have to tell you, I *hate* people like that. I have been in blizzards in August, and I'm very glad to have my three pound tent, which makes my pack about 40 pounds."

She continues, "I pack light. I wear a man's shirt because they're roomy, have big pockets and long shirttails so you can bathe modestly. It's a cotton polyester — dries quickly — one shirt does me. We stop early in the afternoon, and at the high altitudes things dry quickly. I bring a nylon jersey for the next layer, ski-weight wool sweater, and then a down jacket, and then rain gear. I have shorts and long pants. And we have just enough underwear to launder and allow for a rainy day.

"I believe in being prepared. You should be in good physical shape, eat properly, and have good equipment. Not fancy equipment, I don't go for these things that wick [clothing, usually of synthetic fibers, that conducts perspiration away from your body]. They may be fine, I have them, my kids give them to me for Christmas, but I still go for wool. For food, we usually fix the Rice-a-roni kind of thing. Sometimes we take backpacking foods."

✦ ✦ ✦ ✦ ✦

My boots are moderately heavy. I need the support of an above-the-ankle leather boot. If I didn't need the support, I'd investigate lighter-weight footwear which has less impact on the trail and weighs less. Backpacker Magazine (Dec. 2002) states that reducing the weight of your boots one pound is equivalent to taking better than six pounds off of your back. Try boots on with the two layers of socks you'll undoubtedly be wearing: a heavy outer one of wool and a lightweight inner one of synthetic material. It's best to try shoes on in the evening, since your feet are usually more swollen, and therefore larger, later in the day.

Do not buy boots in a hurry, just before a trip. Not only do you want to do some research on what's available for varying conditions and feet, but you also need a couple of weeks (minimum) to be sure your boots are well broken in, and that your feet are in condition. Modern boots should feel comfortable on day one. The synthetic materials have very little give, so it is your feet that have to do the changing.

If your boots do not fit properly and are not broken in, you are quite likely to end up with blisters, chafing, or black toes. To avoid black toes: bruising under the toenail from toes pressing against the front of the shoe—and subsequent nail loss—be sure you have ample toe room so that your toes do not hit the toe of the shoe on steep downhill stretches.

Not having comfortable shoes can turn an otherwise wonderful backpacking trip into a miserable experience. Chapter twelve, "Either Tortoise or Hare is Fine: Going at Your Own Pace, Training & Staying Healthy" provides additional important information on proper foot care.

You should evaluate *any* suggested list and adjust it as necessary. You may need specialized equipment for other activities (rock-climbing for example), or want items others would consider superfluous (a drawing tablet or a fly-fishing rod for example). Consider your own body metabolism (I sleep cold, but seem to need less food than the daily one-and- a-half pounds usually suggested).

Note that almost all outdoor clothing available now is fast-drying and wicks moisture away from your body. I avoid cotton because it holds moisture. Since most outdoor clothing is designed to be layered, buy sizes that allow for it. Down jackets are wonderfully warm and light, unless they get wet; then they are useless until they dry, which may take days. When I carry my down jacket, I also carry my Goretex jacket to wear as an outer layer.

Before you do your final packing, be sure everything fits and is comfortable to wear. And, if your skin is sensitive, wash any new clothing to get rid of fillers that may cause allergic reactions.

On Top of the Basics

Every ounce you add to your pack makes hiking more difficult, but if something sustains you, bring it. Marcy, Betty Lennox, and Sandra find writing poetry or their thoughts so important they wouldn't think of leaving their notebooks at home. I also keep a journal, but carry one piece of notepaper for each day of the trip rather than a bound book. I want to read, so I bring a paperback that I can tear up page by page and throw into the campfire as we go. I "must" have a camera — so I carry one (we're experimenting with a new lightweight model).

✦ Carol

Usually Carol (a slight 110 pounds) carries a thirty-pound pack, and Al has forty-five to fifty. Though they carry most of their foods for the time they will be out, on the longer trips they have hiked out to get replenishments. They carry freeze-dried dinners, but when she is craving fresh apples or baked potatoes, or he is craving a chocolate milkshake, they've been known to hitchhike out to a nearby town. Carol manages to keep the pack weight down by closely scrutinizing every item. She cuts down her toothbrush, and tears the pages off her *Readers' Digest* and burns them as she goes. Because they travel together, Carol and Al share many supplies — including the mini-tube of toothpaste — and can save weight that way also. Their greatest indulgence is their camera, but it is also a source of great pleasure.

✦ Joyce

Joyce adopted ski poles following knee surgery. Her advice to newcomers was to "learn the equipment, and don't carry too much weight." But she carries 35-40 pounds, partly because she wants a camera. Being able to photograph is one of her main reasons for backpacking, so it's a trade-off she chooses to make.

✦ Irene

Irene found that refining the list of what she considers essential has taken a long time. "You want to know what you need, and what you don't need — and you sure don't want to carry any excess," she added. "My sister is a good photographer and has a lot of equipment but when we're backpacking we carry a lightweight disposable camera."

✦ Sharon

Sharon's favorite gear is her backpacker's hammock — not only comfortable for sleeping, but also great for sitting. But one problem with it is that other group members consider, "Hmm, she's out of it, I wonder if it's my turn." Her second favorite is her lightweight campstool. It's especially great for cooking, and in the rain — but you need one for everyone in the group.

✦ Marcy

"But I have to add one more thing — I have to take my harmonica everywhere. That and a good-sized notebook are my luxuries. I'm a writer, and as you remember seeing my notepad, it was pretty thick. I used almost every last page — for journaling, poems, sketches, and pressing flowers."

Tip: Consider using a lightweight umbrella; it will protect again rain and extreme heat.

Tip: Carry a few feet of duct tape wrapped around a pencil or film container, etc. This multi-use item can be used to do everything from a covering a hole in your tent to holding a splint on your finger.

Betty Lennox and Sandra Nicholls on Lake Tahoe to Yosemite backpack

11
Do I Just Stand Here and Shake in My Boots?
Safety in the Wilderness

"Fortune truly helps those who are of good judgement."

Euripides

"Will I be safe?" is an oft-asked question by women considering a backpacking trip. In Shirley MacLaine's, *The Camino: A Journey of the Spirit*, she walks the famous pilgrimage trail across Northern Spain to Santiago de Compostela. People honk their horns, and call to her, "Ultreya!" "What does it mean?" she asks. Her companion Anna replies, "It means moving forward with courage."

Just the act of going backpacking can be a physical challenge to most people. Carrying a full pack, covering long miles over rugged terrain, and going to high altitudes qualifies as demanding physical activity. We go because we want some degree of challenge, and also because we long for the exhilaration of being out in nature. However, most of us are not looking for the risks of "extreme" sports. We'd prefer to hike in relative safety — and return home. While we are hoping to have some degree of adventure on our trip into the backcountry, we're wise women who want to be reasonably prepared for what we will encounter.

So, just as we try to fit in additional pre-conditioning hikes, and look for ways to reduce pack weight, we are interested in knowing how to reduce the chance of personal injury or disease.

Always remember that your backpack is your life support system in the wilderness. So whenever you leave your backpack behind in basecamp — when going for a dayhike, for example — you must still carry everything essential to your survival.

Survival Skills

✦ Betty and her daughter, Susie

The following story contains numerous lessons. From the example of two experienced backpackers forgetting essential gear and making potentially life-threatening errors in navigation, we are reminded that errors can be easily made and quickly compounded in the wilderness. Checklists of essential gear are invaluable. As we read Betty's account of their activities after they realized they were in trouble, we can observe that their calmness and resourcefulness played a large part in helping them survive getting lost in the wilderness.

In August of 1992, Betty and Susie, set out from Carson Pass in Northern California to Lake Alpine, a 25-mile round trip.

The first night's stop was Camp Irene on the Mokelumne River. They quickly ran out of matches; each thought the other had some. The two rangers they encountered didn't have any either. But the two campers did manage to get a Wilderness Permit — which they hadn't obtained earlier because they had gotten to the area too late in the day to get one. With these few details worked out — it was to be granola and cold tomato soup for dinner that night — they settled in for the evening.

Up the next morning at 5:30, they were soon underway; Betty knew it was a good eight and a half miles to Lake Alpine that day. They hiked along but after a while they found the "ducks" (trail-markers) were fewer and farther between. They were spending a lot of time "duck hunting," — often removing their packs to scout around. They were encountering lots of brush and no obvious trail. Soon they were traveling cross-country.

"We came out at the base of a huge granite outcropping with steep, rough sides, shelves and crevices. We scrambled to the top and looked around. Below, we could see the stream that we knew we had to get to. In the absence of any ducks, we figured a way to get down and slid all the way. Susie's ragged seat of her pants is evidence of the roughness of the ride.

"Then we saw a monstrous boulder that blocked our way jutting out into the water — completely impassable." They struggled up the granite again.

They stopped to drink cold cocoa. Which way to go? They continued to clamber up and down, "duckless and hopeless."

Hope was rekindled. Betty continued, "We came to a spot on the river where we stopped and had lunch, after spotting a duck on the cliff above. A search revealed a few more, and we finally arrived at what we thought was what the book described as the 'drinking pool.'" But they could find no more ducks. In despair, they decided they'd just have to sit there and wait to be rescued. There was no possibility of retracing their steps.

Finally they noticed a duck above them that indicated the trail went up. They decided to give it one more try. Perhaps they could still make it to Alpine — though a day late. They bushwhacked their way as far as they could go, which wasn't far. Studying the map, they considered that they might be on the wrong side of the creek. They descended to the creek again, not sure at that point which one it was.

They decided to stay put, and hope to be rescued. They set up camp. "People won't worry about us too much until tomorrow morning," recorded Betty in her journal. "Then let's hope they get a search party out."

Of Monday, Betty recorded in her journal "We got up about 6:30 after a good night's sleep in spite of our worrying about the people who were worrying about us. We wished we could tell people we were okay, just lost. We went down to the river and Susie put the red poncho out on a flat boulder in the river and wrote "S.O.S." with little rocks. Then she took my space blanket and put it on another rock with the shiny side up."

They decided it was time to start rationing their food. "We had breakfast — a bit of granola, sugar, and the stale old dry milk that's tasting better every day. Also had one and a half apricots — that's the end of the apricots."

"We went back by the river to wait and started reading the book Susie brought: Mark Twain's, *Letters from the Earth*. "It was very funny, but somewhat blasphemous. It does pass the time and gives us stuff to talk about." They played word games — expressions with pairs of consonants from B to Z: "Black and blue, safe and sound," etc.

"Then we made Raimen by putting it in a can with water, spices, and butter. We set it in the sun, hoping it would soak up enough to be edible. It was fine; we ate half of it for lunch.

While we were waiting for it to stew up, Susie put my yellow windbreaker on a rock across the river.

"In the afternoon, we read some more of Terrible Twain and then went for a swim." Susie swam in the buff in the river, certain that help would come as soon as they were in the river, but no. Dinner was a bit of trail mix, a small piece of cheese, and Tang-barely-flavored-water.

"It's Tuesday, August 11th, the third day of being lost."

Betty writes in her journal, "At 6:15 a.m., we heard a chopper! We jumped up, and saw the chopper. We frantically began to wave everything, and jump up and down and holler."

Susie was down by the stream and Betty was up at the clearing. The helicopter made three passes to the east, up-river.

Betty recorded more, "We thought they saw us, but apparently not. We each ate a teaspoon of the remaining granola for breakfast.

"The rush of adrenaline had an astounding effect on all my stiff joints; I don't seem to be very stiff anymore. We were both elated and…

"Hey, what's that up there!! The chopper again! And they're coming right towards us! Praise the Lord!!"

"9:15 a.m. They got bigger and bigger, louder and louder. We scurried to clear the open space thinking they were going to land there, but they just hovered about 40 feet above us, and let Brian [a member of the crew] down on a rope with his medical pack. I threw my arms around him. He said the thing they noticed was me in the clearing, flapping the red space blanket.

"Then the rest of the crew took the helicopter to a better landing spot about a quarter-mile away. Susie and Brian went down to retrieve my blue poncho which was spread out on a rock across the river and my yellow windbreaker that Susie had tied around a tree. She had hopped over big boulders and crossed the river to put both in place earlier this morning — even though she was in a somewhat weakened condition from so little food.

"While Susie and Brian were gone, the other four men of the crew came walking through the bushes. Kyle, Sean, Greg, and John were from the Naval Air Station in Fallon, Nevada. All these young men were perfectly wonderful to us, seemed so glad they'd found us, and were very concerned for our welfare.

"The helicopter created the 'Wind from Hell.' When we went to gather up our stuff, some of it was a bit far afield. My journal was stuck up in a bush from all the wind. The crew carried our packs. We walked through some rugged terrain to the helicopter.

"Quite an experience, riding in a helicopter. Never saw so many dials, buttons, and levers. It's a very exacting job; each man has his special responsibility. The pilot handed us earplugs because of the noise. They gave us a peanut butter sandwich. It was very exciting."

Back at Carson Pass, Betty and Susie were greeted by another group of well wishers at the kiosk who took a report from them. The sheriff at Carson Pass had some knowledge of the area and thought they had probably gotten onto an abandoned Indian trail — one that probably hadn't been used in a hundred years. That would account for all the ducks they kept discovering in the extremely rough terrain.

Undaunted, the next year Betty and her friend Sandy decided to try the hike again, this time by starting from the opposite direction — Lake Alpine to Camp Irene. They were in a tiny store near the trailhead. The shop's owner said, "You two ladies going into that canyon alone? That's for experienced hikers only. Why, last year this lady and her daughter got lost in there!" But a woman ranger Betty and Sandy talked to encouraged them, "It's the '90s, go for it." The new trip was successful.

Water Crossings

Joyce's story of her experience crossing wild water during an Alaska backpack trip demonstrates one of the most important techniques for safe crossings.

✦ Joyce

"We were on my third Alaska trip, an eight-day backpack near Rainbow Mountain. Rain had been heavy throughout the trek. We were due to be picked up in the wilderness by a bush pilot the following day, and we came to a large river that had to be crossed. By the time we had waded halfway out, the water was mid-chest. So we backtracked and walked a mile upstream. Once again it was too deep. We hiked another mile upstream, and this time, luckily, we found a stream where we could cross. It was now late, but we were able to camp by the river, build a fire and warm ourselves."

Choose the conditions:

- Don't cross if the conditions are unsafe; look for another place where you can cross safely. In Joyce's case, this required three attempts.
- Don't attempt to cross where you'd be unable to recover from a slip or fall.
- Narrow, deep streams are more dangerous than wide, slow moving ones; be particularly careful of the outer edge of curves. Choose a place where the stream divides.

- If the water is from snowmelt, do your crossing early morning before the sun warms the snow uphill. If the water is in canyonland, wait for storm waters to recede.

  Use Proper Techniques:

- If you are carrying a pack, **unbuckle** the belts before you start across.
- **Wear** water shoes, water socks, sandals, or your boots (you can take off socks or liners to keep them dry) so you can cross more quickly and not stub your toes.
- Never **tie** anyone to a rope.
- Use your walking poles, or a stout branch, to help **maintain balance.**
- Walk diagonally downstream; link arms (not hands) with partners.
- If you fall during a dangerous crossing, get rid of your pack, get on your back with your feet pointing downstream, and try to get to calmer water.
- And, Joyce's second bit of wisdom, "After the crossing, warm yourself. Get out of your wet clothing, get dry, drink something warm, eat some carbs, and keep moving."

Early Stages of Altitude Sickness

The altitude is a consideration any time you exceed 8,000 feet. This is because the atmospheric pressure decreases with increases in altitude, making less oxygen available. And when the body is starved for oxygen, it sets off a chain reaction of physical responses to deal with the situation. "Breathe faster" from the brain; "beat faster" from the heart. Less oxygen to the brain also increases the time that thinking requires.

Bottom line: it's noticeably harder to breathe the higher you go. Your heart rate will increase; your reaction time will slow. The body adjusts to the difference over time, but most backpackers don't want to wait several days or weeks to adjust. They want to drive to the higher elevation and set out right away. This can be risky, the more so the higher the starting point.

Between 8,000 and 12,000 feet, most people will experience the aforementioned shortness of breath with exertion. They may suffer headaches, minor swelling of hands and feet, or nausea. They may have difficulty sleeping, a loss of appetite, and feel run-down. Usually these symptoms will clear up with rest. Rarely, but importantly, they may encounter acute mountain sickness (AMS) such as high-altitude cerebral or pulmonary edema. Here are some points to ponder, and some suggestions for dealing with these difficulties:

- Be physically fit for backpacking — training should include strength training and aerobic conditioning.
- Arrive earlier than your scheduled hiking departure time. Give yourself time to acclimate. A day or two is best; overnight is the minimum.
- If ascending and descending — particularly in the early days — sleep at the *lower* elevations.
- Drink plenty of water or other fluids (do not count diuretics such as caffeinated tea and coffee).
- Plan rest days, especially if you are continuing to ascend. At elevations exceeding 5,000 feet, go up no more than 2,000 to 3,000 feet per day.
- Some suggest a very high-carbohydrate diet.
- If someone in the party is suffering from AMS, (for which there are prescription drugs to aid during descent), there is no alternative to going to a lower elevation. Her life may depend on it.

✦ Jeannine

Jeannine Burk's experience with a trip into the Sierra to climb Mt. Whitney contains pearls of wisdom. "Our party got as far as Kearsarge Pass and everyone except my mom and I decided against continuing. Mom was just under five feet tall, weighed less than 100 pounds and was carrying a drawstring bag with her gear. But she taught me how to pace myself, to pause when I needed to, and to ignore the hikers going by like gangbusters (who were soon out of breath)."

Hypothermia

Hypothermia is a potentially life-threatening condition where the body's core becomes too cold. It occurs when the body is losing heat faster than it can replace it — when you are too cold, too long — and the body attempts to protect the brain and heart. In the early stages, shivering may actually warm the body. In later stages, shivering may stop as the person experiences difficulty walking and possibly becomes incoherent. Clearly, the first step in preventing hypothermia is to know when it strikes, and to avoid those situations.

Some surprising facts that may save a life:

- Hypothermia not only happens at below-freezing temperatures, but also can occur when the air temperature is 40-80 degrees, if the body's core temperature is cooled too much by wet or windy conditions.
- Alcohol is *not* recommended because, though it makes you *feel* warm, it dilates the blood cells and brings them closer to the skin's surface causing further heat loss.
- Because backpacking often involves strenuous exercise, sometimes in cold and wet weather — conditions that can lead to hypothermia — prevention should focus on keeping warm and dry, eating

properly, staying hydrated, and getting sufficient rest. During a storm, take shelter earlier, rather than later.

- Your clothing is your first line of defense. Wear a hat; most of your body's heat is lost through your head, so keep it — including your ears — warm. I wear two pairs of gloves — a lightweight pair that lets my fingers move for lighting my camp-stove, zipping my sleeping bag, and taking photographs — and an outer pair that is warm and water-repellant. However, if you need more protection, be aware that mittens are warmer than gloves.

- Wear *layers* of clothing; select inner layer clothing that wicks moisture away from your core, and outerwear that sheds water.

- Select backpacking gear that is appropriate to the area you are exploring. A backpacker used to the weather in one area may be unfamiliar with the conditions of another. The three-season tent and the down sleeping bag that can withstand the common afternoon thunderstorms of the Sierra Nevada may not be the gear of choice for a week of misty fog, drenching rain, or sleet in Washington's Olympic Peninsula, Alaska, or Maine.

The treatment of hypothermia includes:

- Get the person to shelter — out of the wind and wet, and off the cold ground.
- Remove wet and tight clothing and boots and replace with dry clothing. Cover the head.
- Get the person into a dry sleeping bag; warm her with your own body heat.
- If the person is alert, give her warm (preferably sweetened) liquids.

✦ Marcy

Marcy primarily hikes in the Sierra Nevada — where summer afternoon storms are not infrequent, and mountain passes may still be snow-covered in July. "Our first trip of the season was very strenuous. The snow covered the trails from Donahue Pass, south of Yosemite's Tuolumne, all the way to Shadow Lake, where we threw in the towel and hiked out eight miles to Agnew Meadows. There we took the shuttle to my car at Red's Meadow — ten miles further.

"It had been very difficult trying to decide where the trail was, or where it would go. We got very tired and every day turned up new challenges. We got caught in a hailstorm and lightning was very close. We got wet and cold — had to put up the tent in the rain, take off all wet clothes, get in our bags, and huddle close to get warm. Luckily, I had an emergency hand warmer, and that not only warmed up my feet, but dried the whole bottom end of the bag."

✦ Carolyn

On one of her Appalachian hikes, Carolyn found out how quickly hypothermia can occur. She was hiking in Maine. It started to rain and the temperature dropped quickly. She did not stop and change into dry clothes soon enough; she was close to hypothermia. Luckily, she did reach a shelter and a fellow hiker got her some hot tea quickly. She believes his quick response and kindness may have saved her life.

✦ Elizabeth

Elizabeth has had a couple of close encounters with hypothermia. She and her friend, Phyllis, were hiking together. It suddenly started drizzling and they became so cold their teeth were chattering. Phyllis seemed to be approaching hypothermia. Elizabeth took Phyllis into her tent, took off all their wet clothes, and warmed her up.

✦ Doris

Doris is also adamant about being prepared for weather changes. "I have a lightweight tent, three pounds, four ounces. I believe in it. We've had blizzards in August in the Sierra and been very glad. We've had 20-knot winds, and hail.

"It really makes me mad when people say they travel light, that you never need a tent in the Sierra. I beg to differ. The first time I took Ronnie up (and she's very lean and in super shape), we were caught out in a hailstorm going up the face of Seven Gables. We were trying to get off of it, but there was no way. A thunderstorm came up (I believe Seven Gables makes its own weather), so we moved to low places, and scattered so our heat wouldn't be so attractive to the lightning, and scrunched down. Three of the girls put on their wool sweaters.

"Ronnie and I didn't want to put on our sweaters. We wanted to have something warm and dry for when we would be able to retreat after the storm down in the meadow and put up our tents. We thought we would be so clever and have dry sweaters. At any rate, you need to wear wool or warm up the body.

"Well, we both got hypothermia. Now, I'm not skinny, and I was able to eat a granola bar and put on a warm sweater and be okay, but Ronnie just couldn't stop shivering. So I had to bring her into the sleeping bag with me in order to get her warm again. I know it's recommended that you try to get more than one person in there to keep the victim warm, but I don't know if I could get three people in our tent or not. I tried to give her my first aid for hypothermia, a chocolate bar, but she said, 'I can't do this.' It made her nauseous, so she didn't eat it. I think the chocolate warmed me up, but not her.

"So we really would have been in trouble without a tent. The next day, we had to amend our plans because she was so affected. It wasn't that she was cold and shivering one day, and fine the next day. It was a sobering experience."

"My friend Nancy swears by a tarp. 'They're wonderful,' she says. "I've never been so cold in my life as when we all slept under that tarp! The wind was blowing it, there's "gap-osis" on the bottom, people were putting their packs around for a foundation to try to keep the wind from blowing in on us. It was very cold."

Lightning

In the United States, approximately 89 people die of lightning strikes and between 1,000 to 1,500 are injured each year. More than a quarter of the deaths occur in open spaces, fields, and ballparks, 18% under trees, and 13% in water related activities — boating, fishing, or swimming. Backpackers do not contribute greatly to the number of injured, but here are some guidelines:

- To figure out how far away lightning is, count the seconds between the flash and the thunder. Each count of five is equal to one mile — so fifteen seconds means the lightning is about three miles away. The next strike could be closer; look for shelter.
- A mountaintop is dangerous during a lightening storm. Stay below timberline after 11:00 a.m. on stormy days. Don't leave shelter too soon, as strikes can happen after the rain stops and the sky is clearing.
- Certain areas of trees often show signs of previous lightning strikes. Do not take shelter under a lone tree or the tallest tree of a forest.
- Try to **minimize** ground contact, since lightning can travel along the ground. If there's no place to take shelter, use your insulated sleeping pad or bag, and squat on the balls of your feet, preferably on a low boulder. Don't put your hands on the ground.

- If you are fishing or swimming, get away from the water immediately. In a boat, crouch low.
- General recommendations say not to touch metal objects, such as golf clubs, tennis rackets, and bicycles; most backpacks and many tents contain metal. If the count is down to five seconds or less, it may be wise to shelter apart from the backpack.
- Know CPR. You can safely do CPR or mouth-to-mouth resuscitation. The person who was hit does not have an electrical charge after being struck. People who have been struck by lightning can sometimes be revived.

Sun Protection

Sunscreen: For the last few years, we have read numerous studies that conclude that we should wear sunscreen, especially those who are fair-skinned. The major health reason to do so, we've been told, is to protect against ultraviolet rays that may cause the increased incidence of melanoma.

However, some researchers do not agree that sunscreen prevents melanomas. They believe that those who wear sunscreen are more often outdoors, and/or that those wearing sunscreen may have a false sense of security when wearing it and, as a consequence, they stay out longer, or more often, than they would if they were not wearing it.

Make your decisions based on your health giver's advice and your common sense. It seems reasonable to look for other means of protection in addition to using a sunscreen. Keep your skin covered during the most intense sunlit parts of the day.

White tee-shirts permit UV to pass through, so choose darker colors. There are synthetics offered that are advertised to be equal to a SPF20+. A leading consumer ratings magazine did not find all advertised clothing to protect as the manufacturers claimed, but they did suggest that darker and denser fabrics were an aid.

Sunglasses: Lenses made of plastic or polycarbonate offer some protection from ultraviolet (UV) rays from the material itself. Glass offers less protection. Tint alone does not block UV rays. The best protection is from chemicals embedded within the lens, which should block both UV-A and UV-B — two kinds of ultraviolet rays. Lenses coated with a thin film of these chemicals are just as effective but may lose protection if scratched or abraded.

If you want to see if your existing sunglasses offer UV protection, you can take them to an optician to have the UV absorption measured. The measuring is easy to do and may be free. If you need them re-coated, the charge is around $30.

If you buy new sunglasses, look for ANSI (American National Standard Institute) on the label. Buy glasses that block 99% of UV-A and UV-B. If you're going to be at the beach, in snow, on granite walls, or other extremely bright areas, you need glasses that block 75% or more of visible light. Gray or green lenses reduce glare without color distortion. Highly protective sunglasses do not have to have high prices.

When you backpack, an extra pair of glasses is recommended if you are extremely dependent on them. Put them on a cord so you won't loose them.

Insects

Ticks: Lyme Disease & Rocky Mountain Spotted Fever: Ticks are tiny parasitic pests that can be a major nuisance. Backpackers need to be aware of two of the diseases they may carry — Lyme Disease and Rocky Mountain Spotted Fever.

Lyme Disease is caused by bacteria, which are transmitted by the bite of a tick. The disease occurs worldwide (except Antarctica), but its distribution is not even; some areas are much more likely to have outbreaks. It was first identified as a form of arthritis in the woodlands near Lyme, Connecticut — hence its name. Campers, hikers, and backpackers need to take basic precautions in areas likely to be infected, but at the same time they need to be aware that the incidence of Lyme disease is very low.

Even in cases where you are bitten by an infected tick, you have a less than one-percent chance of being infected. In the U.S., approximately 15,000 cases are reported annually, mostly in the Northeast (Maine to Maryland), the Midwest (Wisconsin and Minnesota), and the West (Northern California and Oregon). The tick has to feed on a human for 24 to 48 hours before the bacteria can be transmitted. Also, though its peak season may vary in different locales, it is primarily a summer disease. That's because it is also the peak season for the newly hatched nymphs and the time of year most people are outdoors.

The early symptoms are usually mild and often ignored. However, 80% of cases have a red, raised bulls-eye rash at the site of the tick bite that spreads for several days and can last for weeks. Some of the symptoms are much like more common illnesses. There may be flu-like symptoms like chills, fever, headache, lack of energy, a stiff neck, or joint or muscle pain. After several months, if left untreated, there may be inflammation of the large joints.

In a study, reported in the February 2000 Journal of the American Medical Association, of 678 patients who had been diagnosed as having Lyme disease, 70% of the people, one to eleven years after diagnosis, believed they were cured.

This study was of Connecticut residents diagnosed with Lyme disease compared with a control group of 212 people without the disease. Eighty-five percent of the group diagnosed with Lyme disease had taken antibiotics. Medical tests on both groups showed similar levels of health.

A single-dose antibiotic, which was effective in preventing the disease in 87% of patients, has recently become available. To be effective, it must be given immediately after a deer-tick bite to prevent Lyme disease. Researchers are being cautious, however, because overuse could make the disease resistant to drugs.

The diagnosis, treatment, and study of Lyme disease is difficult, however, because its symptoms may vary a lot from person to person; the current tests for Lyme disease are unreliable and may indicate a person is infected when, in fact, they are not, or vice-versa. In rare cases, those who are not treated promptly may experience recurrent arthritis. Luckily, reliable tests are on the way, which should improve treatment.

To lessen your risks and your worry about Lyme disease while backpacking, hiking, or in your yard, you can take the following precautions:

- Wear long slacks and a long-sleeved shirt with cuffs that button. Tuck the pants legs into your socks or boots. Wear light colored fabrics so that any ticks will be more easily seen.
- Use insect repellant containing DEET on your clothing, including shoes. You can also apply the repellant to your skin in recommended doses, if you are not bothered by it. Permethrin, applied only to clothing, is said to be an excellent repellant and is sold in many areas. Whether or not it should be put on clothes to be worn in the wilderness, where it will eventually be washed into streams and lakes, is another question.

- Walk in the middle of the trail; ticks don't jump. Avoid brushing against tall grasses and underbrush.
- Check for ticks occasionally when you're in likely areas, such as shrubs and wooded areas, and later do a thorough check of your entire body. The nymphs (young) are the most likely to be encountered, and they are only the size of a pinhead. When they become engorged, they will be three to five times larger, which is still very tiny.
- Try to have someone else look at your back and head, and then decide how you want to conduct a thorough search of your dark, moist areas: the back of your knees, under your arms, and your crotch.
- If you find a tick, remove it by grabbing it with a pair of tweezers as close to your skin as possible. You want to avoid squeezing its bloated body. Don't use your fingers. Pull straight out, not twisting. After removing it, wash your hands, the affected area and the tweezers with soap and water. Apply an antiseptic such as rubbing alcohol. You can also use an ice pack if the area itches or is painful.
- It is **not** recommended that you apply petroleum jelly, gasoline, or a hot match. And don't use disinfectant.
- Though Lyme disease has occurred in most states, cases have primarily been in the Northeast and Upper Midwest and on the Pacific coast, usually on the margins where suburban lawns meet the woodlands. In the East, it is chiefly the white-footed field mouse that is the main host; in the West, it is the wood rat. Deer, whose numbers have increased dramatically in the last decade, also help spread the disease.

Rocky Mountain Spotted Fever may have originated in the Rockies in the 1940s, but it is now primarily found in the southern Atlantic states: North Carolina, Virginia, and Maryland, as well as Oklahoma. Rocky Mountain Spotted Fever is caused by the adult dog tick or wood tick infected with an organism, R. rickettsii. The symptoms are severe headache, chills with long-lasting high fever (to 104 degrees) and a pink rash that typically appears within two to six days of the onset of the fever. The rash is usually on wrists and ankles and spreads over the trunk and face within 24 hours; occasionally the rash appears on the palms and soles. Approximately 10% of people with the disease don't get the rash. The medical treatment will normally include a full course of antibiotics.

Mild cases may disappear in a week or two; severe cases require medical treatment, sometimes with hospitalization, because kidney failure, heart failure, pneumonia, and other complications may arise. There is a 20-30% fatality rate, so this is not something to ignore.

The recommended precautions are much the same as for Lyme Disease (above) including: stay out of infested (heavily wooded or sagebrush) areas; wear protective clothing and a repellent such as DEET; at least daily, inspect thoroughly for ticks; remove ticks carefully; wash with soap and water.

Mosquitoes: *West Nile Virus*: According to the Center for Disease Control (CDC), West Nile Virus has now occurred in humans in every state in the U.S., except Alaska and Hawaii. Eighty percent of those bitten by an infected mosquito will show no symptoms. Up to 2 in 10 people may have moderate symptoms (fever, aches, nausea and vomiting within 3 to 15 days of infection). About 1 in 150 people develop more serious symptoms or death. The risk for serious illness is highest for people age 50 and over and for those with compromised health. For updated info, go to www.cdc.gov.

Minimize risks by using a repellent. An Environmental Protection Agency (EPA) approval indicates that an ingredient has been tested for safety and efficacy. For use on *skin and clothing*: products containing EPA-approved DEET or Picaridin as active ingredients are the most effective. For use on clothing, *not skin:* we can add Permethrin. Two recent studies have indicated that oil of lemon eucalyptus (a plant based repellent, which has also been registered with EPA) provided results comparable to DEET against mosquitoes found in the U.S.

Further info from the CDC: use repellents as labels direct and conditions warrant. The concentration of the active ingredient will affect its length of protection (i.e. 23.8% DEET provides an average of 5 hours). Don't apply repellents under clothing; apply a thin layer at first and more later if necessary; don't use repellents over cuts, wounds or irritated skin; don't apply to eyes or mouth, and apply sparingly around ears.

When using sprays, "do not spray directly on face — spray on hands first and then apply to face. This is particularly important when repellents are used repeatedly in a day or on consecutive days. If a rash or other bad reaction from an insect repellent occurs, stop using the repellent, wash the repellent off with mild soap and water, and call a local poison control center for further guidance. When using on children, apply to your own hands first and then put on the child — you may not want to apply to children's hands."

I recommend against the combination sunscreen/bug repellents. We've found that when you need the one, you probably don't need the other. And, whereas I don't mind repeated heavy applications of sunscreen, I like to minimize the use of bug repellents.

Choose clothing that will minimize your exposure to insects — long sleeved shirts, long pants tucked into your socks. Wear light colors rather than dark — they are less attractive to insects. Choose closely-woven fabrics, particularly synthetics. Finally, wear mosquito head coverings and/or clothing. (These items may make hiking hotter and feel confining, but they are sometimes necessary.)

In our tent days, when all else failed, I dove for the tent. Now, I make do with my head net. If you can make it through the dinner hour, when the mosquitoes are most numerous, you're okay.

After you have bug-proofed yourself, you can amuse yourself by conducting your own research on what colors, fabrics, and odors seem to attract more flying insects. I personally find it somewhat amusing to watch them ineptly try to drill through fleece, Levi's, and so forth.

Other Considerations

✦ Kathy

Kathy doesn't worry about animal or people encounters. "Six miles in there's nothing but fellow backpackers." She has seen those with guns and dogs, and it's been suggested she carry a weapon, but she doesn't want the added weight. When she meets some of the eccentrics of the "front country," she ignores them — brushes them off.

✦ Barbara and her women's group

Barbara cautions that even with the best of planning, mishaps and illness can occur. In 1999, her Bay Area women's group went out from Bridgeport, California. They were a couple of days into a pack trip, when a group member became ill. She leaned over as if she was having a stroke. Because they were not in a service area, no one's cell phone worked.

Though they had thought they were prepared for emergencies — being experienced backpackers with knowledge of mountain medicine — they found they weren't able to deal with everything. Initially they wondered if the friend had altitude sickness, but that didn't seem logical since they'd been out a while. After a terrible night, they decided to seek help. At 5:00 a.m., two women hiked four and a half-hours to the trailhead while two others went another direction to try to find a ranger and two remained in camp with the ill woman.

Finally, help was found and a helicopter was brought in to airlift the member to a medical facility. It was found she had experienced a hemorrhage of the lining of the brain. She recovered from this medical emergency that could have occurred anywhere and was unrelated to the trip, but of course it was potentially more serious in the backcountry where help is hours or days away.

✦ Della

In New Hampshire, the most difficult part of the Appalachian Trail in her opinion, Della fell and broke her ribs. That night she shared the shelter with a young man who found it disconcerting each time a ripping pain hit her and she screamed out. So she tried to breathe shallowly and reduce the pain. That concerned the young man too, because then he couldn't hear her breathing. "Are you okay?" he would ask during the night.

She kept going. "The pack didn't hit the broken spot," she commented. But she did reduce her usual daily mileage of 17 or 18 miles to seven or eight for the next three days. Considerately, the young man reduced his pace too, so that he could help her get her pack on and off when she stopped at day's end.

✦ Marcy

Marcy's mishap just proves that it only takes a moment of distraction to have a mishap. "A mile from the parking lot, I was busy patting myself on the back over a very successful trip, no accidents, didn't get into any trouble — when BAM! I fell flat on my face! Pinned down by my backpack. Unfortunately (or fortunately) there was nobody around to help me up, or say, 'Oh, poor baby.' I had to unbuckle my straps and pull myself out from under the pack, drag it to a slight rise in the sage and struggle back into it. One skinned knee and a barked shin. No lasting harm, just God reminding me to be humble!"

Insurance

Your backpacking trips may take you out of the country. In *Stories of World Travel* by Wild Writing Women, contributing author Alison Wright relates the horrific story of a bus accident and her severe injuries, while she was traveling in Laos. The costs of airlifting her back to the United States, and of her brother flying to Laos to help her, were horrendous. Therefore, if you are planning international travel consider the availability of medical care and the value of medical coverage.

✦ ✦ ✦ ✦

Even though I know that statistics indicate that I am safer in the wilderness than driving across the state to the trailhead, I know I will probably continue to cringe when there is a lightning storm, but sing while we drive along the highway. Courage is not being unafraid. It's managing the fear and planning for contingencies.

> Tip: Experts believe that many of the intestional upsets encountered in the wilderness are caused *not* by water-borne parasites, but by inadequate hygiene. Be certain that all group members understand the importance of washing hands after going to the bathroom and before preparing or sharing food. Keep the threads of your water bottle clean. Wash dishes in hot water as often as possible.

12
Either Tortoise or Hare is Fine:
Going at Your Own Pace, Training & Staying Healthy

"Those who don't find time for exercise will have to find time for illness."

old proverb

Older Americans are not only living longer, they are also living healthier. Kenneth Manton, from the Center for Demographic Studies at Duke University, stated that better medical care, diet, exercise, and public health advances have contributed to our significant gains. In addition, he noted that older Americans are better educated, and tend to take better care of themselves than ever before. Christiane Northrup, author of *Wisdom of Menopause*, says we shouldn't slow down, we are "just beginning to hit [our] stride."

Heart Disease and Walking, Hiking, and Backpacking

Heart disease, according the National Center for Disease Control, is the leading cause of death in the United States. However, numerous studies indicate that heart disease rates are significantly less in those incorporating healthy eating and regular exercise into their daily lives. Many studies suggest that walking, particularly brisk walking, is the exercise of choice.

The prestigious New England Journal of Medicine (January 1998) reported that at walking two miles a day cut the risk of death by almost 50 percent for those aged 60 and older.

In 1999, Harvard researchers reported in the New England Journal of Medicine on a study involving 72,488 female nurses ages 40 to 65. Their conclusion — walking at the rate of three miles per hour, or more, thirty minutes a day (at least three hours a week), can reduce women's risk of heart disease up to 40 percent. This is not "casual strolling." Nor, according to JoAnn E. Manson, Professor of Medicine at Bringham and Women's Hospital in Boston (lead author of the study) is it "window shopping at the mall." Brisk walking's benefits are the same as those of other regular vigorous physical activities — such as jogging, stair-stepping, and so forth. This is certainly reassuring to those of us who enjoy walking and hiking, but hadn't been certain that our walking was a strenuous enough form of exercise to afford the protection that aerobics provide.

The Harvard study also indicated that the more walking, the lower the disease risk. Women who walked briskly five hours per week cut their risk of heart disease in half, compared with sedentary women. Women who smoked, were overweight, or had other risk factors for heart disease, also significantly reduced their risk of premature heart disease by regular, brisk walking. (Women who hiked and were smokers, though reducing their risk by hiking, were still at twice the coronary risk as the most sedentary non-smokers.)

Walking is easy, does not require equipment (except for good shoes), and is readily accessible. Walking or hiking is an excellent way to condition for backpacking, and is part of the training conditioning that most of the women I interviewed use. But, since backpacking can be a very strenuous form of exercise, getting a doctor's okay before starting is important.

Foot Care: In addition to carefully selecting the appropriate and well fitting boots as detailed in Chapter Ten, there are several steps of self-care that will keep your feet in good condition for your hike.

- Strengthen your feet gradually (ahead of time) by increasing the length of your hikes over time.
- Further strengthen feet with at-home exercises, such as toe raises (with shoes on, raise onto the ball of your feet), toe circles (point toes and inscribe circles with your toes), and toe flexes (point and flex toes and then, flex and move toes side to side).
- Maintain your weight at a reasonable level.
- Wear orthotics if you bothered by arch conditions such as *plantar fasciitis.*
- Select socks with care. I wear two layers — the lightweight synthetic inner sock, and the Smartwool med-heavy weight wool outdoor sock. Bring an adequate number of socks to change them at least once a day. Three sets will provide one set to wear, with one set of dry socks to wear when one set is drying.
- Put socks on carefully. Take the time to smooth out any wrinkles. Leave toe wiggle-room. I wear my socks wrong side out to avoid the seams rubbing.
- Soak or air-cool your feet frequently if they are getting hot and sweaty. Nothing beats sticking those dogs in a cold stream or lake, but just taking off your boots to cool them in the air is helpful. You can also soak your feet at your campsite by filling a portable basin or emptied bear canister with water.
- Deal with hot spots immediately. Hot spots, which are caused by friction and heat, quickly turn into blisters.

Every athlete seems to have a different preventative treatment: applying Moleskin, adhesive tape, duct tape, powder, lotion, or ointment (such as Vaseline). We prefer using breathable medical tape applied at the first sign of tenderness. You may have to experiment to find what works well for your feet.

- To avoid infection and tearing the skin, it's best *not* to drain a blister. Instead, attempt to cushion it and avoid further irritation.
- If you *do* have to drain a blister, use a sterilized needle to go into the skin *near* it. Then go into the blister itself from inside, rather than going directly into the blister from the top. We've found this prevents the skin above the blister from peeling off to leave a raw area.

Knee Care Guidelines

Even women in excellent health otherwise may have joint problems as they age. The cartilage in our joints decreases and bones may become more brittle. While genetically we may be susceptible to some degeneration, there are steps we can take that seem to be helpful in slowing, sometimes arresting, joint problems.

Knee problems, because of our physiology, affect more women than men; the knee is the most common site of joint problems as we age. But, according to experts, there are three preventative measures that we can take: controlling weight, keeping exercise to a reasonable level, and getting medical advice when pain persists. The follow is a compilation of measures that can reduce your risk of pain or injury — and keep you on the trail many additional years. Fitness centers, your doctor, or other medical allies can recommend other important leg strengthening exercises.

- Stretch before and after exercise.
- Exercise and strengthen the supportive muscle around your knee. Strong leg muscles not only let you hike

with less tiring, they also support the comparatively weak knee. An added benefit to women backpackers: having strong thigh muscles makes squatting easier to pee and poop. *Wall sits* are worthwhile. Start by standing with your heels about one foot from the wall, your feet shoulder width apart, your arms by your sides. Bend your knees so you end up with your back against the wall, and slide down until your knees are at a 90 degree angle (less for beginners). Hold for 15-30 seconds, rest for 30 seconds, repeat three times.

- Alternate and vary exercise routines. Jogging and running put stress on the knee joints and cartilage. If you do these activities, alternate with other activities to let muscles heal. Avoid hard surfaces. A paved surface is *ten* times harder on your joints than a dirt path.
- Maintain a reasonable weight. Every extra pound you carry is added pressure on knees and feet. Researchers at the Boston University found that a loss of 11 pounds in medium-height women was associated with a roughly 50 percent reduction in the risk of developing osterarthritis.
- Obtain adequate calcium in your diet from foods and supplements to help prevent osteoporosis.
- Consider glucosamine supplement. Although there are many variables that can affect joints, many people (myself included) have found immediate improvement after adding glucosamine to their daily diet.
- Carry medication to reduce joint inflammation. Sometimes, I take ibuprofen *before* a hike to minimize swelling. Those who take aspirin as a preventative for heart problems may find it also reduces inflammation.
- Use trekking poles or a hiking stick. They reduce the impact to your knees, hips, and feet many-fold. Europeans have used poles for decades, and they are becoming increasingly popular in the United States. I find them invaluable when going up and down mountain trails (and they help with balance when

fording rivers). Added benefit: more exercise for your upper body, especially those underarms that wave back at you. The poles that have shock absorbers are less jarring to wrists, arms, and shoulders; some collapsible models will fit in luggage.

- Wear orthotics when indicated. Shoe inserts may help not only feet, but also — since everything starts with the feet — may help knees and hips stay in alignment.
- Wear elastic knee supports, which can be helpful for stabilizing the knee. These can be purchased over the counter.
- Reduce your packweight. I can not overemphasize the importance of keeping what you carry to the minimum you can with safety. Carrying a heavy pack not only makes your trip harder than it needs to be, it also takes its toll on your body.

When I started backpacking, in my late 40s, I wasn't sure how my body would respond. Having injured my knees skiing in my early 40s, I was concerned that backpacking would be cause my knees problems to resurface. Amazingly, my knees cause me fewer problems today then they did fifteen years ago. My doctors have routinely told me to keep walking.

I believe that backpacking has been good for me, too. As I've gotten older, I've acquired a number of aged related degenerative problems — episodes of lower back pain, knee cartilage problems, hip joint bursitis, and plantar fascitiis… But, interestingly, when I am hiking and backpacking, I have much few problems than when I am home and more sedentary.

The Partnership for Taking Charge of Your Health

Those of us in our fifties and beyond remember doctors making house calls. When the doctor arrived on our doorstep, black bag in hand, we knew we were going to be taken care of. Doctors today rarely make house calls. When we visit our medical provider, we may not have the sense of connection we had once upon a time with our general practitioner.

Today, we have to be more pro-active in regard to our health care. We have to do some homework: follow relevant medical research, reports, and treatments as reported by the media. When we need to visit the doctor for routine or urgent appointments, we need to keep in mind that doctors are often rushed and the time allotted for an appointment may be short. So, we have to be prepared to ask questions of our medical providers and not wait for information to be offered. Sometimes we have to doggedly fight to get past the "gatekeepers." We have to insist on being seen in a timely manner, to have a second opinion, or to be referred to a specialist. Remember, it's "the squeaky wheel that gets the grease."

Pro-active also includes taking measures and increasing responsibility for staying health and fit. Certainly it makes a lot of sense (and may be of critical importance if an emergency arises) to be in good physical health before venturing into the wilderness. That said, lots of women go backpacking (this author included) in less than prime condition.

Most of us have busy lives, with so many demands on our time that we often postpone looking after our health. That makes it important to consider the level of difficulty of the trip you are planning to be certain it's a good match.

Our Methods for Staying Active

Though good health is partly a measure of good luck and good genes, our lifestyle choices also play a significant part. Many diseases can be controlled or slowed by diet and exercise. Backpacking is for most people an occasional event, not a weekly one. Therefore, women who take on this demanding exercise, usually find it necessary to keep in shape with other year-round activities. Perhaps some of the following stories will inspire you to add something new to your exercise plan.

✦ Jeannine

Jeannine found a unique method of getting and staying fit. When she returned home to Los Angeles after a summer working in Alaska's Denali National Park, she resumed local walks. When that began to get boring, she decided to set a goal. She would walk all the streets north of Sunset Boulevard starting at the beach. She began to mark off the streets as she continued. She became more intrigued, and after she had walked every block of every street north of Sunset, she began doing those below Sunset. Finally, she had covered the area from the beach to downtown. Then, she walked all the streets above Wilshire, and a large number of the ones below the boulevard.

"Climbing the hills was at least as much exercise as stair stepping, and a lot more interesting. Whenever I was in town, and not traveling out of the country, I loaded up my fanny pack with a water bottle and my lunch and set out for several hours of walking," said Jeannine.

Over the course of several years, she visited a wide variety of neighborhoods, each with its own personality representing the cultural diversity of Los Angeles — Russian, Latin, and Armenian to name a few. Some neighborhoods were wealthy (Bel Air and Beverly Hills), some were "arty" with fascinating architecture, outdoor sculpture or gardens, and some (like the beachfront canals of Venice) were being rediscovered.

Not only did Jeannine benefit from achieving her original goal of staying fit by walking, but she also gained tremendous pleasure from discovering her city's neighborhoods.

Going at Your Own Pace

In backpacking, as in much of life, it is wise to know your strengths and your limitations. Newcomers to backpacking should start slowly and choose a companion or group that will allow people to travel at their own pace. Veteran hikers may have to change their expectations as they get older. Many of the women of this book who started backpacking in their twenties have found ways to modify their trips in order to continue them.

There are several options for modifying trips including going at a slower pace, using pack animals, and planning less demanding trips by looking for shorter routes, lower elevations, or added layover days.

✦ Kathy

"Backpacking does not need to be about speed," stated Kathy. Though she thinks she is slow, her pace has not kept her from backpacking, nor from writing her widely respected trail guides.

✦ Sylvelin

Sylvelin has found it necessary to slow down. Luckily, she has found people to travel with who are not "peak-baggers," and whether they are younger, the same age, or older, she finds companions with whom she can hike comfortably. "I'm not a competitive hiker. I've had problems with an Achilles tendon, and the next time out, I plan to just accept minor aches and pains."

Sylvelin planned her 1998 trip as a "compromise." Her trip to the Audubon Summer Camp in the southern part of the Sierra Nevada allowed her to drive to the trailhead at

10,000 feet and then hike on fairly level terrain to the permanent camp of platform tents.

✦ Grace

Grace took a novel approach when she bought, and began to raise, llamas. She believes that acquiring these pets will allow her ten additional years of backpacking. Not only does she get plenty of exercise as she hikes in the Sierra throughout the summer, she also keeps fit the rest of the year with the daily care of her llamas.

Don't Let Up!

As anyone who has packed on more than one occasion will testify, the wilderness can be a mighty force to be reckoned with — accidents happen, nature roars — and it's important to have a little reserve energy (as well as extra food, water, and warm clothing).

Researchers tell us that strength begins to decrease in the 30's, with a rapid decline coming in the 50's. Intuitively we in our 40's, 50's, and 60's or older know this, because we have observed our acquaintances, co-workers, and friends starting to develop health problems at an alarming rate. We have also noticed that a lot of these problems are related to decreasing fitness. If you're like me, you have experienced or observed a vicious circle — we experience a sports injury, we have to ease up, and muscles weaken in the interim.

The good news is that we can increase our muscle strength by 15-30% by doing weight training — no matter what age we are, or how long we've been inactive.

✦ Kathy

Kathy Morey keeps fit during the "off" season by going to the gym several times a week, bicycling on Bishop's trails, and snowshoeing and skiing near her home in Mammoth.

✦ Frandee

Frandee Johnson doesn't really need to exercise or train for backpacking per se, because she is active in sports year-round. She skis in the spring, gets to the mountains in the summers, and goes to the deserts of Utah in the fall. Someone asked one time how she prepared for a climb of Mt. Rainier, and her reply was "I'm just active."

✦ Joyce

Joyce's trips are relatively short — three to seven days — and she always feels ready for them because she hikes, cross-country skis, and bicycles throughout the year.

✦ Irene

Irene stays in shape by hiking throughout the year. She also does water aerobics. When she is getting ready to go backpacking, she puts on her pack with some weight added and does some additional miles.

✦ Carolyn

As Carolyn hikes once or twice a week, she figures she's always ready to go. She believes she was in better condition when she was getting ready for the Appalachian Trail; to keep in shape for that trip (which was completed over a three year period) she took three-day, 50 mile hikes regularly. Of the difficulties of the AT, she said, "I never felt like giving up, I just kept rolling along. "

✦ Marcy

Marcy doesn't train. "Now that's a good idea!" she responded to my inquiry. But since she works at a gym, she regularly uses equipment for aerobics and weight lifting. "I lost five pounds on this last backpack. I was very pleased about that. I've kept it off too, so far. It turned into muscle, but I think the ratio is slipping back the other way."

✦ Carol

Before Carol and Al Messenger started backpacking, a backpacker told them to prepare for their hikes by walking, especially on hills. But, when you live in Ohio there are none, and it's hard to duplicate the conditions of a mountainous region. It's also an unusual sight to see a backpacker there, so Carol had more than one person ask, "Staying long?" "We trained for the Appalachian by putting bags of birdseed in our backpacks and walking up and down the street. It wasn't the same, but it was a help," Carol said. Recently, a trail near their home, the Buckeye Trail, has been improved, and so the couple has been enjoying the new route while keeping in shape.

Carol's recommendation for someone starting out is a simple, "Go for it, you'll like it!"

✦ Laurie

Laurie had problems with shin splints on both the Appalachian and the American Discovery trails. In Virginia, she solved this by getting the weight off — by taking a day off for rest and by slack-packing [someone takes your pack on ahead by car or otherwise]. These solutions also helped her in both North Carolina and Tennessee when she had problems with her knees.

Make It *Your* Trip:

The underlying theme of the stories I collected was to honor yourself. This can be accomplished by three measures: planning a trip that will feel rewarding to you, preparing adequately for the trip, and setting out on your journey. Firstly, make certain that the trip you are considering will be pleasurable to you. Your trip will not be much fun if you select a partner who wants to hike 20 miles a day and you want to sketch and paint in the meadow, so negotiate compromises ahead of time. Secondly, find a method for getting into condition for going on the trip you desire and make it one that fits your schedule and your interests. Finally, enjoy the trip as it unfolds. Don't worry about keeping up with others; if your partner likes to travel faster than you do, either get a head start or ask him/her to wait at designated spots (this should include all forks in the trail).

You may find it difficult (this author still struggles) to internalize the underlying message that you should go at your own pace, but it's important. Consider the following: first, trying to keep up with someone stronger or faster is unpleasant at best, dangerous at worst. It's unpleasant to "beat up" on yourself for not measuring up to someone else and it's not fun to be so focused on "catching up" that you don't have time to enjoy your surroundings. It's dangerous to push yourself to the point where you don't take time to drink needed water, or to cause yourself stress injuries, or to reach a state of exhaustion. Sometimes, I have to remind myself that pushing too hard is perhaps more selfish — especially if it makes me more irritable or tired than I would otherwise be.

Finally, going at the rate that is comfortable for you demonstrates that you value yourself — mentally, physically, and spiritually. As we discussed in the first chapter on why we backpack, older women bring a lot to backpacking and they gain many rewards from it. We must remember how important we are. We help others — let others help us. We listen — let our requests be heard. I think for many women, these are the most important lessons that we can learn.

Frandee Johnson in a field of columbine,
Rawah Wilderness, Colorado, 1999.

13
What's This Funny Little Blue Line on the Map?
Where to Backpack: Trails & Organizations

"Nothing comes from doing nothing."

William Shakespeare

◆ Doris

Doris Klein, who turned 76 in 2002, hikes two or three times a week. "I have three hiking groups. I instigated a hiking group for the Bay Area Ridge Trail in 1990. I did it once a month for four years, but when my husband died I was so busy I had to drop something so I dropped that and only do it two or three times a year now. I also have my Thursday group here, which is an outgrowth of the YMCA group.

When the Bay Area Ridge Trail had a dedication of a section that runs halfway between Benicia and Vallejo, 150 people attended the event. Added Doris, "I was so impressed with the interest that Benicians were showing that I trotted over to the Recreation Department and said, 'Would you like me to start a hiking program for you?'"

From that event came Doris's third hiking group. "They said, 'Sure, go ahead,' — after they ran it through their lawyer and my insurance agent. That's been fun. Last year, we closed out the registration at 125. I was horrified to think that they'd all come at once. They never do, we never have more than 30-35. That's still too big, but usually not as many as that come. This year, we stopped at 70, and we're averaging about 20-22 people on Saturdays.

"I'm taking a couple of people from that group backpacking. They're in their 40s. Most of the Jane Muirs are getting older; I don't know how much longer they're going to want to do it. The new ones seem just as excited and entranced with what I have to show them as the other gals, what we've been doing for 17 years now."

Organizations

Non-profit, environmentally-based organizations, such as the Sierra Club or the Nature Conservancy, offer a way for women to get into backpacking, and also provide logistical support and companionship for more-experienced hikers.

If a woman is interested in backpacking, she likely is also interested in hiking. Hiking obviously helps keep us in condition year round, ready for the occasional backpack trip. Living in the San Francisco Bay Area, I have numerous non-profit groups to choose from when I want to hike. When you are selecting a group to hike with, you probably will have comparable options. Hiking clubs in the Bay Area generally fall into the following categories.

Local hiking clubs: Our local Berkeley Hiking Club, founded in 1922, accepts newcomers for a modest fee and seldom advertises. Most people learn of the club's existence by word-of-mouth. Its stated purpose, "To draw together, in mutual consideration, persons interested in hiking to develop an appreciation of the out-of-doors; to foster the preservation and extension of them [the outdoors] and to furnish such recreation as may seem desirable."

This is the sort of club that friends can start on their own and expand later by spreading the word informally or by attaching themselves to their local recreation center.

Regional hiking clubs: The next level of hiking organizations is one such as our Bay Area Ridge Trail. These are organizations that have a specific goal that requires resources beyond what a handful of participants can provide. Trail acquisition is an extremely expensive proposition — money is needed for dealing with a variety of governmental agencies, as well as buying the land itself. Organizations also require money for staff and land restoration and upkeep. In the case of our Bay Area Ridge Trail organization, their goal is to complete a ridgeline trail surrounding San Francisco Bay. The hikes they lead are not only to share their love of the outdoors, but also to increase awareness of an important resource that may be lost, and to garner support for the trail's completion.

Agencies' recreational hikes: In addition, we have a number of city, county, or regional recreation departments that include hikes in their activities. Occasionally these agencies offer instruction in preparing for backpacking, and then lead backpack trips.

National organizations: Finally, I can join organizations such as the Wilderness Society, Nature Conservancy, or the Sierra Club, which have a broader focus yet offer opportunities to hike, sometimes backpack, into parks and lands in the U.S. and, in the case of the Sierra Club, worldwide. The Sierra Club has both local and national offices, which have different focuses. I can call my local office and find out about local outings or I can call the national offices and find out about national or international travel.

The other established organizations, such as Nature Conservancy, lead trips into current holdings and into areas they hope to protect.

Commercial outings: Beyond the non-profits, a wide variety of organizations and companies offer tour and outdoor trips for women craving outdoor adventure. You can find listings at: www.backpack45.com (our website), at: www.backpacker.com (by *Backpacker Magazine),* and in the advertising section of *Sierra* (the Sierra Club magazine), for starters. Undoubtedly, you will find additional trips listed in your local newspaper's travel section.

How to Select a Trip

I find that while sifting through the offerings, I go through a couple of stages. The initial phase is excitement and stimulation. It all sounds great, I want to do it all, and I want to experience it all now. The next phase is less fun, but there are ways to reduce the stress of this second phase. Recognize that part of the stress comes from being overwhelmed by so many choices. It's worth holding off a few days, considering the following questions, and narrowing your focus before you request various catalogs from vendors. Receiving too much mail is daunting.

Where do you want to go? Most of us have a mental "wish list" of where we want to go. However, when you are seriously considering a trip to, say, Africa, it is wise to narrow the search to a few of its parks or regions. Sometimes political realities can cause one to reconsider a destination. I had visions of backpacking the Inca Trail in Peru in 2000, but found the information provided by the U.S. Tourism unsettling. We opted for a tour of Peru and Bolivia (and highly recommend the tour company — Adventures Abroad). Going on a tour was completely different than our usual mode of travel, yet did include a short hike on the Inca Trail in Machu Picchu.

Why are you going? Many tour companies have a focus, or a choice of focuses. If you begin your selection process with your main goals, finding the best match will be easier. Do you want to learn about photography while you are backpacking? Do you want to hike into an area where you'll find hot springs and massage? Do you want to scale a mountain? Perhaps you want to combine backpacking and kayaking? There are companies that will accommodate any of these interests. Alternatively, if you are willing to pay the price, they will create the unique trip of your dreams.

When and how much time do you have? Some trips require a large investment in time and money, or are only available certain times of year. Obviously, these considerations will play an important factor in your planning. We enjoy the desert, but are not keen on hiking there in the heat of summer. Therefore, we go to Baja California, the deserts of California, and the Southwest during the late fall, winter, or early spring. We have yet to get to Paria Canyon, though it is high on the list of places I'd like to explore, because we haven't had time during the best seasons — when it's not unbearably hot, and there's minimal risk of flash floods.

Do you have time to handle the logistics? If you want to go on a trip, and you can find a group that is going when and where you want to go, you may find it easier to join them than handle all the trip details yourself. This is especially important to consider when permits or guides are required.

Who will be on this trip? The group dynamics are part of what makes groups interesting, but there *will* be interaction. Large groups (let's say 20) provide many opportunities for meeting with new people. They can be great for the "people person" who can roll with the punches and won't be overly bothered if there's a complainer or similarly negative personality in the crowd.

A large group tends to divide into smaller groups or couples, and come together for shared experiences — meal times, for example. Even the more independent traveler may still be happy traveling with a large group if the group's schedule allows some flexibility, such as allowing individuals to dayhike solo and return to the group's base camp at night.

On the other hand, if you are one who prefers punctual departures and doing things on your own, perhaps you would prefer traveling with a smaller group with a specialized focus.

The second consideration is whether the group will be based on such things as gender, marital status, or sexual orientation. Though there are more trips available for heterogeneous groups of travelers, there are an increasing number of trips available with other options.

Why go with women only? For many, it feels like a safe, supportive environment. When women hike and backpack together, they experience the outdoors, and the new situation, in a less competitive environment. For beginners, it's especially valuable; they learn from each other, as well as from their own experiences. Everything from the tasks learned (pitching a tent), to the challenges (climbing the trail), to surviving the risks (crossing icy streams) build expertise. They return home with more confidence in themselves, and more enthusiasm about outdoor adventuring.

In addition, women-with-women trips can break down traditional roles. The logistics of setting up camp — where to put the tent, how to light the stove, and who should wash the dishes — will need to be settled by whose turn it is, who knows how, or who prefers which chore. Likewise, it's best if everyone can read the map, knows how to pump her own water, and knows how to deal with a blister or splinter.

Where does your money go when you pay for a trip? *What is the organization's philosophy?* I'm concerned about the impact my travel makes whether it's local or international. To that end, I support the rerouting of trails away from sensitive areas in the Sierra that would otherwise be destroyed by overuse. I don't believe that every piece of land our government owns should be accessible to me. And I prefer to travel with organizations that use part of their fees for environmental causes, use local guides when appropriate, and consider the impact of tourism on the cultures and areas visited. You can usually quickly tell from a company's literature whether or not it seeks to minimize its impact on a local economy.

Seasoned Women Advise

✦ Sharon

"Especially for beginners or anyone on a weekend trip, go to Emigrant Wilderness, California. There's no permit required, no quota, and fires are allowed," recommends Sharon.

✦ Frandee

"For others considering backpacking or wanting another challenge, join a mountain club. You get to go and you meet other people with similar interests," Frandee's advice that parallels her outdoor experience.

✦ Kathy

"Go with experienced people," offers Kathy to beginners.

✦ ✦ ✦ ✦ ✦

We live in an incredible world with the freedom and means to travel to an amazing number of places. Though in some respects it used to be easier to pick up and go because fewer people backpacked and sites were not overflowing with people, it is now easier to find transportation and access to exotic locations. With the wealth of information available on parks, trails, and tours, you should be able to find a trip tailor-made to your requirements.

Our Major Trails

American Discovery Trail (ADT): The United States' first coast-to-coast trail is vastly different from the John Muir, the Pacific Crest, the Appalachian, and all the other major ones. It's being called a "slice of America" because it does not attempt to go quickly from Point A to Point B, but often meanders extensively so that it can pass through the nation's most scenic and historical sites. Traveling from east to west, the ADT actually splits into a northern and southern route in Cincinnati, Ohio and rejoins in Denver, Colorado. The trail travels through major cities, including Cincinnati and San Francisco, and 14 national parks, including the Chesapeake & Ohio Canal and Utah's Canyonlands, Capital Reef, and Arches.

It traces parts of the Pony Express National Historic Trail in Nebraska, and the Old Spanish Trail in Colorado. It visits points of interest such as the Capital's attractions in Washington, D.C., and curiosities such the nation's largest hairball — a basketball-sized blob found in the stomach of a cow and now kept in a Garden City, Kansas museum. One 70-mile stretch of the trail in West Virginia features 10 train tunnels; luckily, for hikers, the trains no longer run.

This new, 6,365-mile trail extends from Cape Henlopen State Park, Delaware to Pt. Reyes National Seashore, California. The trail is made up of footpaths, sidewalks, paved and dirt roads, road shoulders, and rail-trails. It was initially conceived of by *Backpacker*; the American Hiking Society (AHS) quickly came on board. The American Discovery Trail travels through 15 states and the District of Columbia, often linking previously existing East-West trails such as the Katy Trail of Missouri and the Colorado Trail. It can be covered by horseback, bike, or foot.

Few have hiked the entire trail — which would take almost a year — but as word spreads, increasing numbers are traveling portions of it on foot, horseback, or bicycle. Laurie Foot and her late-husband Bill (d.1999) covered the entire southern route in 1997, and completed the bypassed northern section the following year. Though the majority of their mileage was on bicycles, 700 miles of the first trip was on foot. By so doing, Laurie became the first woman over 45 to complete the journey. Brian Stark, aged 24, spent 238 days running the trail east to west in 1998.

While approximately 10% of the U.S. population lives within 20 miles of the trail, it is not well known. If sponsors of the trail who are attempting to have the trail designated the "National American Discovery Trail" by Congress are successful, it would put the trail on the map and authorize trail markers. Then millions of Americans would have a new trail linking them, and a means to explore our country more intimately — on foot — rather than from a car in the fast lane. Info: American Discovery Trail Society, P.O. Box 20155, Washington, DC 20041-2144, phone 1-800-663-2387 or 703-753-0149, or website: www.discoverytrail.org, or, e-mail: adtsociety@aol.com.

Appalachian Trail (AT): The Appalachian Trail is a 2,160-mile trail that has been traveled in part or total by millions of hikers and backpackers. It was the first National Scenic Trail, and it links federal, state, and local parklands of 14 states. It runs from Mt. Katahdin, Maine (its highest point at 5,267', which is the sixth highest peak in New England) to Springer Mountain in Georgia. It winds through the valleys, forests, and mountains of the eastern Appalachians. The Appalachian Trail Conference (ATC) is a private, non-profit organization that was formed in 1925 by Benton MacKaye and a small group of individuals and public agency leaders for the purpose of creating this continuous footpath. The original path was completed in 1937, while the years 1937-1984 were ones in which the emphasis was on creating a protective buffer zone on either side of the trail. The years from 1984 to present have been largely concerned with managing the trail as authorized by the National Park Service.

✦ Carolyn

Carolyn says that generally her favorite place is above the timberline for the views. She found the Appalachian Trail is very different from place to place. In New Hampshire, in Mt. Washington and the White Mountains, there were switchbacks that seemed to go straight up-and-over boulders. It was a shock to the knees for those used to the more gradual approaches found in Georgia. The Smokies and Virginia were relatively flat. Her usual higher mileage days were cut in such terrain — one day was only a six-mile day.

To accommodate the Appalachian Trail hike, Carolyn took summers off from her work of task assessment with manufacturers. She hiked the Appalachian Trail over a two and one-half year period — less than a week was done as day hikes. She credits this achievement due to the incredible amount of help given by everyone along the way. She used many different ways of hiking each section. Sometimes she would get a shuttle to one end of a hike, and then hike back to her waiting car. Other times she would "key swap" with someone hiking the other direction (they would trade car keys and at trips' end, they would meet and exchange cars). When she wanted a lift into town, or to be picked up somewhere, she could always count on the network of other hikers or nearby residents. She relied extensively on the ATC publication, The Thru Hikers' Companion. Updated annually, it gives names and phone numbers of people and places along the way.

✦ Irene

Irene is hard pressed to name a favorite part of the AT. "What I'm on is my favorite," Irene said, "they're all special." She liked everything from the beautiful woods — being enclosed in them — to the meadows with grasses and flowers. Her sister Sharon especially likes the so-called "balds" (mountain tops without trees), unless there is lightning or rain.

This did not mean that it was without effort. In some sections of the trail, "You get beat to death going down through one ravine and then the next. The Appalachian Trail is up and down, up and down."

She normally stayed in the shelters, or in her tent (which she loved). Most of the shelters are near water, so they found that they didn't need to carry more than what they'd need to drink during the day.

✦ Della

Another "rule" Della made for herself was about where she would sleep. She thought that camping outside was more in the spirit of the trip, and so her first choice was sleeping under the stars (which was also her favorite place on clear nights) or her tent. Then, in descending order, she would choose a trail shelter, a hostel, a motel, or a bed and breakfast. Shelters on the Appalachian Trail are usually three-sided structures and maintained to some degree, but often animals such as mice or snakes have taken up residence, so they are not wildly popular.

✦ Laurie

Bill and Laurie's Appalachian backpack was the "traditional" route of South to North, and it took five and one-half months. While it was difficult to name a favorite section — as each area has its appeal and the variety is part of the pleasure — Laurie mentioned Virginia because the closest section of the trail runs within one-fourth mile of their house. She also liked New Hampshire and Maine because of their remoteness.

The ATC says that three to four million people hike some part of the AT every year. In 2001, almost 3,000 people set out to thru-hike the trail and approximately 550 succeeded — walked its entire length in one continuous journey. Most thru-hikers do the Appalachian Trail in approximately five months and plan to finish before the October 15th closing date. Those who have been involved with it, have been touched by its magic — and part of that magic has been created by, "The legacy of the volunteer maintainer, whose faithful stewardship of his or her section of trail has been the heart and soul of the Appalachian Trail" (1996, The Appalachian Trail Conference.)

Volunteers have always been crucial to the Appalachian Trail. Thousands have helped with its maintenance — clearing brush, building and repairing trail sections, and maintaining shelters and rock walls. Sometimes the work projects have been massive. In October, 2002, a new mile-long elevated boardwalk and a suspension bridge were opened in Vernon township, New Jersey to hikers — allowing them to avoid the previous trail section that had forced them to walk two and a half miles on the edge of a highway.

The National office can be contacted on the Web at www.atconf.org. The four regional offices are: (New England) atc-nero@atconf.org; (Mid-Atlantic) atc-maro@pa.net; (Central SW Virginia) atc-varo@atconf.org; (Tennessee, North Carolina, Georgia) atc-gntro@atconf.org.

Buckeye Trail: Today, in Hocking Hills State Park, Ohio, is the Grandma Gatewood Trail. It's a beautiful six mile stretch of that state's Buckeye Trail. The Gatewood section passes through gorges shaded by hemlock, two impressive caves, and four waterfalls. Archaeological evidence indicates that the area encompassed by Hocking Hills was first inhabited more than 7,000 years ago. The Wyandot, Delaware, and Shawnee people extensively visited or lived in the area in the mid 1700s. The first land acquisition for Hocking Hills was in 1924 and was for 146 acres including Old Man's Cave.

Contact: Hocking Hills State Park, 20160 State Route 664, Logan, OH 43138. (740) 385-6185. www.ohiodnr.com/parks/parks/hocking.htm.

Continental Divide National Scenic Trail: The Continental Divide Trail is 3,200 miles of rugged trail following the length of the Rocky Mountain from Mexico to Canada. It was established in 1978 and is under the jurisdiction of the U.S. Forest Service. Officially designated is the 795 miles that run from Canada through Montana and Idaho to Yellowstone Park. It is open to backpackers, hikes, pack and saddle animals, and in portions, to off-road vehicles. Info: Continental Divide Trail Society, 3704 N. Charles St. #601, Baltimore, MD 21218, (410) 235-9619, e-mail address: cdtsociety@aol.com.

✦ Frandee

Frandee decides where to go by studying the guide books — the same guide books that encourage others to go, which she says leads to trouble, since they cause others to go where you wanted to be alone. It's always a question whether to keep a favorite place to yourself or not. If you tell others, word may spread and it may no longer be the private paradise you remember. She also recognizes that if others don't know about a special place, they won't fight to protect it down the line when a developer or other interests come along.

✦ Jan

Jan, too, has mixed feelings about today's backpacking. "I've seen the numbers change," she commented. Of her first trip to Rocky Mountain National Park years ago, she said, "There was no one else there. It was the first day of school, plus there were no campers, no retirees. Things pretty much were shut down September to May. Now there is no quiet time. You need permits, and usually you'll have company at the campsites. There is so much information on places to hike that one loses the pleasure of discovery."

On the other hand she knows the local mountains so well that she can always find a secret place — but she's not telling.

Florida National Scenic Trail: One of our newer trails, the Florida trail is the only one that travels through a sub-tropical climate. As such, it is particularly suitable for winter hiking and camping, when many of our other national trails are covered with snow. The Florida trail was conceived by James A. Kern who formed the Florida Trail Association in 1964. The plan is to extend from Big Cypress National Preserve in South Florida, through the state's three national forests, to the Gulf Islands National Seashore in the western panhandle. Completed it will be 1,300 miles, presently approximately 700 miles are officially open. Established in 1983, now under the jurisdiction of the U.S. Forest Service.

Contact: Florida Trail Association, P.O. Box 13708, Gainesville, FL 32604, (904) 378-8823.

Ice Age National Scenic Trail: The Ice Age trail is 1,000 miles that follows the rugged chain of moraine hills of Wisconsin. The moraine hills are the remnants of our last ice age. As the glaciers that covered the northern portion of our country melted and receded, they left behind rocks as well as glacier-carved lakes, streams, and forests. Ray Zillmer had the idea for this trail in the 1950's, and it was further publicized by Rep. Henry Reuss. It was established in 1980, and is under the jurisdiction of the National Park Service. About half of the trail is open to public use; some sections of it are popular for marathons and ski events.

Contact: National Park Service, Ice Age National Scenic Trail, 700 Rayovac Dr., Suite 100 Madison, WI 53711 (608) 264-5610.

Isle Royale National Park: This wild north woods park on the shoreline of Lake Superior is an archipelago 45 miles long and nine miles wide. It has 165 miles of hiking trails — and no roads. Hiking can be slow going — especially through the numerous ponds and swamps. Camping and fishing are popular activities. Visitors who are extremely lucky may see moose, even wolves. Insects, according to the official website, are to be expected; they are part of the Isle Royale experience. Mosquitoes — usually most prevalent in June and July — are described as bugs with small hypodermic needles attached. Because of the relative isolation of Isle Royale — accessible only by boat or float plane — influence by the outside has been limited. It is home to a U.S. Biosphere Reserve.

Contact: Isle Royale National Park, 800 East Lakeshore Drive, Houghton, MI 49931. (906-482-0984). www.nps.gov/isro.htm.

John Muir Trail (JMT): The John Muir Trail is largely a subset of the Pacific Crest Trail. It is 210 miles that passes through unsurpassed mountain vistas of the Sierra Nevada. This California trail extends from Tuolumne Meadows (in Yosemite) to Kings Canyon at elevations of 5,000 feet to 14,600 feet (peak of Mt. Whitney). Compared to other mountain ranges, during the summer months it has the mildest, sunniest weather in the world. However, even during those short months, one needs be prepared for rain, hail, lightning, and be able to ford (or otherwise negotiate) swift rivers.

Because of its spectacular scenery and weather, the John Muir Trail is heavily used, so much so that permits are required, and sometimes have to be applied for months in advance. The hike to Mt. Whitney from its closest trailhead (Onion Valley) is extremely popular. While reservations are taken up to six months in advance, trail quotas are often filled within a few hours. But even though you will encounter many people in a day, because of the Sierra's vastness and remoteness, it is easy to drop off the trail and find solitude in places of great beauty.

Natchez Trace National Scenic Trail: The Natchez Trace trail is an historic route that commemorates an ancient path used first by game and Native Americans. Later it was used by explorers, boatmen, post riders, and military men — including General Andrew Jackson after his victorious Battle of New Orleans. The Trace trail is 110 miles of the Natchez Trace Parkway (450 miles). The four developed trail segments are open to hiking and equestrians. The Parkway runs from Natchez, Mississippi to Nashville, Tennessee and was established in 1983.

The Natchez Trace Trail is under the jurisdiction of the National Park Service. Contact: Natchez Trace National Scenic Trail, 2680 Natchez Trace Pkwy., Tupelo, MX 38802 (601) 680-4004.

North Country National Scenic Trail: The North Country Trail is more than 4,500 miles of segmented trails that extend from the Adirondack Mountains of New York to the Missouri River in North Dakota. The terrain is diverse. The eastern end is the Adirondacks, the Pennsylvania hardwood forests, Ohio's farmlands and canals, the shorelines of the Great Lakes, the rugged mountains and forests of Wisconsin and Minnesota, the plains of North

Dakota. More than 2,000 miles of this scenic trail is open for public use. Established: 1980.

Contact: National Park Service, North Country National Scenic Trail, 700 Rayovac Dr., Suite 100, Madison, WI 53711 (608) 264-5610.

Pacific Crest Trail: The Pacific Crest Trail runs 2,650 miles along the Western United States, from the Mexican border to Manning Park at the Canadian border. It ranges from 40 to 180 miles from the Pacific Ocean as it travels through California, Oregon, and Washington. Its highest point is 13,200 feet at Forester Pass in the Sierra Nevada, the lowest 140 feet on the Columbia River. As one hikes the trail, one can encounter blazing heat one day, snow and sleet the next. It was built over a period of 30 years by legions of government employees and volunteers. Both groups are still of incalculable value in maintaining the rugged and heavily used trail.

Whereas the East Coast's Appalachian Trail was built to go up one hill and down another, that style of trail would be impossible for the significantly greater elevation of the Pacific Crest Trail. Ordinary people and pack animals would be unable to follow it. So the trail wends its way through the higher peaks by the means of "switchbacks" (zigzagged paths).

It was designed for fair weather usage, which may mean a very small window of time in the west. Thru-hikers must carefully plan their travel dates because it will take three and a-half to five months to complete the trail. Leaving too early in the year, backpackers may encounter the previous season's snowpack. Losing the trail and avalanche dangers are real considerations. Alternately, by starting too late in the year, one may run into blizzard conditions.

Because much of the Pacific Crest Trail is buffered from civilization and its development by towering mountains, vast evergreen forests, and arid desert, it remains more natural and wild than the Appalachian Trail. The PCT was planned to avoid towns, yet with planning, one can find a rustic resort, ranger station, or post office where one can pick up food and other provisions along the route.

The PCT is also a National Scenic Trail (it and the AT were the first two trails designated such in 1968). It is administered by the National Forest Service, the National Park Service, and the Bureau of Land Management, depending on the area of interest.

Potomac Heritage National Scenic Trail: The Potomac Heritage trail as established and proposed is 700 miles along the Potomac River. It is a trail that combines history and recreation. One existing segment is a 184 mile towpath (boats were towed along the canal by workers, or machinery) along the Chesapeake and Ohio Canal of Washington, D.C. and Maryland. Two other segments are in place — 18 miles of the Mt. Vernon Trail in Virginia, and the 75- mile Laurel Highland trail in Pennsylvania.

Established in 1983, the Potomac Heritage trail is under the jurisdiction of the National Park Service, National Capital Region, Land Use Coordination, 1100 Ohio Drive SW, Washington, D.C. 20241. (202) 819-7027.

Tip: Always leave trip details with someone back home. Explain your route, your destination, and your expected return time. If you are driving to a trailhead, leave your car license number, too.

Epilogue:
End of the Trail

"A well spent day brings happy sleep."

Leonardo da Vinci

We backpack for many reasons. Some are for the mind — to break away from city life, to learn new skills, and to problem solve challenges encountered only in a wilderness setting. Others are physical — to feel your body get "leaner and meaner" each day as you add muscle mass, and to feel attuned to nature when bathing in a frigid alpine lake and sunbathing on a granite rock. Still others are spiritual or transformational — witnessing alpine glow, watching a meteor shower, discovering more about yourself, or enjoying the camaraderie of your companions.

The women who have shared their stories throughout this book may have traveled on various trails, but they have all traveled on a common path. We have many different ways of talking about this path — "the journey is the goal, "living in the moment," or "stopping to smell the roses," but we intuitively know that it is frequently found and traveled in the wilderness.

Though we acknowledge that "living in the moment" may be stressful — like when you realize you're lost, or you're chasing away a bear, or you need to cross a swollen river — and it can be pleasurable — when you spot a deer, when you hear the roar of the river, or when you smell the pines — it is definitely the time when one feels most alive.

As the women in this book have demonstrated, backpacking is an activity in which women of all ages can participate and excel. In great part, that is because backpacking requires perseverance — a quality that women usually have in great measure.

Defining Success

For me, examining my motivations for backpacking and how I define a successful trip is an ongoing self-dialogue. We don't necessarily escape our ingrained ideas about success and winning just because we are in a different setting — and much or our judgement about success or failure is based on other's definitions. The roots that have brought many of us to this point are worth considering — our frontier ethic, the "dog eat dog" mentality of the workplace, and our battles as women to gain equal rights.

Backpacking, like most sports and outdoor activities, is dominated by men. And, though it is not a competitive sport in the sense that running a marathon is, it's obvious that many participants (usually men) are greatly motivated by being first or fastest. If we as women judge ourselves by male standards and measurements, we may conclude that we are somehow lacking. It is wiser to follow the examples provided by the women of this book who are motivated by personal goals. They aren't necessary attempting to be the first to climb a mountain or the fastest to finish a hike, they are just attempting to complete a climb or hike. The first challenge is, therefore, to *set your own goals.*

These personal goals should be ones that will provide great satisfaction when achieved — or even attempted. The second step is to *savor your successes* rather than allowing them to lose their shine by immediately setting new, and more difficult, goals. Thirdly, when you do set new goals, *use your previous successes to remind yourself of your personal strength and endurance.* Remember, *go at your own pace* — you are presumably also there to see the wildflowers, not just the tops of the mountains.

Backpacking — after the first couple of miles in — is about endurance; this implies a sizable length of time. How much more fulfilling if each moment is noticed not just the final ones. This leads us back to Chapter One's themes of physical challenge, mental exercise, and spiritual insights. It's about the initial shock of jumping into an alpine lake, the shared experiences with friends or lovers, the late night confidences, and the shared camp chores, and the sense of personal accomplishment — negotiating a stream crossing without getting soaked, scaring away a visiting bear, and carrying a heavy pack up a steep trail.

Every portion of that trail is cause de celebre. We strive and thrive in an environment most people only dream of entering. We endure lightening storms and hailstones as well as sweaty packs and blistered feet. Our beds in the wilderness are not all that comfortable (even if we dig a hip hole), our food may be hearty, but it isn't necessarily gourmet, and the toilet is behind a shrub. This is fun? Yes, because we stretch and grow when we move out of our comfort zone. For a time, we leave behind the trappings of a culture convinced that more is better. We experiment with stripping our possessions to the minimum, and in the process, we discover that strength comes from within.

Fran Smith in the East Bay hills, San Francisco Bay Area, CA

Appendix
Expanded Profiles (by first names)

Barbara P. was 60 years old at the time of her interview. She is a medium-tall woman, with gray hair, fit, who lives in the San Francisco Bay Area with her husband. Two of her four daughters are enthusiastic backpackers when time allows, and two are enthusiastic mothers.

Betty Lennox has backpacked in the Sierras many times. Years back, she regularly covered 40-mile segments of the Pacific Crest Trail. The first trips were with her son and other family members or friends and started near the California/Mexican border. She continued year after year doing trips, snagging others to accompany her, until they got to the point where the Mojave Desert was coming up. Then the trips moved to the Desolation Valley and Yosemite areas where her explorations still continue.

What was once her grandfather's ranch is now Shelter Cove, a resort area on the north coast of California. In fact as a girl, she enjoyed many a day riding through the area on horseback.

Carmen Borrmann is one of the original Marching Mothers, an Orinda, California women's backpacking group.

The name of the group may sound militaristic, but this group seems anything but. In fact, when asked to describe themselves, one of the attributes they were first to mention was that they are non-competitive. Sis Curtis, whose interview is later, belongs to the same group.

In the earlier years of their marriage, **Carol Messenger's** main outdoor activity was bicycle riding. She has ridden across the United States both from east to west and north to south plus many miles on other long tours. "But, Al hates riding a bike and thus we were spending many weeks, and even months apart. This is not a good thing. In fact, it looked like divorce might be the only solution to happiness."

So they took up backpacking and began walking the Appalachian Trail together as a section hike. It was a "ten-year plan" which they finished in 9 years — from 1987-1995. Carol was 57 at completion. The first year they completed 200 miles, but they upped the ante after that, and so were able to finish earlier.

Carol was an American history and high school teacher when the trip started so long weekends, Easter break, and summers were the available times. Their backpacking and hiking continued after the AT — numerous 50 trails in Ohio, a 70 mile trip in Pennsylvania, the Buffalo River in Arkansas, and a reunion in England with a friend made while on the AT. At the time I talked to Carol in 1999 she was 61. She says she has three more goals: to go to Hawaii (the last of the 50 United States to see), to see the Pyramids of Egypt, and to sing at Carnegie Hall.

When **Carolyn Ebel** was living in northwest Virginia, she led numerous hikes for the Sierra Club. Then, she moved to Tennessee in 1991, where she became increasingly interested in the Smokies. She lives only 79 miles away, making it relatively accessible. "I have had some hiking experience, having completed the AT as well as the Smokies.

I'm head of the 900 Miler Club of the Great Smoky Mountain National Park and have hiked 28 of the 40 high points (over 6,000') of North Carolina, Virginia, and Tennessee." In addition, she has climbed 37 of the United States' highest points to date." She plans to climb another four. In the Southwest, she has reached the highest points in New Mexico, Arizona, and Colorado, but in 1999, when she attempted the highest point in Utah, even though she had given herself three days to acclimate, she got sick from the altitude, and had to turn back. "I figure I don't belong there," she added.

Debbie Collins has enjoyed hiking, camping, and backpacking with friends and family from the time she entered college. While living in Seattle, she went on her first backpack trip with her geology class to Mt. Rainier. Later she worked in Sun Valley, Idaho for a season where she also went backpacking with friends.

Debbie is a long time friend who I met at the start of a Sierra Club trip to Baja California, Mexico. Whale watching is not very good in December on the peninsula, so most of our time was spent traveling, hiking, and getting acquainted.

Debbie's love and concern for nature does not end when she steps off the trail. As both student and teacher, Debbie continually seeks ways to protect the earth: creative reuse, recycling, organic gardening, and using natural products. Whether it is through her art, dance, or by soaking in hot springs, Debbie enjoys feeling her spiritual connection to the Earth.

Della Powell was a "tomboy." When she was little, what she liked most was playing outside all day. What she liked least was her mom calling her home to dinner. When she became an adult, she married, and raised a son. Family vacations were often tent camping trips next to the car. Her career was 32 years working in the lab of a large hospital.

And as much as she loved her job, for many of those years she felt she was "pulling time in prison" because what she wanted was to be outside.

My interview with Della Powell was by phone as she lives in Virginia. I loved doing this interview. Della was fun to talk to, spirited, open, and filled with enthusiasm about her love of the outdoors, and her adventures in completing the Appalachian Trail.

Doris Klein "I was always a country girl. I grew up in Wyoming, and I just loved the wide-open spaces — it was just bred into me. We lived kind on in the prairies, close to Montana, rode horseback to school, skated on the river, all that sort of thing.

I started backpacking in 1972. My son, Chris, was the occasion for that. He was a Boy Scout, and I would make sure he was properly prepared, with what I thought was needed, poor soul, — including a heavy jacket and soft shoes. We were good friends with a sailing family from the yacht club who were also mountaineers. Oftentimes the wife would go up in the mountains with our kids, while her husband was sailing. One time my son said to her, 'Gee, mom would enjoy this,' and so one day she asked me. I was hooked; I was really hooked. I love it."

She frequently hikes and leads trips cross-country, no doubt finding trails too tame, and over-populated. In her leisure time she donates time to the Bay Area Ridge Trail — an organization working to complete a 400-mile trail which will encircle San Francisco, San Pablo, and Suisun Bays. When Doris leads interested hikers on the trail, they quickly learn that this will not be a stroll, they'll have to scramble to keep up with her. "Women who backpack are gutsy women, and I like gutsy women," jokes Doris.

Elizabeth Wagner of Orinda, California is now in her seventies, and no longer backpacks. She no longer saw the point and gave it up when she observed that one of the major areas where she used to hike, near her summer cottage in Northern California, had been dissected by roads.

Emma "Grandma" Gatewood (October 25, 1887-June 4, 1973). When she accomplished her first thru-hike of the Appalachian Trail in 1955, she gained national prominence. Long distance hiking was a rarity at that time, and an older woman hiking such a great distance, and solo, was unheard of.

Emma was born in a log cabin in Gallia County, Ohio — the eighth of fifteen children. She went to a one room schoolhouse through the eight grade, then helped full time on the family's farm until she married at nineteen. She never learned to drive a car, and as transportation was not always available, she always walked.

While raising eleven children, she worked in the fields, ran the household, and kept flower and vegetable gardens (from which she canned and preserved much of their food). She was well known regionally for her knowledge of herbs and flowers, and her skill in practical nursing. Later she remarked that she hadn't taken up long distance hiking earlier because she couldn't just take off when she had children to tend to. Living on a farm and raising a family through the Depression and W.W.II combined to shape a no-nonsense, resourceful, determined woman. When people advised her not to go on various hikes — and there were many to follow her first Appalachian Trail hike — her response was that since she was still able to paint her house and chop her firewood she was certainly able to hike.

Fran Smith grew up in Colorado and enjoyed family camping trips, trips with the Girl Scouts, and stays at their cabin. This was the Depression era, and vacations were not luxury trips. After she and Vic married, and had their three children, they moved to California and began trips into the Sierra. These family-hiking trips began in the early 1970s. They investigated Yosemite's Glen Aulin with its Waterwheel Falls, and Mt. Hoffman. They hiked the High Sierra loop from cabin to cabin. In time, their minister suggested backpacking trips with the youth groups. They traveled with pack animals, the hikers carrying their personal belongings, and the mules carrying food, water, and sleeping bags. "This was real 'community living' and everyone slept out under the stars," with Fran not remembering rain in the 10 years they did this.

Fran's first experience with backpacking, where she and her husband Vic were totally on their own, was in 1979. It was a weekend trip. They climbed Mt. Conners in Yosemite, all 12,500 feet of it. Fran was 53 years old. Twelve years later, in 1991, the entire family went on a backpacking trip and set out for Mt. Dana at 13,053 feet. Four of the five in the party made it. The next year, Fran and Vic climbed Mt. Dana again.

Her advice to women beginning this activity, "Stay trim, do practice hikes, and do it while you're young." But would she do it again? Perhaps asking about her 1998 trip up Mt. Whitney only three months afterwards was too soon – she wasn't certain. But she does want to see more of the Sequoia backcountry.

Frandee Johnson lives in Boulder, Colorado and is a co-founder, and vice-president, of Great Old Broads for Wilderness, an advocacy group formed in 1989 to lobby for acquiring and protecting wilderness areas. They were involved in the acquisition of the Escalante area of Southern Utah before it was "discovered" and became a National Monument under the Clinton administration. Now that it is a monument, the Great Old Broads is continuing to lobby to make sure that it is managed as a wilderness — no grazing, no mining, no off road vehicles.

Frandee has led hikes with the Colorado Mountain Club. She has been backpacking in many parts of the United States including Colorado, Utah, Montana, and Alaska. The Brooks Range was her first Alaska trip, and as her younger son lives there, she has returned several summers. Frandee, now in her sixties, continues to be overwhelmed by the beauty of her adopted state. Two of Frandee's long-time hiking companions are Joyce Gellhorn and Jan Robertson (whose interviews will follow).

Grace Lohr (the Llama Mama) gives her dad the credit for introducing her to the outdoors when she was a child. She grew up in Southern California, and when she was young, her dad bought a pre-WWII bus and converted it to a motor home. The family toured the U.S. one summer, and then parked on the eastern side of California (near Mineral King) for weeks on end. While her dad lazed around the campground, the kids were free to run and play outdoors all day.

Irene "Tag Along" Cline and her sister, Sharon (18 years her junior), were both raised in Southern Indiana, Evansville, on the Ohio River. They didn't camp or backpack as youngsters, but Irene always liked playing "boys' games, not girls' games."

When she was in school, Irene's school counselor gave her an interest test, which indicated that she should find a job that was "out-in-the-field" and "working with people," but there weren't outdoor jobs for women in that era. So Irene became a teacher. When she married, she followed her husband from place to place – living in Ohio, Texas, and Missouri. She taught every grade from 1-9, but mostly junior high level. Because her husband didn't like the outdoors, it was Irene who took their children — two sons and a daughter camping and fishing.

It took months to catch up with Irene for a phone interview. Hiking the AT was not the last of her adventures. She continues to go on day hikes three times a week near her home in Winston-Salem, North Carolina, as well as go on longer vacations. In 1999, at the age of 80, she went hut to hut on the England's "Coast to Coast" trail. And, in 2000, she did the "top of the bridge walk" in Sidney, Australia and a parachute jump (in tandem) while in Queenstown, New Zealand.

Isabella L. Bird was 41 when she climbed Longs Peak. Her doctor had prescribed travel for her health. With that first trip a pattern developed: she traveled from home in England to exotic lands, came home and wrote about her adventures, grew restless and ill, and went on another trip. Unlike most European travelers of her day, she did not insulate herself from the people and their lifestyles: in the U.S. she learned to drive wagons, in Hawaii she rode astride as the local women did, and in Asia, she rode elephants and stayed in huts. All told, she wrote a dozen volumes.

Jan Robertson was raised in St. Louis, Missouri, but from the time she was two, she and her family spent much of the summer in the mountains. They rented cottages in the early years; eventually they built a cabin. This was the "polio era," a time when families with the means to do so would escape the city, and avoid public swimming pools. Mothers and children would spend their summers at a vacation spot; fathers would come and go as work allowed.

Jan is the author of *The Magnificent Mountain Women — Adventures in the Colorado Rockies.* Her book relates both historical and contemporary accounts of dozens of women who courageously ventured into the mountains of Colorado. She often hikes with Joyce Gellhorn and Frandee Johnson.

Jeannine Burk grew up near Ashland, Oregon, later moved to Los Angeles where she lived for nearly 25 years, and has recently returned to Oregon. As a child, she treasured being allowed to sleep outdoors with the stars, and roaming the hills near home. The family owned a peach ranch, and she remembers the difficult work picking peaches and working in a packing plant one summer as a teenager. Weekend picnics in town might be enjoyed at Ashland's Lillith Park, and vacations could take them to Northern California. Always her question was, "I wonder what's over that hill?"

Her father differed from most men of that area and generation in that he did not hunt. Her mother, Bertha Florence, had a lifelong love of nature, and at seventy-five, went with Jeannine on a rafting trip down the Colorado River in the Grand Canyon. When friends teased Jeannine that she was trying to get rid of her mother, her mother replied, "If I'm going to die, I'd rather die in the wilderness."

Through the remainder of the 1970s, when she was in her late thirties and early forties, Jeannine backpacked frequently. With the Sierra Club, she hiked much of the John Muir Trail and enjoyed the Yosemite high camps. In her late forties, she and her mother climbed the Grand Canyon's strenuous Angel Trail. She packed in Arches National Monument, Utah. Jeannine's last backpacking trip was when she was fifty-three; in 1988, she spent the summer working, hiking, and backpacking in Denali National Park, Alaska.

Jenny Jardine of LaPine, Oregon is the youngest person interviewed for this book. It was the only interview completed entirely by e-mail. Jenny grew up in San Jose, California as part of family that camped and backpacked together often. Her mom and dad were schoolteachers. Summers, as well as Christmas and Easter holidays were spent in the mountains as much as possible. "Yes, I have always liked — loved — the outdoors. This love was something that Mom and Dad, but especially Mom instilled in all five of us kids at a very early age. And not just a love of the outdoors, but a respect for all natural things."

Jenny's husband Ray is often called the father of minimalist backpacking. He has published two important backpacking books, *The Pacific Crest Trail Hiker's Handbook* and *Beyond Backpacking — Ray Jardine's Guide to Lightweight Hiking*. He dedicated both to Jenny for her "companionship and constant assistance." Jenny and Ray custom-made their sleeping quilt, backpacks, and tarp (carried instead of a tent) for their backpacking trips of the Pacific Crest Trail.

Following the Jardines' 1987 PCT hike, they did some shorter hikes — mostly in the Rockies of Colorado and in the Wasatch and Uinta Mountains of Utah. In 1989, they hiked the John Muir Trail from Cottonwood Pass to Tuolumne Meadows. Then in 1991, they hiked the PCT again. In 1992, the Continental Divide Trail — north to south. In 1993, the Appalachian Trail — south to north. And in 1994, the PCT again — this time north to south.

In more recent years, they have kayaked and canoed extensively — with explorations of Alaska, Canada, and Baja California. Then, in 2000, they took up skydiving. Since that time, they have both earned "A" licenses and enjoyed hundreds of free-fall expeditions.

Joyce Gellhorn and I played "phone-tag" for weeks. She is a writer in her own right. She has published 80-90 articles, including "Arctic Renewal," which was published in *The World & I* (August 1994), and probably 200 photos. Most have been curriculum materials related to the outdoors and her background in science. Joyce was a high school science teacher until she retired in 1993.

Joyce grew up in the Midwest, near Minneapolis, and was part of a family that enjoyed the outdoors and hiking. She moved to Colorado in the 1950s to go to college, and it was there that she married and began backpacking. She liked it so much that she continued even after her husband had lost interest.

Judy Valentine is a volunteer counselor in California's Napa Valley. She is a very warm and sensitive person — which made interviewing her a delight. She is slight — and like several of the women interviewed — not fitting the stereotypical image of "stocky" woman backpacker.

Judy was born in England and as a little girl moved in Southern California. While her father, brothers, and sisters loved the outdoors, Judy preferred being indoors playing with her dolls and the piano.

When **Kathryn Smick** responded to the otherwise unsuccessful tiny ad I had placed in our local Sierra Club newsletter (looking for women to interview), it was with some caution — she was concerned that I might have been deluged with responses, and would not want to bother talking with her. Needless to say, I jumped at the opportunity. We met at a local coffee shop, and I couldn't help noticing that while she drank the tea I bought for her, she barely touched the pastry. "So that's how she stays in such good shape," I thought — and hid my croissant until after she was gone. The slight, trim woman sipping tea with me was retired, but still going into work three times a month as a doctor (specializing in the treatment of tuberculosis).

Nowadays, Kathryn gets to share her backpacking adventures with grandchildren. In fact, one of her favorite memories is of a trip she took with her daughter-in-law and her six months old grandson, Johnny.

I interviewed **Kathy Morey** by phone in November 2000. She grew up in a household with adult roles typical of the times. Her father loved to go deer and duck hunting, her mother was an indoor person. Girls did not go on hunting trips. And, much like me, she hadn't really heard of backpacking until she was in her mid-thirties. In the mid-1970s, Kathy found herself divorced and working for Hughes Aircraft which had a hiking club. She had a crush on a guy who worked there. He asked her to go backpacking — couldn't have been because she had a VW bus that would carry lots of gear? Anyway, she rented equipment and boots — and Kathy, the guy, and three of his buddies set out for the Sierras.

As her backpacking knowledge increased, she sent comments and corrections to Wilderness Press. Thomas Winnett, co-author of Wilderness Presses' *Sierra North* and other publications, responded. After a couple of years, to her surprise, Winnett asked her to update trips in their *Sierra South*. Kathy, at age 47, found herself a trail scout. A few years later, she left Hughes, and Wilderness Press asked her to do a series of four books on Hawaii. She has continued to do updates on the guides to the Sierra and Hawaii, and has also published *Hot Showers, Soft Beds, and Day Hikes in the Sierras* (1998). An accomplished photographer, Kathy contributed many of the photographs to the Hawaii series of guides. She began by experimenting with point and shoot models, but now is using a lightweight, automatic 35mm.

Kathy's prefers backpacking June to October — when the days are long, and the weather kinder. Her husband is not able to backpack but they do an annual trip with pack mules. During the "off" season, she keeps fit by going to the gym several times a week, bicycling on Bishop's trails, and show-shoeing and skiing in the ski area near her home in Mammoth.

Laurie (Laurel Ibbotson Foot) Foot lives in Lynchburg, Virginia. It was not until the summer she and Bill married that Laurie went camping. Though as a kid she thought it might be fun, her parents weren't interested. Bill, however, was an Eagle Scout with considerable outdoors experience.

But, soon there was a family, and that "hindered" outdoor trips.

From the time that Laurie learned of the Appalachian Trail, that there was a trail running all the way along the eastern states, she was captivated by it. "Wow, you can hike that whole way!" she said. She and Bill had talked about their desire to do it for years. And then, the "timing was right." Their son was in college, their daughter, 14, was still at home, but her best friend's parents (family friends) offered to let her stay with them.

Marcyn Del Clements lives in Southern California. Ralph and I met her on the John Muir Trail in 1999. We talked for about five minutes. That was followed by a phone interview later that year. Since that time, Marcy and I have been in frequent contact — and shared many stories of backpacking and other travels.

Marcy has always enjoyed the outdoors. "When we were kids, my parents couldn't afford fancy vacations. My mom was very intrepid, however, and took us all camping in our local foothills (the San Gabriels) every summer. There were four little girls. We'd go for weeks at a time, Daddy would come up on the weekends, unfold his beach chair, crack a beer and say, 'AHHHH, this is the life! Huh?' Then my baby sister would crawl into his lap and it seemed like it was the life. I loved the open sky at night, with all the fancy constellations. I took the nature hikes with the resident ranger, became fascinated with everything natural. All of us little girls were more tomboys than the feminine kind."

As a young adult, Marcy discovered backpacking, but then had to give it up. "My husband's back gave out. He had surgery, learned to live with pain, and never played golf or backpacked again. For years it was OK." They went camping and fishing with their kids, and in more recent years have taken trips to exotic bird-watching sites in Kenya (500 new birds the first day), Venezuela, Belize, Brazil, India, and Katmandu, as well as North American sites in Nova Scotia and Maine.

"But the yearning [only] slumbered," added Marcy. The desire to backpack was still there; she has returned to her trips to the mountains: taking numerous trips with her friend Dottie as well as going solo.

Margaret Campbell is an Associate Professor of Religious Studies at Holy Names College, Oakland. Appropriately enough, her biographical information on the college's website lists "The Sierra High Country" as one of her "personal interests." Margaret took up backpacking when a friend of hers, who was experienced, suggested going. "It seemed natural enough," said Margaret. Sort of an extension of all the hiking and camping she had so long enjoyed. Margaret broke her leg four years ago and has not been backpacking since — but continues to car camp.

Marilyn Morris is a resident of Orinda, California. She backpacks occasionally when she can break away from her work with a local law firm.

Sandra Nicholls owns a Bed & Breakfast in Northern California, The Inn at Valley Ford, which keeps her busy much of the year, but she also enjoys backpacking.

Sharon Hanna was raised in Texas, but family vacations were 2,000-mile trips to the cool mountains of Creed, Colorado from the time she was in diapers. Her father had been doing this drive from Houston from the time he bought a Model A. To Sharon, the creeksides of Colorado were like magic, especially coming from the hot, flat, and no trees that describe South Texas and its summers.

Sharon is now in her fifties. She has an outgoing personality, and exudes warmth, enthusiasm, and honesty.

Having finished the restoration of a Georgian flat in San Francisco, she has rented it out, and moved into a craftsman style home in the city. She appeared for our luncheon interview with a delicious fruit salad with curry-flavored dressing. As we talked, I learned that just that morning she had taken a hammer to the pink ceramic tile and two-inch thick grout that were masking the original stone fireplace of her newly acquired home — clearly, a woman of many talents.

Pat G., in the Marching Mothers' 1976 journal, gave **Sis Curtis** this tribute, "Sis identified the most plant and bird life, ran instead of walked the entire way, and stands in danger of having her thyroid supply sabotaged next year. She also holds the record for being the youngest — and looking it."

Sylvelin Edgerton didn't backpack as a youngster, but became interested through her friend Valerie (interview follows). Valerie introduced her to UCLA Mountaineers' Club, and she went with them to Picacha Diablo (Devil's Peak) — a 10,154 foot mountain inland from San Felipe, Baja California — which was a favorite of rock-climbers while she was in college. She also went on trips with them to Yosemite and the Grand Canyon.

This was followed by an 18-year hiatus while she was living in New England. She did only one backpack while living there, but continued day hikes.

Valerie Cooley has hiked with Sylvelin (above). Valerie enjoyed picnicking and the usual family outings as a youngster, but didn't learn much about the outdoors until she became a college student at UCLA. She liked San Onofre, near the Marine Base, where the gorgeous people seemed to hang out. One day she noticed a particularly gorgeous guy — with his ear glued to the radio listening to the first rock climb of Yosemite's Half Dome.

Her involvement with UCLA's hiking and climbing lead to her continuing interests in hiking, camping, and backpacking. Valerie has a great sense of humor. During our interview, we discovered we had several mutual interests. Besides backpacking, we were both involved in folk music, folk dancing, had studied Sociology, and knew Jeannine Burk (interview earlier).

Acknowledgements

Many thanks to the wonderful and amazing women whose stories inspired this book, and me. Their talents and accomplishments were a constant source of support and inspiration. I appreciate being able to use Desiree's poem, *The Highest & the Deepest*; thanks also to her mother, Diane Abad, for permission to use it.

Thanks also to the members of my writer's group led so capably by Rose Offner. I would never have been able to carry this project through to completion without the support of friends Melanie Clark, Denise Roessle, and Joan Olson. Helene Goldberg, psychotherapist, helped me when I despaired of ever finishing this project and by reminding me to take time to enjoy my successes. Dr. Richard Teel, Marin County chiropractor, not only adjusted my body when I overdid working in my garden, but also strongly supported my walking. Brad Newsham, who read my manuscript in its final stages and gave me enthusiastic support to see the project through. Valuable research assistance was provided by Laurie Potteiger of the Appalachian Trail Council. Editing and invaluable feedback were also provided by Fran Alcorn, Denise, and Eloise Bodine. That having been said, any remaining errors are strictly my responsibility. And, finally, I want to thank my mother, Vivien Bean, for teaching me by her example to travel wherever I wanted.

Happy trails!

Time Line

Details of starred (*) entries follow the Time Line.

B.C. 13,000+	**Ice Age***
to 1850s	**Native Americans***
1838	**Trail of Tears (Cherokee)***
1850s	**Pioneer Women/Westward Movement***
1873	**Isabella Bird* climbs in the Rockies**
1955	**Emma Gatewood – 1st Appalachian hike**
1968	**Pacific Crest Trail – dedicated**
1990-98	**Irene Cline (born 1921) hikes the entire Appalachian Trail**
1970s	**1st U.S. backpacking craze**
2003	**Present day resurgence**

Ice Age: Beringia, also known as the Bering Land Bridge, was exposed during glacial periods allowing people to enter North America from Asia. Theoretically, therefore, people could have come across the land bridge during many periods ranging from 40,000 to 13,000 years ago. Artifacts found in the southwestern United States and South America suggest that humans lived in those locations around 12,000 years ago.

Native Americans: Before the European ages of exploration and settlement, and when the land that we now call the United States was home to hundreds of Indian tribes, tens of thousands of men, women, and children traveled countless miles each year to satisfy such basic needs as: food, water, shelter, and more moderate climate. Probably the best known example of this is the Plains Indians. Before the Spanish introduced the horse, tribes would either follow the buffalo or camp where the animals' migrations would pass by and hunters could slay their prey.

Trail of Tears: In 1838, the United States government took the homes and lands of the Cherokee Nation in Georgia, and forced the men, women, and children to move to Oklahoma. More than 4,000 of the 17,000 Cherokee died as a result of the removal. Both the route and the journey became known as "The Trail of Tears."

The *Legend of the Cherokee Rose* followed: The Cherokee mothers were so saddened that the chiefs prayed for them. A sign, they thought, would lift the women's spirits and give them the strength to care for their children. Prayers brought forth a beautiful new flower, a rose, which grew whereever a mother's tear had fallen to the ground.

Today, the Cherokee Rose grows along the route of the "Trail of Tears" and is Georgia's official state flower. The white rose symbolizes the mothers' tears, the gold center represents the gold taken from the Cherokee lands, and the stem of the rose has seven leaves — one for each of the seven Cherokee clans that traveled the "Trail of Tears."

Pioneer Women: When the Oregon Trail and other important westward-bound trails opened (the great Western Expansion), hundreds of thousands of Americans packed their possessions and provisions and began their journey in search of a new life and lands. (Martha) Alice Parker was one of these brave women. Alice was born March 22, 1846 in Lancastershire, England. In 1856, she sailed with her family to the United States. After traveling to Iowa City, they joined a Mormon "handcart" train.

All of the family's possessions were loaded in their handcart. Initially, it was pushed by Alice's mother, Ann, and pulled by her father, Robert. Later, when her father became ill, Alice helped her mother push the cart. By the time they reached the Salt Lake Valley in September, 1856, they had walked 1,300 miles.

Isabella Bird: Following Isabella's 1873 ascent of Longs Peak in Colorado, Isabella continued her adventurous travels. Subsequently she traveled to Japan, the Malay Peninsula, India, Persia, Kurdistan, Turkey, China, Korea, and Morocco. Though most of her travel was by horseback, she walked when circumstances dictated. Bird died in 1903.

Emma Gatewood: Emma, whose story is also told in this book, was not always sure she liked the publicity she attracted. In her era, she was a novelty — not only for the long-distance hikes she took but also because of her age, that she was a woman, and that she was hiking alone.

View from atop Mt. Whitney, 2002

Susan's Clothing and Sundries

___ Kelty backpack weighing 4.9 pounds. I love this old, garage sale purchase, but because of its weight, it is currently #1 on my priority list for replacing to reduce weight.

Upper Body:

___ 300 weight, Polarguard fleece *or* down jacket

___ Waterproof jacket (Goretex) — fits over fleece jacket

___ Midweight synthetic long-sleeved undershirt (black). Can also be worn as outerwear.

___ Patterned sportsbra, wicking, supplex, that doubles as halter and swim top

___ l long sleeve blouse, Intera/polyester

___ Additional blouse, long *or* short sleeve, synthetic

___ Lightweight wool sweater, turtleneck, slip-on (optional)

Head:

___ Fleece hat — dark color, covers ears

___ Fabric, brimmed hat — for protection from the sun. Has coverage for the back of the neck.

Hands:

___ 1 pair liner gloves, synthetic (for added warmth and/or sun protection). Since liner gloves are thin and lightweight, they offer protection, but allow the dexterity to operate a camera, zippers, etc.

___ 1 pair wool gloves (mittens are warmer, but don't have the dexterity.

Lower Body:

___ Fleece pants with zippers at the bottom of legs. I found I needed to replace the zippers provided with longer ones so that they would go over on my boots without having to remove my boots!)

___ Rainpants (coated nylon)

___ 1 pair lightweight slacks with leg zippers for converting to shorts

___ 1 pair additional light-weight, light-colored slacks (light colors are less attractive to insects) *or* 1 pair shorts

___ 2 or 3 pair underpants, dark color, fast-dry, seamless (could wear swimming)

Feet:

___ Hiking boots, Vasque, treated with water repellent.

___ 2 pair Smartwool outer socks (Wool keeps your feet warm even when it's wet, and provides cushioning).

___ 2-3 pair liner socks (synthetic for wicking and fast drying)

___ Tevas (for crossing streams and for campsite wear). The increasingly popular water shoes worn by kayakers and other water sportswomen look interesting, which I may change to. They'd definitely save weight. Some people use sneakers, running shoes, or other sandals — you'll just want to be sure what you choose has decent tread and will dry quickly.

Miscellaneous:

___ Bandanna — large enough to use as scarf over head or face

___ Mosquito net head covering

___ Sunglasses

___ Prescription glasses — I wear one, carry the other (regular lens and sunglasses).

Backpacking Essentials from A to Z

A Acclimate

B Baby Wipes & Bear Canisters

C Compass

D Dehydrated food

E Energy Bars

F Filter

G GORP (Good Old Raisins & Peanuts), Ground cover

H Head coverings

I Iodine tablets & Insulated sleeping pad

J Jerky

K Knife

L Llama, Layer, Lighten

M Maps & Matches

N No-Doz (supplies caffeine), Needle (Blisters & making repairs), Nuts

O Organize

P Pen or Pencil

Q Quality, no quantity

R Rest, Rinse, Ropes

S Sterilize, Sleeping bag, Soup

T Toilet Paper & Trekking Poles

U Umbrella

V Vitamins & Vegetables

W Water, Wick, Whistle, Waterproof ,Walk at your own pace

X eXamine your boots before you leave

Y Yogurt-covered raisins

Z Zip-Lock bags

Sources and Suggested Readings

"Great ideas need landing gear as well as wings."

C. D. Jackson.

Bears and other Creatures:

Bear Attacks, Their Causes and Avoidance, Stephen Herrero, Lyons & Hittleman. Bantam Books, NY: 1985.

Food:

Wilderness Cuisine: How to Prepare and Enjoy Fine Food on the Trail and in Camp by Carole Latimer. Wilderness Press, CA: May 1991.

General Information:

Backpacker – The Magazine of Wilderness Travel. Subscription address: Backpacker, P O Box 7590, Red Oak, Iowa 51591-0590. Web address: www.backpacker.com.

The Sierra Club Wilderness Handbook, edited by David Brower, Sierra Club, Ballantine Books, Inc., NY: 1968.

Guide Books and History:

The Backpacker's Handbook, 2nd edition, by Chris Townsend. Ragged Mountain Press, ME: 1996.

The Complete Walker IV by Colin Fletcher with co-author Chip Rawlins. Knopf, New York: 2002. *Field and Stream* called the original edition, "the Hiker's Bible."

Harper & Row's Complete Field Guide to North American Wildlife, (Western Edition). compiled by Jay Ellis Ransom. Harper & Row, NY: 1981.

Hiking the Triple Crown: Appalachian Trail - Pacific Crest Trail - Continental Divide Trail - How to Hike America's Longest Trails by Karen Berger. Mountaineers Books, WA: March 2001.

Magnificent Mountain Women, The, Adventures in the Colorado Rockies by Janet Robertson. University of Nebraska Press, NE: 1990

Mammals of the Pacific States by Lloyd G. Ingles. Stanford University Press, Stanford, CA: 1965.

The Pacific Crest Trail Hiker's Handbook, Innovative Techniques and Trail Tested Instruction for the Long Distance Hiker by Ray Jardine. Adventure Lore, LaPine, OR.: 1996

Sierra South, by Thomas Winnett, Jason Winnett, Kathy Morey, and Lyn Haber. Wilderness Press, Berkeley, CA: 1993

Sierra North by Thomas Winnett and Jason Winnett. Wilderness Press, Berkeley, CA: 1985

Health and First Aid:

Fixing Your Feet, Prevention and Treatments for Athletes, Second Edition by John Vonhof. Footwork Publications, Fremont CA: 2000. www.footworkpub.com

Lightweight Backpacking:

Beyond Backpacking — Ray Jardine's Guide to Lightweight Hiking by Ray Jardine. Adventure Lore, LaPine, OR: 2000.

Memoirs/Personal Accounts::

A Lady's Life in the Rocky Mountains by Isabella L. Bird. Norman, University of Oklahoma Press, OK: 1960.

Take Me With You — A Round-the-World Journey to Invite a Stranger Home by Brad Newsham. Travelers' Tales, San Francisco, CA: 2000.

Women's Adventure Travel:

Flying South by Barbara Cushman Rowell. Ten Speed Press, Berkeley, CA: 2002

Rowing to Latitude by Jill Fredston. North Point Press (Division of Farrar, Straus and Giroux), NY: 2002

Women's Tours:

Adventures in Good Company – The Complete Guide to Women's Tours and Outdoor Trips by Thalia Zepatos. The Eighth Mountain Press, Portland, OR: 1994.

Index

About the Author

Susan Alcorn has backpacked more than 600 miles in the Sierra Nevada since her mid-life plunge into backpacking and continues to hike several hundred miles each year. She has hiked more than 500 miles in Spain and France on pilgrimage trails — including the *Camino de Santiago*. Her interest in finding other women backpackers in their forties and beyond led her to almost three dozen women who backpack with zest.

She has recently retired from teaching. During her career, she enjoyed leading hundreds of elementary school students on study trips that emphasized learning about, caring for, and enjoying the natural world.

Susan is an accomplished photographer who prefers to travel light when venturing into the wilderness — but rarely fails to bring her camera. Her multi-media shows — combining slides and a musical background — have been enjoyed by people of all ages including students, community organizations, and attendees at backpacking clinics.

She has published three previous books as well as numerous magazine and newspaper articles. Susan lives in Northern California with her husband Ralph — and they hike, backpack, and travel as often as they can.

Her twice-monthly newsletter on hiking and backpacking "tales and tips" is available, free, by request at: **backpack45@yahoo.com.** Visit Susan Alcorn's website at: **www.backpack45.com.**

Shepherd Canyon Books
25 Southwood Ct.
Oakland, CA 94611

Visit us at: **www.backpack45.com** to:

- order additional copies,

- gain information about our titles,

- and learn more about women's backpacking tours

   and trips.

Order Form

Please send me _____ copies of *We're in the Mountains, Not over the Hill* at $14.95 each.

Book order: $ _____
Sales tax (Calif only): _____
Shipping : _____
Total: _____

My check/money order for $ _____ is enclosed.

Please charge my credit card: ☐ Visa ☐ MasterCard

Account number

_____

Expiration date

_____

Name on card

_____

Signature

_____

Send to:
Name

_____

Address

_____

City, State, zip

_____

Mail form to:
Shepherd Canyon Books
25 Southwood Ct.
Oakland, CA 94611

510-339-3441 *or* 866-219-8260
www.backpack45.com

CA Sales Tax	
per book	
7.25%	$1.08
U.S. Shipping:	
Book Rate	
1st Book	$1.99
Each Add'l	$1.00
Priority Mail	
1st Book	$3.99